FOREST MANAGEMENT AND ECONOMICS

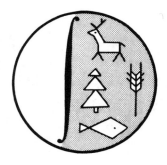

BIOLOGICAL RESOURCE MANAGEMENT

A Series of Primers on the Conservation and Exploitation of Natural and Cultivated Ecosystems

Wayne M. Getz, Series Editor
University of California, Berkeley

FOREST MANAGEMENT AND ECONOMICS

A Primer in Quantitative Methods

Joseph Buongiorno

University of Wisconsin, Madison

J. Keith Gilless

University of California, Berkeley

MACMILLAN PUBLISHING COMPANY
NEW YORK

Collier Macmillan Publishers
LONDON

Macmillan Publishing Company
866 Third Avenue, New York, NY 10022

Collier Macmillan Canada, Inc.

Printed in the United States of America
Printing: 1   2   3   4   5   6   7   8   9   10
Year: 7   8   9   0   1   2   3   4   5   6

Library of Congress Cataloging-in-Publication Data

Buongiorno, Joseph.
   Forest management.

   (Biological resource management)
   Includes bibliographies and index.
   1. Forest management—Mathematical models.
2. Forest management—Linear programming.   3. Forest
management—Data processing.   I. Gilless, J. Keith.
II. Title.   III. Series.
SD387.M33B86   1987   634.9′28   86-21665
ISBN 0-02-948740-4

For my parents–J.B.

Contents

Preface

This book started from a set of notes for a course taught for many years at the University of Wisconsin, Madison. The course is designed for senior undergraduates, although a few graduate students in forestry and other disciplines often take it. Like the course, this book is meant mostly for undergraduates. These students have little patience for theory; they chose forestry to walk the woods, not to dissect arcane equations, nor to waste their young years staring at computer terminals. Smart undergraduates are willing to study abstract methods and principles only if they can see clearly their application in the woods.

Having learned this, not without a few stinging failures, we used a teaching mode in which no more than one lecture would deal with methods or principles before considering an application. In fact, wherever possible, the method and the application evolved together, the application almost calling for a method to solve the problem being posed.

The book follows the same pattern. It is meant to be a book in forest management and economics, not a book in methods only. The mathematics used are kept to a minimum. Proofs of theorems and detailed descriptions of algorithms are avoided. Heuristics are used instead, wherever possible. Nevertheless, mathematics are used freely if they describe a particular concept more succinctly and precisely than long verbosities.

The book does not assume any specific preparation in mathematics or other sciences. Nevertheless, the material presented does require, by its very nature, a certain level of mathematical maturity. This should not be a problem for most forestry seniors, of whom a fair knowledge of mathematics and statistics is expected.

The end of Chap. 8 is the only part of the book that requires elementary linear algebra. However, all the matrix definitions and operations needed are presented in App. A. This material can be taught in less than one lecture. It would be a pity if that little extra effort stopped anyone from studying thoroughly what is perhaps the oldest, and certainly the most pleasing, form of forest management.

Modern quantitative methods are inseparable from computers. Again, many forestry students now take formal courses in computer science. Nevertheless, a knowledge of computers is not required to understand and use the methods discussed in this book. Most of the problems can be done with existing computer programs, the best of which are very easy to use.

Formal computer programming is required only in Chaps. 13 to 15, dealing with simulation methods. There, short programs written in BASIC are presented. We hope that they will awake the curiosity of those students who have not yet had programming. Operating a computer and using others' programs is a great experience, but writing your own programs is bliss. We have summarized the rudiments of BASIC programming in App. B. The reader can use this as refresher material, or as an introduction to programming that is sufficient to understand the programs used in these chapters, and to do the related problems. Simulation is such a powerful management tool that we hope that this will be only the beginning for more extensive studies of programming techniques.

In fact, our objective in planning the book was to awaken the curiosity of students, to expose them to many different methods and to show, with a few examples, how these methods can be used in forest management. The emphasis throughout is not on how particular quantitative techniques work, but rather on how they can be used. For example, we do not want to teach how linear programs are solved, but rather how forestry problems can be expressed as linear programs. The task of a forest manager is not to solve models but rather to express managerial problems in model forms for which there are solutions.

Consequently, this book is more about the art of model formulation than about the science of model solution. Like any art, mastering it takes a long apprenticeship. We feel that this is best accomplished by exposing students to many different models. There is a too-frequent syndrome that consists of casting every problem in the mold of the technique that one knows best. Being aware of different approaches should help ensure that the best method is selected for each particular problem.

The decision to discuss many different methods meant that each application had to be a simplification of models used in actual decision making. We feel that this is the most appropriate approach for classroom instruction. The students should spend the short time they have learning the principles of a method rather than the intricate details of its actual application in the field. Nevertheless, the longest problems at the end of each chapter are realistic enough to give the student a good idea of the power and limitations of each method, and of the time needed for formulating and solving a practical problem.

Also, several of the references at the end of each chapter describe large-scale applications. In choosing these references we have favored those that would be easier to read by undergraduates. A few more advanced works are cited to guide graduate students in further studies. Still, these references are not meant to be complete bibliographies.

We thank our students for having served as involuntary, though sometimes vocal, guinea pigs for the successive versions of the material presented in this book. We also warmly thank our colleagues who have reviewed the initial drafts and provided suggestions for improvement: Larry Davis, David Klemperer, and James Hotvedt. We specially thank Alan McQuillan for reading the entire final draft. It was Sarah Greene who induced us to start the book; she and Sheila Gillams edited it. Much of the art work was done with superior care by Jean Holland. Our publisher, Greg Payne, helped us towards a timely completion, and Steve Bedney guided the final production. We are grateful to all.

Joseph Buongiorno
J. Keith Gilless

FOREST MANAGEMENT AND ECONOMICS

Chapter 1

Introduction

1.1 SCOPE OF FOREST MANAGEMENT

Forest management is the art and science of making decisions with regard to the organization, use, and conservation of forests. Such decisions may involve the very long-term future of the forest or the day-to-day activities. They may deal with very complex forest systems or with simple parts. The geographic area of concern may be an entire country, a region, or a single stand of timber. This book deals mostly with the *economic* effects of decisions within the forest, but a few topics deal with other effects and with forest industries. Some of the management problems that we shall consider include:

> Scheduling harvests on an even-aged forest so that either the volume produced or the discounted value of all returns is maximum. While achieving this, one must satisfy various constraints regarding the pattern of timber output over time and the structure of the forest left at the end of the planning horizon (Chaps. 4 to 7, and 14).

> Predicting the effect of various constraints and management policies on the value of a forest (Chaps. 6 and 7).

> Determining the cutting cycle, cutting intensity and residual diameter distribution to maximize timber production or revenues from a selection forest (Chaps. 8 and 13).

> Planning the production of a pulp mill so that goals on revenues, employment, and pollution are met (Chap. 9).

Designing a road network that is as cheap as possible while providing adequate access to various projects and ensuring that timber and recreational goals are met (Chap. 10).

Scheduling forest plantations that are subject to fire hazards and scheduling slash burns (Chaps. 15 and 11).

Allocating funds to projects to save an endangered species (Chap. 12).

Ranking alternative investment projects in such a way that those selected maximize the contribution to private or public wealth (Chap. 16).

Forecasting how demand, supply, and the price of pulpwood in a paper-producing state are likely to change (Chap. 17).

1.2 THE NATURE OF MODELS

In making decisions of this kind, forest managers use models. *Models* are abstract representations of the real world that are useful for purposes of thinking, forecasting, and decision making.

Models may be very informal, mostly intuitive, supported by experience and information that are not put together in any systematic manner. Nevertheless, in the process of thinking about a problem, pondering alternatives, and reaching a decision, one undoubtedly uses a model that is a very abstract representation of what the real-life problem is. Most decisions are made with this kind of informal model. The results may be very good, especially for a smart, experienced manager, but the process is unique to each individual and is difficult to learn.

More concrete models have long been used by foresters. Some are physically very similar to what they represent. For example, a forest hydrologist may use a sand-and-water model of a watershed that differs from the real watershed only with respect to scale. Water, or a liquid of higher density, is made to flow at varying rates to simulate seasonal variations in precipitation and flooding. The resulting erosion is observed, and various systems of dams and levees can be tested using the model.

A forest map is an example of a more abstract model. There is very little physical correspondence between the map and the forest it represents. Nevertheless, maps are essential in many forestry activities. Few decisions are made without referring to them.

This book is about *mathematical models*. These are much more abstract than maps. Here, no visual analogy is left between the real world and the model. Reality is captured by symbolic variables and by formal algebraic relationships between them.

Mathematical models are not new in forestry. Biometric relationship between a stand's volume per acre, its species, its age, and the site conditions of the land on which it grows have long been expressed in terms of tables or mathematical functions. Forest economists have developed formulas to calculate the value of land in terms of its expected production, market value of its outputs, its management costs, and interest rates; these investment models are fundamental in forestry decision making, and we shall study them in detail in Chap. 16. However, most of the mathematical models discussed in this book deal with broader questions than do the specialized models just mentioned and can tackle problems with a very large number of variables and relationships. This makes them well-suited to real-life managerial situations.

1.3 SYSTEMS MODELS

Forest-management problems involve many different variables. Some are biological, such as the growth potential of a particular combination of soil and species; some are economic, such as the price of timber and the cost of labor; and others are social, such as the environmental laws that may regulate the treatment of a forest. Often these variables are interrelated; changes in one may influence the others.

All such variables and the relationships that tie them together constitute a *system*. Because of the complexity of forestry systems, foreseeing the likely consequences of a particular decision is not an easy task. For example, to respond to a high demand for timber, the manager of a national forest may feel that the current volume cut should be increased, but the law states that national forests must be managed for a nondeclining flow of timber. Will an increase in the current harvest level force future production to decline?

In such situations, models help managers predict the consequences of their actions. In a sense, a model is a device that brings the real world to the laboratory or to the office. The manager can carry out experiments with the model that would be impossible in reality. For example, one can try many patterns of harvest on a model of the forest and observe the consequences of each, a thing that is totally impossible with the real forest. It is this ability to experiment, predict, and choose that makes forest-systems modeling such an exciting field.

Some of the first systems models, and the methods to solve them, were developed during World War II to assist in military operations. This led to a body of knowledge that is often referred to as *operations research*. After the war, operations research methods began to be applied successfully in industry, agriculture, and government. The Operations Society of America and the Institute of Management Science were created, and universities established academic departments in this field. The first applications of operations research to forest management date from the early 1960s. Their number has been growing rapidly since then. The Society of American Foresters now has a working group on the subject. A similar group has been started within the Institute of Management Science to study applications of the methods to forestry and forest industries.

Most of the quantitative methods presented in this book are thus part of the field of operations research, but investment and econometric models have an even longer history within economics. To date, many systems models therefore combine the methods of operations research with those of economics.

1.4 THE ROLE OF COMPUTERS

Although systems models are formulated with mathematics, mathematics alone cannot make them work. The reason is that only very simple mathematical models have exact analytical solutions. For example, a simplistic model of the growth of a deer population in a forest would state that the growth proceeds at a rate proportional to the number of animals. This relationship can be expressed as a simple equation whose solution gives the population size as a function of time. In fact, however, the growth of the population is also a function of the amount of food available in the forest, which itself changes at a rate that depends on the way the forest is managed, and so on. To model these relationships properly, one needs a system of equations for which there are no exact solutions, only approximate ones.

This example is typical of the situations of systems models. By their very nature, they do not have exact solutions. They must be solved by numerical methods–that is, essentially by trial and error. But the number of trials can be decreased considerably by algorithms. *Algorithms* are calculation procedures that ensure that, starting from a rough approximation, a good solution is approached within a reasonable number of steps.

Algorithms have long been used in approximating solutions to equations, but the power of algorithms has been increased immensely by digital computers. The advent of computers is a scientific revolution akin to the discovery of differential and integral calculus. Problems that could not even be considered a mere 50 years ago are now solved routinely in a few seconds on a digital computer. For example, computers can determine the optimal solution to a problem that has several thousand variables and constraints. The search for optimality is a recurring theme in operations research and is a feature of several of the models studied in this book.

1.5 GOOD MODELS

The availability of powerful, inexpensive computers is not without its dangers. In forestry, as in other fields, it has often led to the development of awkward, expensive, cumbersome models. Like the good maps alluded to above, the best models are the *simplest*, given the question that must be answered. Too many times, models have been sought that could "do everything." Rather, much can be gained by defining precisely the managerial problem to be solved and by limiting the model strictly to that problem.

In this respect, one can recognize three elements in model development: problem definition, model building, and model implementation. Although this book is mostly concerned with model building, the other two elements are also essential to the development of a successful model, for there is a close relationship between problem definition, model building, and model implementation. What kind of model can be built influences to some extent how the problem is defined, and so does the manner in which the model will be implemented. Regardless, too little time is usually spent on precise problem definition. A well-defined forest-management problem is more than half-solved.

ANNOTATED REFERENCES

Duerr, W. A., D. E. Teeguarden, N. B. Christiansen, and S. Guttenberg. 1979. *Forest resource management: Decision-making principles and cases.* Saunders, Philadelphia. 612 pp. (Chapter 7 discusses the taxonomy and use of models in forest management, and Chap. 8 discusses the use of informal decision models.)

Dykstra, D. P. 1984. *Mathematical programming for natural resource management.* McGraw-Hill, New York. 318 pp. (Chapter 1 gives an overview of management science and models, especially mathematical programming, in natural resource management.)

Eden, C., S. Jones, and D. Sims. 1983. *Messing about in problems: An informal structured approach to their identification and management.* Pergamon, Oxford. 124 pp. (Guide to ways of thinking about problems that complement the quantitative methods discussed in this book.)

Field, R. C. 1984. National Forest planning is promoting U.S. Forest Service acceptance of operations research. *Interfaces* 14(5):67–76. (Account of recent increase in U.S. Forest Service reliance on and acceptance of operations research methods.)

Forgionne, G. A. 1983. Corporate management science activities: An update. *Interfaces* 13(3):20–23. (Survey of the extent of usage, areas of application, and effectiveness ratings of operations research methods in American corporations.)

Harrison, T. P., and C. A. de Kluyver. 1984. MS/OR and the forests products industry: New directions. *Interfaces* 14(5):1–7. (Discussion of current trends and major issues in the use of operations research methods in forestry.)

Holmes, S. 1976. Introduction to operations research as applied in forest products industries. *Forest Products Journal* 26(1):17–22. (Nontechnical review of operations research techniques in use by forest industries.)

LeMaster, D. C., D. M. Baumgartner, and R. C. Chapman. 1981. *Forestry predictive models: Problems in application.* Washington State University Cooperative Extension, Pullman. 116 pp. (Collection of papers illustrating the range of forestry problems addressed using mathematical models.)

Martin, A. J., and P. E. Sendak. 1973. Operations research in forestry: A bibliography. U.S. Forest Service General Technical Report NE-8. Northeastern Forest Experiment Station, Upper Darby. 90 pp. (References for more than 400 applications of operations research to forestry and forest industries.)

Valfer, E. S., M. W. Kirby, and G. Schwarzbart. 1981. Returns on investments in management sciences: Six case studies. U.S. Forest Service General Technical Report PSW-52. Pacific Southwest Forest and Range Experiment Station, Berkeley. 14 pp. (Case studies documenting the value of operations research methods to the U.S. Forest Service.)

Chapter 2

Principles of Linear Programming: Formulations

2.1 INTRODUCTION

This chapter is an introduction to the method of linear programming. Here, we shall deal mostly with simple examples showing how a management problem can be formulated as a special mathematical model called a linear program. We shall concentrate on formulation, leaving the question of how to solve linear programs to the next chapter.

Linear programming is a very general optimization technique. It can be applied to many different problems, some of which have nothing to do with forestry or even with management science; nevertheless, linear programming was designed (and is used primarily) to solve managerial problems. In fact, it was one of the first practical tools devised to tackle complex decision-making problems common to industry, agriculture, and government.

For our immediate purpose, *linear programming* can be defined as a method to allocate limited resources to competing activities in an optimal manner.

This definition describes well the situation faced by forest managers. The resources with which they work—be they land, people, trees, time, or money—are always limited. Furthermore, many of the activities that managers administer compete for these resources. For example, one may want to increase the land area that is growing red pine, but then less land will be available for aspen. Another may want to assign more of her staff to prepare timber sales, but then fewer people will be available to do stand improvement work. She could hire more people, but then she would have too little money.

No matter what the course of action chosen, managers always face constraints that limit the range of their options. Linear programming is designed to help them choose. Not only can the method show which alternatives are possible ("feasible" in linear-programming jargon), it can also help determine the best one. But this requires that both the management objective as well as the constraints be defined in a precise mathematical manner. Finding the best alternative is a recurring theme in management science; most of the methods presented in this book involve optimization models.

The first practical way of solving linear programs, the simplex method, was invented by George Dantzig in the late 1940s. At first, by hand and with mechanical desk calculators, only small problems could be solved. Now, using computers and linear programming, one can routinely solve problems with thousands of variables and hundreds of constraints.

Linear programming is by far the most widely used operations research method, although simulation (which we shall examine in Chaps. 13 to 15) is also becoming a very effective method. Linear programming has been and continues to be used intensively in forest management. Some of the most widely used forest-planning models to date in industry and on national forests use linear programming or its close cousin, goal programming (examined in Chap. 9).

2.2 FIRST EXAMPLE: A POET AND HIS WOODS

This first example of the application of linear programming is certainly artificial, too simple to correspond to a real forestry operation. Nevertheless, it will suffice to introduce the main concepts and definitions. Later on we will use this same example to discuss the graphic and simplex methods of solving linear programs.

Anyway, the story is romantic.

Problem Definition

The protagonist is a congenial poet-forester who lives in the woods of northern Wisconsin. Some success in his writing allowed him about 10 years ago to buy a cabin and 90 acres of woods in good, productive condition.

The poet needs to walk the beautiful woods to keep his inspiration alive. But the muses do not always respond, and he finds that sales from the woods come in very handy to replenish a sometimes empty wallet. In fact, times have been somewhat harder than usual lately. He has firmly decided to get the most he can out of his woods.

But the arts must go on. The poet does not want to spend more than half his time in the woods; the rest is for prose and sonnets.

Our poet has a curious mind. He has even read about linear programming: a method to allocate scarce resources to optimize certain objectives. He thinks that this is exactly what he needs to get the most out of his woods while pursuing his poetic vocation.

Data

In order to develop his model, the poet has put together the following information:

> About 40 acres of the land he owns are covered with red-pine plantations. The other 50 acres contain mixed northern hardwoods.
>
> Having kept a very good record of his time, he figures that since he bought these woods he has spent approximately 800 days managing the red pine and 1500 days managing the hardwoods.
>
> The total net income he got for this effort during the same period was $36,000 from the red-pine land and $60,000 from the hardwoods.

Problem Formulation

To formulate his model, the poet-forester needs to choose the variables to symbolize his decisions. The choice of proper decision variables is critical in building a model. Some choices will make the problem far simpler to formulate and solve than will others. Unfortunately, there is no set method for choosing decision variables. Choosing is part of the art of model building, which can only be learned by practice.

But we can offer him sound advice: "Look at the objective. Its nature will often give some clue as to what the decision variables should be."

We noted above that his objective is to maximize revenues. But this has a meaning only if the revenues are finite; thus, we must talk about revenues per unit of time, say per year (meaning an average year, like any one of the past 10 enjoyable years that the poet has spent on his property). Formally, we write the objective as:

Maximize Z = dollars of net revenue per year

The revenues symbolized by Z arise from managing red pine or northern hardwoods, or both. Therefore, a natural set of decision variables is:

X_1 = number of acres of red pine to be managed
X_2 = number of acres of northern hardwoods to be managed

These are the unknowns. We seek the values of X_1 and X_2 that make Z as large as possible.

Objective Function The objective function expresses the relationship between Z, the revenues generated by the woods, and the decision variables X_1 and X_2. To write this function, we need an estimate of the yearly revenues generated by each type of woods. Since the poet has earned $36,000 on 40 acres of red pine and $60,000 on 50 acres of northern hardwoods during the past 10 years, the average earnings have been $90 per acre per year (90 $/a/y) for red pine and 120 $/a/y for northern hardwoods. Using these figures as measures of the poet's expected earnings during the coming years, we can now write his objective function as:

$$\max Z = \underset{(\$/y)}{90} \underset{(\$/a/y)(a)}{X_1} + \underset{(\$/a/y)(a)}{120} \ X_2$$

where the units of measurement of each variable and constant are shown in parentheses. A good modeling practice is always to check the homogeneity of all algebraic expressions with respect to the units of measurement. Here, Z is expressed in dollars per year; therefore, the operations on the right of the equal sign must also yield dollars per year, which they do.

To complete the model, we must determine what constraints limit the actions of our poet-forester and then help him express these constraints in terms of the decision variables X_1 and X_2.

Constraints   Two constraints are very simple. The area managed in each timber type cannot exceed the area available; i.e.:

$X_1 \leq 40$ acres of red pine

$X_2 \leq 50$ acres of northern hardwoods

A third constraint is set by the fact that the poet does not want to spend more than half his time, let us say 180 days per year, managing the woods. In order to write this constraint in terms of the decision variables, we note that the time he has spent managing red pine during the past 10 years (800 days on 40 acres) averages 2 days per acre per year (d/a/y). Similarly, he has spent 3 d/a/y on northern hardwoods (1500 days on 50 acres). Therefore, in terms of the decision variables X_1 and X_2, the total time spent by the poet-forester to manage his woods is:

$$\underset{(d/a/y)(a)}{2 \ X_1} + \underset{(d/a/y)(a)}{3 \ X_2}$$

and the expression of the constraint limiting this time to no more than 180 days is:

$$\underset{(d/y)}{2X_1} + \underset{(d/y)}{3X_2} \leq \underset{(d/y)}{180}$$

Note that northern hardwoods are cultivated under a selection system; this has taken the poet more time per acre, especially to mark timber sales, than has the even-aged red pine. But, on the other hand, the hardwoods tend to return more revenue per acre, as reflected in the objective function. Therefore, the choice of the best management strategy is not obvious.

The last constraint needed to complete the formulation of the problem states that none of the decision variables may be negative; i.e.:

$$X_1 \geq 0 \quad \text{and} \quad X_2 \geq 0$$

Final Model

In summary, combining the objective function and the constraints, we obtain the complete formulation of the poet-forester problem as: Find the variables X_1 and X_2, which measure the number of acres of red pine and of northern hardwoods to manage such that

$$\max Z = 90X_1 + 120X_2$$

Subject to:

$$
\begin{aligned}
X_1 &\le 40 \\
X_2 &\le 50 \\
2X_1 + 3X_2 &\le 180 \\
X_1, X_2 &\ge 0
\end{aligned}
$$

In the next chapter we will learn how to solve this problem. But before that, let us study another example.

2.3 SECOND EXAMPLE: PULP-MILL MANAGEMENT

The purpose of this second example is to illustrate the formulation of a linear-programming model that, in contrast to the poet's problem, involves a minimum objective function and constraints of the greater-than-or-equal-to form. Also, in this problem we move away from the strict interpretation of constraints as limits on available resources. Here, some of the constraints will express management objectives.

Problem Formulation

This story deals with a pulp mill operating in a small town in Maine. The pulp mill makes mechanical and chemical pulp. Unfortunately, it also pollutes the river in which it spills its spent waters. This has created enough turmoil to change the management of the mill completely.

The previous owners felt that it would be too costly to reduce the pollution problem. They decided to sell. The mill has been bought back by the employees and local businesses, who now own the mill as a cooperative.

The new management objectives are to maintain at least 300 people employed in the mill and to generate at least $40,000 of gross revenue per day; it is estimated that this revenue will be sufficient to pay the operating expenses and yield a return that will keep the mill competitive in the long run. Within these limits, everything should be done to minimize pollution.

A bright forester who has already provided shrewd solutions to complex wood-procurement problems is asked to suggest an operating strategy for the mill that will meet these objectives. She feels that it can be done by linear programming. Toward this end, she has put together the following data:

Both chemical and mechanical pulp require the labor of one worker for about 1 day, or 1 workday (wd), per ton produced.

The chemical pulp sells at some $200 per ton, the mechanical pulp at $100.

Pollution is measured by the biological oxygen demand (BOD). One ton of mechanical pulp produces 1 unit of BOD, and 1 ton of chemical pulp produces 1.5 units.

The maximum capacity of the mill to make mechanical pulp is 300 tons per day; for chemical pulp, it is 200 tons per day. The two manufacturing processes are independent; that is, the mechanical pulp line cannot be used to make chemical pulp.

Given this data, our forester has found that the management objectives and the technical and financial data could be put together into a linear program. This is how she did it:

Objective Function The objective function to minimize is the amount of pollution, Z, measured here by units of BOD per unit of time, say per day (BOD/d). A natural choice for the decision variables is then: X_1 = amount of mechanical pulp produced in tons per day (t/d), and X_2 = amount of chemical pulp produced (t/d). And the expression of the objective function is:

$$\min Z = \underset{\text{(BOD/d)}}{1} \quad \underset{\text{(BOD/t)(t/d)}}{X_1} + \underset{\text{(BOD/t)(t/d)}}{1.5 \ X_2}$$

where the units of measurement are shown in parentheses. Verify that the objective function is homogeneous in those units.

Constraints One constraint expresses the objective to keep at least 300 workers employed. In terms of the decision variables, this is:

$$\underset{\text{(wd/t)(t/d)}}{1 \ X_1} + \underset{\text{(wd/t)(t/d)}}{1 \ X_2} \geq \underset{\text{(workers)}}{300}$$

A second constraint states that at least $40,000 of gross revenue must be generated every day; i.e.:

$$\underset{\text{($/t)(t/d)}}{100 \ X_1} + \underset{\text{($/t)(t/d)}}{200 \ X_2} \geq \underset{\text{($/d)}}{40{,}000}$$

Two other constraints refer to the fact that the production capacities of the mill cannot be exceeded; i.e.:

For mechanical pulp: $X_1 \leq 300$ (tons per day)
For chemical pulp: $X_2 \leq 200$ (tons per day)

Finally, the quantity of mechanical and chemical pulp produced must be positive or zero: $X_1, X_2 \geq 0$.

In summary, the final form of the linear program that models the dilemma of the pulp-making cooperative is to find X_1 and X_2, which measure the amount of mechanical and chemical pulp produced daily, such that:

$$\min Z = X_1 + 1.5X_2$$

subject to:

$$
\begin{aligned}
X_1 \quad + X_2 &\geq 300 \\
100\,X_1 + 200\,X_2 &\geq 40{,}000 \\
X_1 \quad\quad &\leq 300 \\
X_2 &\leq 200 \\
X_1,\, X_2 &\geq 0
\end{aligned}
$$

A Note on Multiple Objectives

In this example, despite the fact that there were several management objectives, only one of them appeared in the objective function. The other objectives were expressed as constraints. This arrangement corresponds to a rule that is absolute and not peculiar to linear programming. In any optimization problem, only one function can be optimized.

For example, strictly speaking, it makes no sense to say that we want to maximize the amount of timber that a forest produces and the recreational opportunities offered in the same forest. As long as timber and recreation conflict (i.e., as long as they use common resources), we must choose. Either we maximize timber, subject to a specified amount of recreational opportunities, or we maximize recreation, subject to a certain volume of timber production.

One of the teachings of linear programming is that we must choose which objective to optimize. Later, we shall study methods designed to handle several objectives with more flexibility. Goal programming is one such method —but even in goal programming (as we shall see in Chap. 9), the optimized objective function is unique.

2.4 GENERAL STANDARD FORMULATION OF THE LINEAR PROGRAMMING MODEL

Any linear program may be written in several equivalent ways. For example, as in the poet's problem, the pulp-mill problem can be rewritten as a maximization subject to less-than-or-equal-to constraints, as follows:

$$\max(-Z) = -X_1 - 1.5X_2$$

subject to:

$$
\begin{aligned}
-X_1 \quad - X_2 &\leq -300 \\
-100\,X_1 - 200\,X_2 &\leq -40{,}000 \\
X_1 \quad\quad &\leq 300 \\
X_2 &\leq 200 \\
X_1,\, X_2 &\geq 0
\end{aligned}
$$

If there were an equality, say $X_1 + X_2 = 300$, it too could be replaced by two less-than-or-equal-to constraints:

$$X_1 + X_2 \leq 300 \qquad \text{and} \qquad -X_1 - X_2 \leq -300$$

If a variable, say X_2, were free to take negative values, it could be replaced by the difference between two nonnegative variables $X_{2,1}$ and $X_{2,2}$, for if $X_2 = X_{2,1} - X_{2,2}$ (where $X_{2,1}$, $X_{2,2} \geq 0$), then we could have $X_2 \geq 0$ (if $X_{2,1} \geq X_{2,2}$) or could even have $X_2 < 0$ (if $X_{2,1} < X_{2,2}$).

In a linear-programming problem, the objective function may be maximized or minimized, constraints may be in either direction or even in strict equalities, and variables may be free of sign. Still, the problem can be recast in the following *standard form*: Find the values of n variables $X_1, X_2, \ldots, X_n$ (referred to as decision variables, or activities) such that the objective function Z be maximum. The objective function is a linear function of the decision variables; i.e:

$$Z = c_1 X_1 + c_2 X_2 + \cdots + c_n X_n$$

where $c_1, \ldots, c_n$ are all constant parameters. Each parameter c_j measures the contribution of the corresponding variable X_j to the objective function. For example, if X_1 increases (decreases) by 1 unit, then, other variables remaining equal, Z increases (decreases) by c_1 units.

The values that the variables can take in trying to maximize the objective function are limited by constraints. The constraints have the following general expression:

$$a_{1,1} X_1 + a_{1,2} X_2 + \cdots + a_{1,n} X_n \leq b_1$$
$$a_{2,1} X_1 + a_{2,2} X_2 + \cdots + a_{2,n} X_n \leq b_2$$
$$\vdots$$
$$a_{m,1} X_1 + a_{m,2} X_2 + \cdots + a_{m,n} X_n \leq b_m$$

where $b_1, b_2, \ldots, b_m$ are constants. These constants may measure the amounts of resources available. For example, assume that b_1 is the land area that a manager can use and b_2 the amount of money available to spend. In that case, each $a_{i,j}$ is a constant that measures how much of resource i is used per unit of activity X_j. For example, keeping to our interpretation of b_2 and assuming that X_1 is the number of acres planted in a given year, $a_{2,1}$ is the money needed per acre planted.

Within this interpretation, the product $a_{i,j} X_j$ is the amount of resource i used when activity j is at the level X_j. Adding these products up over all activities leads to the following general expression for the total amount of resource i used by n activities:

$$R_i = a_{i,1} X_1 + a_{i,2} X_2 + \cdots + a_{i,n} X_n$$

In linear programming, R_i is referred to as the row activity i in symmetry with X_j, which is the column activity j.

The formulation is completed by the addition of the nonnegativity constraints. These state that all variables must be positive; i.e.:

$$X_1, X_2, \ldots, X_n \geq 0$$

The standard linear-programming model can be expressed in a somewhat more compact form by using the Greek capital letter sigma (Σ) to indicate summations. The general standard linear-programming problem is then to find X_j ($j = 1, \ldots, n$) such that:

$$\max Z = \sum_{j=1}^{n} c_j X_j$$

subject to:

$$\sum_{j=1}^{n} a_{i,j} X_j \leq b_i \qquad \text{for } i = 1, \ldots, m$$

$$X_j \geq 0 \qquad \text{for } j = 1, \ldots, n$$

2.5 ASSUMPTIONS OF LINEAR PROGRAMMING

Before proceeding to study the solutions and applications of linear programming, it is worth stressing the assumptions that it makes. A linear-programming model is a satisfactory representation of a particular forest-management problem when all these assumptions are warranted. They will never hold exactly, but they should be reasonable. The determination of what is reasonable or not is part of the art of management and model building. Keep in mind that bold assumptions are often more useful in understanding the world than are complicated details.

Proportionality

In a linear program it is assumed that the contribution of any activity to the objective function is *directly proportional* to the level of that activity. As the level of the activity increases or decreases, the change in the objective function due to a unit change of the activity remains the same. For example, in the poet-forester problem the contribution of red-pine management to revenues is directly proportional to the area of red pine being managed.

In a similar manner, in linear programming the amount of resource used by each activity is directly proportional to the level of that activity. For example, the time the poet must spend managing his land is directly proportional to the area being managed. If, as the managed area increased, each additional acre took an increasing amount of time, then the linear-programming model would not be valid, at least not without some modification.

Additivity

The linear-programming model assumes that the contribution of all activities to the objective function is just the *sum* of the contribution of each activity. Similarly, the total amount of a resource used by all activities is the sum of the amount used by each individual activity considered independently. This means that the contribution of each variable does not depend on the level of the others.

Thus, regardless of what the poet-forester does with his northern hardwoods, it is assumed that he will always get $90 per acre from each acre of managed red pine and that it will continue to take him 2 days per acre per year to manage it.

Divisibility

The linear-programming model assumes that all activities are continuous and can take any positive value. This means that the model is not generally suited to situations in which the decision variables are *integers*. For example, some models use variables that may take only the integer values 0 or 1 to represent yes or no decisions: Should we build this bridge or not?

For some problems that involve integer variables, it may be enough to compute a continuous solution by ordinary linear programming and then round the variables to the nearest integer. But this is not always suitable.

We will study programming models that use integer variables in Chap. 10.

Determinism

The linear-programming model is deterministic. In computing a solution, it does not take into account that all the coefficients in the model are only approximations.

For this reason, it is useful when using linear programming to compute not only one solution, but several; each solution corresponds to different (but reasonable) assumptions regarding the values of the parameters. This kind of work is known as *sensitivity analysis*. Its object is to show how sensitive a solution is to changes in the values of parameters. In order to arrive at good decisions, one should carefully examine those parameters which have the most impact.

Most of the models presented in this book are deterministic. Stochastic models—that is, models in which the random nature of some parameters is considered explicitly in calculating a solution—will be examined in Chap. 11, which deals with network analysis, and in Chap. 15 on simulation.

2.6 CONCLUSIONS

The two examples used in this chapter have shown the flexibility of linear programming. Problems involving the optimization of a specific objective that is subject to constraints can be cast as linear programs. The objective may be to minimize or maximize something. The constraints may represent the limited resources that the manager can work with, but they may also refer to objectives.

Formulating a forest-management problem in a way that it can be solved by linear programming is not always easy. It takes a lot of ingenuity and practice, plus some courage. To be understood, the world must be simplified; this is what models are all about. Linear programming is no different: it makes some drastic assumptions. But the assumptions are not so critical as to render the method useless. On the contrary, we shall discover in the forthcoming chapters that linear programming is so flexible that it can be applied to a wide range of forest-management problems, from harvest scheduling and multiple-use planning to investment analysis. There is almost no limit except our imagination.

PROBLEMS

2.1. Several management problems are listed below. What kind of objective function would be appropriate in a linear-programming model for each? What kinds of decision variables? What kinds of constraints?

   (a) A farmer wants to maximize the income he will receive over the next 20 years from his woodlot. The woodlot is covered with mature sugar maple trees that could be sold as stumpage or managed to produce maple syrup.

   (b) The manager of a hardwood sawmill wants to maximize the mill's net revenues. The mill can produce pallet stock, dimension lumber, or some combination of the two. Pallet stock commands a lower price than dimension lumber, but it can be produced from less expensive logs, and the mill's daily capacity to produce pallet stock exceeds its capacity to produce dimension lumber.

   (c) A logger wants to minimize the cost of harvesting a stand of timber. She can use mechanical fellers, workers with chainsaws, or some of both. Leasing and operating a mechanical feller is more expensive than hiring a worker with a chainsaw, but a worker does less work. On the other hand, mechanical fellers cannot harvest some of the largest and most valuable trees in the stand.

2.2. Consider the linear-programming model of the poet and his woods in Sec. 2.2. If he had received $50,000 over the last 10 years from managing his red-pine plantations and $30,000 from managing his hardwoods, how would the coefficients of X_1 and X_2 change in the objective function? Suppose the poet found pruning to have a particularly inhibiting effect on his literary endeavors, and two-thirds of the time devoted to managing hardwoods had to be spent pruning. If he wanted to limit the time he spent pruning to not more than 70 days per year, what constraint would have to be added to the model? If one-half of the time devoted to managing red-pine plantations had to be spent pruning, how would this constraint have to be further modified?

2.3. Consider the linear-programming model of pulp-mill management in Sec. 2.3. The mill management might prefer to maximize gross revenues while limiting pollution to not more than 300 BOD per day. Reformulate the model to reflect this new management orientation, leaving the employment and capacity constraints unchanged.

2.4. Consider the linear-programming model of the poet and his woods in Sec. 2.2. If the poet decided to manage 25 acres of red pine and 35 acres of hardwoods, how much income would he receive from his lands each year? What would the row activity in the time constraint be, and what would this mean?

2.5. Consider the linear-programming model of pulp-mill management in Sec. 2.3. If the mill's management decided to produce 150 tons of chemical pulp and 190 tons of mechanical pulp per day, how much pollution would result? What would the row activity in the revenue constraint be, and what would this mean? What would the row activity in employment constraint be, and what would this mean?

2.6. A logger wants to maximize net revenues per hour of operation of her four tractors and six skidders. From her records, she estimates her net revenue per hour of operation for a tractor at $3, and for a skidder at $6. Only 18 people trained to run logging equipment are available in the local labor market. This limits her operations, since it takes two people to run a skidder and three to run a tractor. Formulate this problem as a linear program. Define the units of all variables and coefficients in the model. What values may each variable take? Is this problem an ordinary linear program?

2.7. A logging concern must allocate logging equipment between two sites in the manner that will maximize its daily net revenues. They have determined that the net revenue of a cord of wood is $1.90 from site 1 and $2.10 from site 2. At their disposal are two skidders, one brancher, and one truck. Each kind of equipment can be used for 9 hours per day, and this time can be divided in any proportion between the two sites. The equipment needed to produce a cord of wood from each site varies as shown below. Formulate this problem as a linear program. Define the units of all variables and coefficients in the model. (*Hint*: You will need two variables and one constraint for each kind of equipment.)

EQUIPMENT HOURS NEEDED TO PRODUCE A CORD OF WOOD

Site	Feller	Brancher	Truck
1	0.30	0.30	0.17
2	0.40	0.15	0.17

ANNOTATED REFERENCES

Davis, L. S., and K. N. Johnson. 1986. *Forest management*. McGraw-Hill, New York. (The "steers and trees" problem in Chap. 6 and the "Jerry Wilcox" problem in Chap. 15 are simple linear programs to allocate work to two competing land management activities.)

Duerr, W. A., D. E. Teeguarden, N. B. Christiansen, and S. Guttenberg. 1979. *Forest resource management: Decision-making principles and cases*. Saunders, Philadelphia. 612 pp. (The resort management problem in Chap. 10 is another simple example of resource allocation to two competing land management activities.)

Dykstra, D. P. 1984. *Mathematical programming for natural resource management*. McGraw-Hill, New York. 318 pp. (The cattle ranching problem in Chap. 2 is another simple example of a linear program with only two variables.)

Foster, B. B. 1969. Linear programming: A method for determining least cost blends or mixes in papermaking. *Tappi* 52(9):1658–1660. (Determines the least-cost blend of pulpwood species that will produce a paper with certain characteristics.)

Hanover, S. J., W. L. Hafley, A. G. Mullin, and R. K. Perrin. 1973. Linear programming and sensitivity analysis for hardwood dimension production. *Forest Products Journal* 23(11):47–50. (Determines the size and grade of lumber that will maximize the profits of a sawmill subject to technological and contractual constraints.)

Hillier, F. S., and G. J. Lieberman. 1986. *Introduction to operations research*. Holden-Day, Oakland. 888 pp. (Chapter 3 covers the basics of formulating linear-programming models.)

Kotak, D. B. 1976. Application of linear programming to plywood manufacture. *Interfaces* 7(1) Part 2:56–68. (Optimizes the wood mix used by a plywood mill.)

Little, R. L., and T. E. Wooten. 1972. Product optimization of a log concentration yard by linear programming. Department of Forestry, Clemson University, Clemson. Forest Research Series No. 24. 14 pp. (Sorting logs for resale into the mix of highest value, such as poles, veneer logs, chips, etc.)

Taha, H. A. 1982. *Operations research: An introduction*. Macmillan, New York. 848 pp. (Chapter 2 covers the basics of formulating linear-programming models.)

Chapter 3

Principles of Linear Programming: Solutions

After a forest management problem has been formulated as a linear program, the program must be solved to get the most desirable management strategy. This chapter deals with two different methods of solution. The simplest procedure is graphic, but it can be used only in very small problems; computers use a more general technique, the simplex method. After an optimum solution has been obtained, one can explore how sensitive it is to the values of the parameters in the model. We shall study duality, a powerful method of sensitivity analysis in linear programming.

3.1 GRAPHIC SOLUTION OF THE POET'S PROBLEM

Large linear-programming models that represent real managerial problems must be solved with a computer. However, the small problem that we developed in Sec. 2.2 for the poet-forester can be solved with a simple graphic procedure. The technique for solving it illustrates well the nature of the general linear-programming solution.

Recall the expression of that problem:

$$\max Z = 90X_1 + 120X_2 \qquad \text{dollars per year}$$

subject to:

$$X_1 \qquad \le 40 \text{ acres of red pine}$$
$$X_2 \le 50 \text{ acres of hardwoods}$$
$$2X_1 + 3X_2 \le 180 \text{ days of work}$$
$$X_1, X_2 \ge 0$$

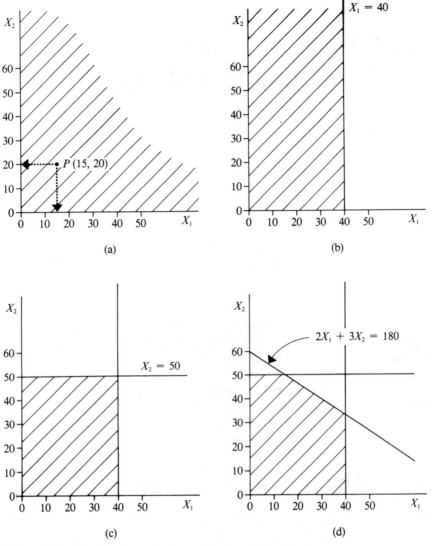

Figure 3.1   Graphic determination of the feasible region.

where the variable X_1 is the number of acres of red pine that the poet should manage and X_2 is the number of acres of northern hardwoods. The object is to find the values of these two variables that maximize Z, which measures the poet's annual revenue from the property. There are 40 acres of red pine on the property and 50 acres of hardwoods, and the poet has 180 days per year to manage his forest.

Because the problem has only two decision variables, it can be represented in a diagram, as in Fig. 3.1(a). The number of acres of red pine is measured on the horizontal axis and that of hardwoods on the vertical axis.

Each point on this diagram represents a management option. For example, the point P in Fig. 3.1(a) corresponds to the decision to manage 15 acres of red pine and 20 acres of hardwoods.

However, given the resource constraints, not all points on the diagram correspond to a possible (feasible) choice. The first task in solving a linear program is to find all the points that are feasible; among those points, we will then seek the one or more that maximize the objective function.

Feasible Region

Since both X_1 and X_2 cannot be negative, only the shaded portion of Fig. 3.1(a) can contain a feasible solution. In addition, the constraint $X_1 \leq 40$ means that a feasible point (X_1, X_2) cannot lie to the right of the vertical line $X_1 = 40$. The result is shown in Fig. 3.1(b), whose shaded area contains only the values of X_1 and X_2 that are permissible thus far. Next, the constraint $X_2 \leq 50$ eliminates all the points above the horizontal line $X_2 = 50$; the feasible region now consists of the points within the shaded rectangle in Fig. 3.1(c).

The last constraint is set by the poet's time: $2X_1 + 3X_2 \leq 180$. Only the points that lie on one side of the line $2X_1 + 3X_2 = 180$ satisfy this restriction. To trace that straight line on our figure, we need two of its points. For example, if $X_1 = 0$, then $X_2 = 60$. Similarly, if $X_2 = 30$, then $X_1 = (180 - 90)/2 = 45$. To find on which side of the line $2X_1 + 3X_2 = 180$ the feasible region lies, we check for one point: for example, the origin. At the origin, both X_1 and X_2 are zero and the time constraint holds; therefore, all the points on the plane that are on the same side of $2X_1 + 3X_2 = 180$ as the origin satisfy the poet's time constraint.

In summary, the feasible region is represented by the shaded polygon in Fig. 3.1(d). The coordinates of any point within that region satisfy simultaneously the land constraints, the poet's time constraint, and the nonnegativity constraints. In the next step we shall determine which point(s) in the feasible region maximize the objective function.

Optimum Solution

To find the optimum solution graphically, we first determine the position of the line that represents the objective function for some arbitrary value of the objective. For example, let $Z = \$1800$ per year. All the combinations of X_1 and X_2 that lead to these returns lie on the line:

$$1800 = 90X_1 + 120X_2$$

This line has been traced in Fig. 3.2. Many of its points lie in the feasible region. Therefore, it is indeed possible for the poet to get this income from his property, and there are many ways in which he can do it. But could he get more? For example, could he double his income? This question is readily

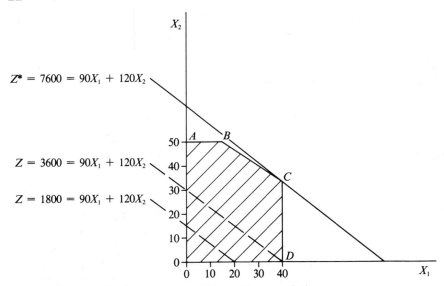

Figure 3.2 Graphic determination of the optimum solution.

answered by tracing the line:

$$3600 = 90X_1 + 120X_2$$

Again, there are many points on this line that are feasible. Note that this line is parallel to the previous one, but farther from the origin.

It is clear that the optimum solution will be obtained by drawing a straight line which is parallel to those we have just traced, which has at least one point within the feasible region, and which is as far from the origin as possible. Thus, the optimum solution must correspond to point C in Fig. 3.2.

The optimum solution can be approximated by reading the coordinates of C on the graph ($X_1 = 40$, $X_2 = 33$). A more precise solution can be obtained by solving the system of equations of the two lines that define C; i.e.:

$$X_1 = 40 \quad \text{and} \quad 2X_1 + 3X_2 = 180$$

Therefore, the optimal value of X_1, which we write as X_1^*, is:

$$X_1^* = 40 \text{ acres}$$

Substituting X_1^* in the second equation leads to:

$$X_2^* = \frac{180 - 80}{3} = 33.33 \text{ acres}$$

Therefore, the best strategy for the poet is to cultivate all the red pine he has. Of the hardwoods, he should manage approximately 33 acres, leaving the rest idle.

The optimum value of the objective function (i.e., the maximum revenue that the poet can obtain from his land) is then:

$$Z^* = 90X_1^* + 120X_2^* = 7600 \text{ dollars per year}$$

3.2 GRAPHIC SOLUTION OF THE PULP-MILL PROBLEM

The problem of the cooperative owning the pulp mill (as described in Sec. 2.3) consisted of finding X_1 and X_2, the daily production of mechanical and chemical pulp, such that:

$$\min Z = X_1 + 1.5X_2 \qquad \text{(pollution, BOD units per day)}$$

subject to:

$$
\begin{aligned}
X_1 \quad + X_2 &\geq 300 && \text{(employment target, workers)} \\
100X_1 + 200X_2 &\geq 40{,}000 && \text{(revenue target, dollars per day)} \\
X_1 \quad\quad &\leq 300 && \text{(mechanical pulping capacity, tons per day)} \\
X_2 &\leq 200 && \text{(chemical pulping capacity, tons per day)} \\
X_1, X_2 &\geq 0
\end{aligned}
$$

The graphic solution proceeds as follows: There are only two decision variables in the problem; these are measured along the axes of Fig. 3.3. We first determine the possible values of X_1 and X_2 (feasible region) and then find the point in this region that minimizes the objective function (optimum solution).

Feasible Region

The nonnegativity constraints (X_1, $X_2 \geq 0$) limit the possible solution to the positive part of the plane defined by the axes in Fig. 3.3.

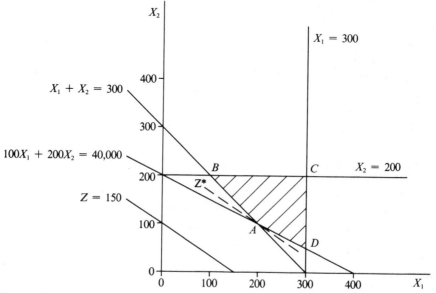

Figure 3.3 Graphic solution of the pulp-mill problem.

In addition, the employment constraint ($X_1 + X_2 \geq 300$ workers) limits the solution to the half plane to the right of the boundary line $X_1 + X_2 = 300$, which goes through the points ($X_1 = 0$, $X_2 = 300$) and ($X_2 = 0$, $X_1 = 300$). This can be verified by observing that for any point to the left of that line, say the origin, the employment constraint is not satisfied.

The feasible region is limited further by the revenue constraint ($100\,X_1 + 200\,X_2 \geq 40,000$ dollars per day). The boundary line of this constraint goes through the points ($X_1 = 0$, $X_2 = 200$) and ($X_2 = 0$, $X_1 = 400$). For the origin, the constraint is false; therefore, the feasible region lies to the right of the boundary line.

Finally, the possible solutions must satisfy the capacity constraints ($X_1 \leq 300$ tons per day of mechanical pulp, and $X_2 \leq 200$ tons per day of chemical pulp). Thus, the feasible area lies below the line $X_2 = 200$ and to the left of the line $X_1 = 300$.

In summary, the feasible region is inside the polygon $ABCD$ in Fig. 3.3. The figure shows that any solution to the problem requires the production of at least some of either kind of pulp, or both. More precisely, all objectives can be achieved simultaneously only if at least 100 tons per day of mechanical pulp are produced (point B in Fig. 3.3) and at least 50 tons per day of chemical pulp (point D).

Optimum Solution

The optimum solution is determined graphically by first finding the slope of the family of straight lines that correspond to the objective function. This is done by drawing the objective function for an arbitrary level of pollution, say $Z = 150$ units of BOD per day. The corresponding line, of equation $150 = X_1 + 1.5X_2$, goes through the points ($X_1 = 0$, $X_2 = 100$) and ($X_2 = 0$, $X_1 = 150$).

At the origin, $Z = 0$; thus, the value of the objective function decreases, the closer the line $Z = X_1 + 1.5X_2$ is to the origin. Consequently, the point in Fig. 3.3 that leads to the smallest possible value of Z while satisfying all the constraints is A.

The coordinates of A can be read directly from the graph. Alternatively, one can solve the system of equations that define the coordinates of A; namely:

$$X_1 + X_2 = 300 \qquad \text{and} \qquad 100\,X_1 + 200\,X_2 = 40,000$$

We eliminate X_1 by first multiplying the first equation left and right by 100 and then subtracting it from the second. This leads to:

$$X_2^* = \frac{10,000}{100} = 100 \text{ tons per day of chemical pulp}$$

Substituting this result in the first equation then gives:

$$X_1^* = 200 \text{ tons per day of mechanical pulp}$$

The value of the objective function that corresponds to this optimum operating strategy is

$$Z^* = X_1^* + 1.5X_2^* = 350 \text{ units of BOD per day}$$

This is the minimum amount of pollution that the pulp mill can produce while satisfying all other objectives.

3.3 THE SIMPLEX METHOD

The graphic method that we have used to solve the two previous examples is limited to cases in which there are at most two or three decision variables in the model. For large, practical problems, a more general technique is needed. The *simplex* method is an algebraic procedure that, when programmed on a computer, can at reasonable cost solve problems with thousands of variables and constraints.

This section will give only an overview of the method. The objective is to show the principles involved rather than the laborious arithmetic manipulations. The principles of the simplex are straightforward and elegant. The arithmetic is best left to a computer.

Slack Variables

The first step of the simplex method is to transform all inequalities in a linear-programming model into equalities. This is done because equalities are much easier to handle mathematically. In particular, a lot is known about the properties and solutions of systems of linear equations.

As an example, let's recall the formulation of the poet's problem (Sec. 2.2): Find the areas of red pine, X_1, and of hardwoods, X_2, to manage such that:

$$\max Z = 90X_1 + 120X_2 \qquad \text{dollars per year}$$

subject to:

$$X_1 \qquad\quad \le 40 \text{ acres of red pine}$$
$$X_2 \le 50 \text{ acres of hardwoods}$$
$$2X_1 + 3X_2 \le 180 \text{ days of work}$$
$$X_1, X_2 \ge 0$$

The first constraint can be changed into an equality by introducing one additional variable, S_1, called a *slack variable*, as follows:

$$X_1 + S_1 = 40 \qquad \text{and} \qquad S_1 \ge 0$$

Note that S_1 simply measures the area of red pine that is not managed. We proceed in similar fashion with each constraint and obtain the following transformed model: Find X_1, X_2, S_2, S_2, and S_3 such that:

$$\max Z = 90X_1 + 120X_2$$

subject to

$$
\begin{aligned}
X_1 &+ S_1 &&= 40 \\
X_2 &+ S_2 &&= 50 \\
2X_1 + 3X_2 &&+ S_3 &= 180 \\
\end{aligned}
$$
$$ X_1, X_2, S_1, S_2, S_3 \geq 0 $$

where S_2 and S_3 are the slack variables measuring unused hardwoods land and unused poet time, respectively.

Basic Feasible Solutions

Let us return to the geometric representation of the feasible solutions for this linear program. For convenience, it is reproduced in Fig. 3.4. The feasible region is the entire area inside the polygon $OABCD$. The equations of the boundary lines are shown in the figure.

A *basic feasible solution* of this linear program corresponds to the corners of the polygon $OABCD$; we shall call these corners the *extreme points* of the feasible region. For example, extreme point O corresponds to the basic feasible solution:

$$ (X_1, X_2, S_1, S_2, S_3) = (0, 0, 40, 50, 180) $$

since at O, $X_1 = X_2 = 0$, and thus, from the constraints, $S_1 = 40$, $S_2 = 50$, and $S_3 = 180$. Similarly, the extreme point A corresponds to the basic feasible solution:

$$ (X_1, X_2, S_1, S_2, S_3) = (0, 50, 40, 0, 30) $$

Note that in each basic feasible solution there are as many positive variables

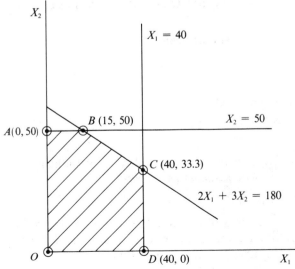

Figure 3.4 Extreme points and basic feasible solutions.

as there are constraints. Positive variables are called *basic variables*, while those equal to zero are nonbasic. In this example there are always three basic variables and two nonbasic. Verify that this is true for the basic feasible solutions corresponding to extreme points *B*, *C* and *D*.

This property of basic feasible solutions is general. In a linear program with n variables (including slacks) and m independent constraints, a basic feasible solution has m basic variables and $n - m$ nonbasic ones.

Theorem of Linear Programming

The fundamental theorem of linear programming, which we give without proof, states that if an optimum solution exists, then at least one basic feasible solution is optimum.

This theorem implies that in a linear program there may be one, many, or no optimum solution. The theorem is fundamental because it means that to solve a linear program, one needs to consider only a *finite* number of solutions —the basic feasible solutions that correspond to the extreme points of the feasible region.

Since the optimum solution of a linear program is a basic feasible solution, it has exactly as many positive variables as there are independent constraints. If a problem has 10 independent constraints and 10,000 variables, only 10 variables in the optimum solution have positive values; all the rest are zero.

There may be even fewer positive variables if all constraints are not independent. Assume that there are 10 constraints in a program and that we get only 8 positive variables in the optimal solution; then, two of the constraints in the model must be redundant. Two constraints result necessarily from the others; therefore, they can be omitted from the model without altering the results. We shall use redundancy in Chap. 6 to reduce the size of a forest-management problem considerably.

Solution Algorithm

Given the theorem of linear programming, a possible solution procedure (an algorithm) would be to calculate all the basic feasible solutions and find the one that maximizes or minimizes the objective function. But this is impractical for large problems because the number of basic feasible solutions may still be too large to examine all of them, even with a fast computer.

The simplex method uses, instead, a *steepest-ascent* algorithm. This algorithm consists of moving from one extreme point to the next adjacent extreme point of the feasible region in the direction that improves the objective function most.

The process can be visualized in this way: Think of the feasible region as a mountain, the peak of which corresponds to the optimum solution. A climber is lost in the fog and can barely see her feet. To reach the summit, she proceeds cautiously but surely. Keeping one foot fixed at one point, she moves

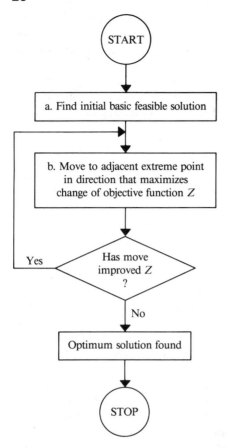

Figure 3.5 Flow chart for the simplex algorithm.

the other foot around her to find the direction of the next step that will raise her the most. When she has found it, she moves in that direction. If no step in any direction lifts the climber, she has reached the summit.

The flowchart in Fig. 3.5 summarizes the various steps of the simplex method. Step (a) consists of finding an initial feasible solution. In step (b) we move from one extreme point to an adjacent extreme point in the direction that maximizes the change in the objective function Z. If step (b) has improved the objective function, step (b) is repeated. The iterations continue until no improvement in Z occurs, indicating that the optimum solution has been obtained in the penultimate iteration.

Example

To illustrate the principles of the simplex method, we will solve the poet's problem by following the steps just described (see Fig. 3.6).

Step a: Find an initial basic feasible solution. The simplest one corresponds to point O in Fig. 3.6, that is:

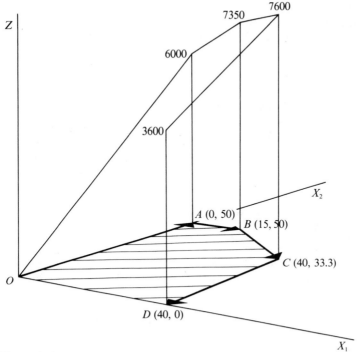

Figure 3.6 Iterations of simplex algorithm.

Nonbasic variables: $X_1 = 0$, $X_2 = 0$
Basic variables: $S_1 = 40$, $S_2 = 50$, $S_3 = 180$
Objective function: $Z_O = 0$

In this initial solution the three slack variables are basic.

Step b1: Since the coefficient of X_1 in the objective function is $90 per acre, while the coefficient of X_2 is 120, the objective function increases most by moving from O in the direction of OX_2 to the adjacent extreme point A, which corresponds to the new basic feasible solution:

Nonbasic variables: $S_2 = 0$, $X_1 = 0$
Basic variables: $X_2 = 50$, $S_1 = 40$, $S_3 = 30$
Objective function: $Z_A = 6000 per year

In the movement from extreme point O to A, the variable X_2 that was nonbasic has become basic, and the variable S_2 that was basic has become nonbasic. This is general; the algebraic equivalent of an adjacent extreme point is a basic feasible solution with one single different basic variable. The steepest ascent chooses as the new basic variable the one that most improves the objective function.

Since the value of the objective function for this new basic feasible solution is higher than the last one, we try another iteration.

Step b2: From extreme point A we now move in the direction OX_1, since this is the only way the objective function may be increased. The adjacent extreme point is B, corresponding to the following basic feasible solution:

Nonbasic variables: $S_2 = 0$, $S_3 = 0$

Basic variables: $X_1 = 15$, $X_2 = 50$, $S_1 = 25$

Objective function: $Z_B = \$7350$ per year

Step b3: Since the last iteration has increased Z, we try another one. The only way the objective function may be increased is by moving to the adjacent extreme point C, which corresponds to the basic feasible solution:

Nonbasic variables: $S_1 = 0$, $S_3 = 0$

Basic variables: $X_1 = 40$, $X_2 = 33.3$, $S_2 = 16.7$

Objective function: $Z_C = \$7600$ per year

Step b4: The last iteration having increased the objective function, we try another one. The next adjacent extreme point is D, corresponding to the basic feasible solution:

Nonbasic variables: $S_1 = 0$, $X_2 = 0$

Basic variables: $X_1 = 40$, $S_3 = 100$, $S_2 = 50$

Objective function: $Z_D = \$3600$ per year

This iteration has decreased the value of the objective function; therefore, the optimum solution is the basic feasible solution corresponding to extreme point C, as reached in the previous iteration.

3.4 DUALITY IN LINEAR PROGRAMMING

Every linear programming problem has a symmetrical formulation that is very useful in interpretating the solution, especially in determining how the objective function changes if one of the constraints changes slightly, everything else remaining equal. This symmetrical formulation is called the *dual* problem. It contains exactly the same data as the original (primal) problem, but rearranged. This different way of looking at the same data yields very practical information.

General Definition

Recall the standard formulation of the linear programming problem given in Chap. 2: Find X_1, X_2, ..., X_n, all nonnegative, such that:

$$\max Z = c_1 X_1 + c_2 X_2 + \cdots + c_n X_n$$

subject to:

$$a_{1,1}\,X_1 + a_{1,2}\,X_2 + \cdots + a_{1,n}\,X_n \le b_1$$
$$a_{2,1}\,X_1 + a_{2,2}\,X_2 + \cdots + a_{2,n}\,X_n \le b_2$$
$$\vdots$$
$$a_{m,1}X_1 + a_{m,2}X_2 + \cdots + a_{m,n}X_n \le b_m$$

The dual of this problem is a linear program with the following characteristics:

It has as many variables (dual variables) as there are constraints in the primal; all dual variables are positive or zero.

The objective function of the dual is minimized (it would be maximized if the primal problem were a minimization).

The coefficients a_{ij} in each column of the primal problem become coefficients in corresponding rows of the dual (first column becomes first row, second column second row, etc.).

The coefficients of the objective function in the primal become the coefficients on the right-hand side of the constraints, and vice versa.

The direction of the inequalities is reversed.

Consequently, the dual of the standard linear program given above is: Find $Y_1, Y_2, \ldots, Y_m$, all nonnegative, such that:

$$\min Z' = b_1 Y_1 + b_2 Y_2 + \cdots + b_m Y_m$$

subject to:

$$a_{1,1}\,Y_1 + a_{2,1}\,Y_2 + \cdots + a_{m,1}Y_m \ge c_1$$
$$a_{1,2}\,Y_1 + a_{2,2}\,Y_2 + \cdots + a_{m,2}Y_m \ge c_2$$
$$\vdots$$
$$a_{1,n}Y_1 + a_{2,n}Y_2 + \cdots + a_{m,n}Y_m \ge c_n$$

Duality is symmetrical in that the dual of the dual is the primal. This can be verified readily by applying the definition to the dual and thus recovering the initial formulation.

Applications of Duality

The duality theorem, one of the most important of linear programming, states that a solution of the dual exists if and only if the primal has a solution. Furthermore, the optimum values of the objective functions of the primal and of the dual are *equal*. In our notations, $Z^* = Z'^*$. We shall see the usefulness of this theorem in the following two examples.

Dual of the Poet's Problem Recall the linear-programming model we formulated for the poet who wanted to find what area of red-pine plantations and hardwoods he should manage (X_1, X_2) in order to maximize his annual revenues (Z) while spending no more than half his time in the woods:

$$\max Z = 90X_1 + 120X_2 \quad \text{dollars per year}$$

subject to:

$$X_1 \quad\quad \leq 40 \text{ acres of red pine}$$
$$X_2 \leq 50 \text{ acres of hardwoods}$$
$$2X_1 + 3X_2 \leq 180 \text{ days of work}$$
$$X_1, X_2 \geq 0$$

Applying the duality definition leads to the following dual problem:

$$\min Z' = 40Y_1 + 50Y_2 + 180Y_3$$

subject to:

$$Y_1 + 0Y_2 + 2Y_3 \geq 90$$
$$0Y_1 + Y_2 + 3Y_3 \geq 120$$
$$Y_1, Y_2, Y_3 \geq 0$$

Shadow Prices We know from Sec. 3.3 that the optimum value of the objective function for the primal problem is $Z^* = \$7600$ per year. The duality theorem states that the optimum value of the objective function for the dual must be equal; thus:

$$Z'^* = Z^* = \$7600 \text{ per year}$$

Thus, Z', the objective function of the dual, is measured in dollars per year. In addition, we know the units of measurement of the coefficients of the objective function in the dual because they were coefficients in the right-hand side of the primal. Consequently, one can infer the units of measurement of the dual variables by making the objective function of the dual homogeneous in its units. This leads to:

$$Z' = 40 \quad Y_1 \quad + 50 \quad Y_2 \quad + 180 \quad Y_3$$
$$(\$/y) \quad (a)(\$/a/y) \quad (a)(\$/a/y) \quad (d/y)(\$/d)$$

where a, y, and d refer to acre, year, and day, respectively. Verify that with these units for Y_1, Y_2, and Y_3 the two constraints of the dual are also homogeneous in their units.

Consequently, Y_1 expresses the value of using red-pine land in terms of dollars per acre per year. Similarly, Y_2 is the value of using hardwood land, and Y_3 is the value of the poet's time in dollars per day. In linear programming, Y_1, Y_2, and Y_3 are called *shadow prices*.

The qualifier "shadow" reminds us that these prices have nothing to do with market prices. For example, Y_3 is not the value of the poet's time on the free market; it is only an implicit value that reflects the activities in which the poet can engage (in this problem), i.e., managing red pine and hardwoods. The duality theorem indicates that when all resources are allocated in an optimal manner, the total implicit value of the resources is equal to the annual returns.

The shadow prices are very useful in getting the most out of the solution of a linear program. To see this, assume that the dual of the poet's problem has been solved. Designate the value of the shadow prices at the optimum by Y_1^*, Y_2^*, and Y_3^*. Then the expression of the objective function of the dual problem at the optimum is:

$$Z'^* = 40\ Y_1^* + 50\ Y_2^* + 180\ Y_3^*$$
$$\text{(\$/y)}\quad \text{(a)(\$/a/y)}\quad \text{(a) (\$/a/y)}\quad \text{(d/y)(\$/d)}$$

Thus, if the red-pine land that is available changes by a small amount k while the amounts of hardwoods land and poet's time remain fixed, the objective function would change by $k \times Y_1^*$ dollars per year.

To obtain the shadow prices, it is not necessary to solve the dual separately. The simplex method gives the optimal and dual solutions simultaneously. These are printed together by most computer programs. The optimum value of the shadow prices for this example are:

$Y_1^* = 10$ (red pine, $/a/y)

$Y_2^* = 0$ (hardwoods, $/a/y)

$Y_3^* = 40$ (poet's time, $/d)

These shadow prices show that one additional acre of red-pine land would increase the poet's annual revenues by $10. On the other hand, extra hardwoods would be worth nothing; this is consistent with the fact that in the optimum primal solution we found that 16.7 acres of hardwoods were not used. Finally, one additional day the poet spends in the woods is worth $40. This should be precious information for the poet to decide whether the financial and aesthetic benefits of versification are worth that much, or more.

In interpreting the dual solution, it should be kept in mind that a shadow price is strictly a *marginal* value; that is, it is useful to predict the change in the objective function that results from a small change in one of the constraints. For example, in the poet's problem the shadow price Y_2^* is zero as long as the hardwood constraint is not binding. The optimum solution found in Sec. 3.3 showed that some 16.7 acres of hardwoods should be left idle; thus, were the poet to sell more than 16.7 acres, the hardwoods constraint would be binding and the shadow price Y_2^* would become positive.

Dual of the Pulp Mill's Problem In using the shadow prices of a linear program, one must keep in mind the direction of the inequalities and whether the objective function is minimized or maximized. As an example of a slightly more involved interpretation of shadow prices, let us recall the pulping example formulated in Sec. 2.3; the primal of this problem was: Find X_1 and X_2, the tonnages of mechanical and chemical pulp produced daily, such that:

$$\min Z = X_1 + 1.5X_2 \quad \text{(units of BOD per day)}$$

subject to:

$$X_1 \quad + X_2 \geq 300 \qquad \text{(workers employed)}$$
$$100\,X_1 + 200\,X_2 \geq 40{,}000 \qquad \text{(daily revenues, \$)}$$
$$X_1 \qquad\qquad \leq 300 \qquad \text{(mechanical pulping capacity, t/d)}$$
$$X_2 \leq 200 \qquad \text{(chemical pulping capacity, t/d)}$$

$$X_1, X_2 \geq 0$$

This primal problem is not in the standard form; as a result, the shadow prices may have negative signs.

The solution of the pulp-mill problem gives the following shadow prices, in absolute values:

$Y_1^* = 0.5$ (BOD units per day per worker)

$Y_2^* = 0.005$ (BOD units per day per dollar)

$Y_3^* = 0.0$ (BOD units per day per ton)

$Y_4^* = 0.0$ (BOD units per day per ton)

We have inferred the unit of each shadow price by dividing the unit of the objective function by the unit of the right-hand-side constant for the constraint to which the shadow price applies.

The two easiest shadow prices to interpret are Y_3^* and Y_4^*. They are both zero because at the optimum solution there is excess capacity for both pulp-making processes. This can be checked in Fig. 3.3. Additional capacity would have no effect on pollution.

The labor constraint, instead, is binding. Its shadow price shows that pollution would increase by 0.5 units of BOD per day for each additional worker that the cooperative would try to employ. Similarly, pollution would increase by 0.005 units of BOD for each additional dollar of daily revenues that the cooperative would like to earn.

In many linear-programming problems, some careful thinking will bring useful information out of the dual solution. Nevertheless, there are situations in which shadow prices are either difficult to interpret or do not have any economic meaning because of the structure of the problem.

3.5 CONCLUSIONS

Linear programs with many constraints but with no more than two decision variables can be solved graphically. This graphic solution illustrates nicely the key steps in finding a solution: First we determine a feasible region: the set of all possible values of the decision variables. Then we find the point within that feasible region where the objective function is highest or lowest.

The simplex algorithm can be applied to a linear program of any size. It uses the fact that if optimum solutions exist, one of them is at a corner point of the feasible region. The simplex method consists, then, in moving from one extreme point of the feasible region to the next in the direction that contributes most to the objective function. When the objective function ceases to increase, the optimum solution has been found.

Computer programs that solve linear programs with variants of the simplex method yield two solutions: that of the original (primal) problem and that of its symmetrical problem, the dual. The dual has one variable for each constraint of the primal. The optimum solution of the dual variables, or shadow prices, have a very useful interpretation: They indicate the change in the objective function that would result from a unit change in the right-hand side of the constraints of the primal.

PROBLEMS

3.1. Consider the problem of the poet and his woods solved in Sec. 3.1. Suppose that the price of hardwood lumber goes up, increasing the return to managing hardwood land from $120 to $180 per acre per year. How would this change the objective function of this problem? Use the graphic solution method to determine the best way for the poet to allocate his time between managing red pine and hardwoods, given this change in his economic environment.

Perform the same analysis, assuming that the return from managing hardwoods goes up only to $135 per acre per year. If there still a unique "best" way for the poet to allocate his management efforts?

3.2. Consider the problem of pulp-mill management solved in Section 3.2. Suppose that the mill installs chemical recycling equipment that reduces the pollution associated with producing chemical pulp from 1.5 to 0.9 BOD units per day. How would this change the objective function of this problem's linear-programming model? Use the graphic solution method to determine the optimum amounts of mechanical and chemical pulp that the mill should produce after this change.

Do the same analysis assuming that the mill invests instead in solid-waste treatment equipment that reduces the pollution associated with producing mechanical pulp from 1.0 to 0.6 BOD units per day.

3.3. Use the graphic solution method to solve the linear-programming model developed for Prob. 2.3.

3.4. Use the graphic solution method to solve the linear-programming model developed for Prob. 2.6.

3.5. Use the simplex algorithm demonstrated in Sec. 3.3 to solve the linear-programming model developed for Prob. 2.6. Compare the graphic solution (Prob. 3.4) and the simplex solutions.

3.6. Use a linear-programming package to solve the pulp-mill management problem solved graphically in Sec. 3.2. Compare the solutions obtained by each method.

3.7. Consider the dual problem of the poet and his woods solved in Sec. 3.4. Change the right-hand-side constant in the time constraint from 180 to 182, and solve the modified problem with a computer. How much does the optimal value of the objective function change? Explain this change knowing that the shadow price for this constraint was $40 per day in the original problem.

3.8. Consider the dual problem of the poet and his woods solved in Sec. 3.4. Change the right-hand-side constant in the hardwood land constraint of the primal from

50 to 55, and solve the modified problem with a computer. How much does the optimal value of the objective function change? Explain this change if the shadow price for this constraint was zero dollars per acre of hardwood land in the original problem.

ANNOTATED REFERENCES

Blanning, R. W. 1974. The sources and uses of sensitivity information. *Interfaces* 4(4):32–38. (Describes four different methods for evaluating the sensitivity of a model to its parameters.)

Hillier, F. S., and G. J. Lieberman. 1986. *Introduction to operations research*. Holden-Day, Oakland. 888 pp. (Chapter 4 gives the details of the simplex solution algorithm, Chap. 5 discusses the theoretical foundations of the algorithm, and Chap. 6 discusses duality theory and sensitivity testing.)

Perry, C., and K. C. Crellin. 1982. The precise management meaning of a shadow price. *Interfaces* 12(2):61–63. (Precise explanation of shadow prices and how they can be used in decision making.)

Taha, H. A. 1982. *Operations research: An introduction*. Macmillan, New York. 848 pp. (Chapter 2 demonstrates the graphic solution of linear-programming models, Chap. 3 gives the details of the simplex-solution algorithm, and Chap. 4 discusses duality theory and sensitivity testing.)

Chapter 4

Even-Aged Forest Management: A First Model

4.1 INTRODUCTION

In the next five chapters we shall study applications of linear programming to timber *harvest scheduling*. Chapters 4 through 7 deal with even-aged forests, Chap. 8 with uneven-aged or selection forests.

Planning the future sequence of harvests on a forest is only one of the numerous tasks of a forest manager, but it is essential. One of the major purposes of forestry is still to produce wood. In fact, this is often the dominant goal for industrial forests. On public forests, an adequate balance between timber, recreation, water, and wildlife is almost always required. The nontimber goals constrain timber production. But within these constraints it is still desirable to organize timber production in the best possible way. Harvest scheduling models help us do that. In Chap. 9 we shall study goal programming techniques that may be used to weigh timber production against other goals.

4.2 DEFINITIONS

Even-aged management deals with forests composed of even-aged stands. In such a stand, individual trees originate at about the same time, either naturally or artificially. In addition, the stand has a specific termination date at which time all remaining trees are cut. That complete harvest is called a clear-cut.

Regeneration of even-aged stands may be done by planting or seeding. The latter may be natural. For example, in a shelterwood system a few old trees are left during the period of regeneration to provide seed and protect the young seedlings. Natural regeneration may continue for a few years after initial planting or seeding. Nevertheless, the basic management remains the same, it leads to a total harvest and a main crop when the stand reaches the *rotation* age. Sometimes, light cuts, called "thinnings," are done in even-aged stands before the final harvest.

An even-aged forest consists of a mosaic of even-aged stands of different age and size called "management units" or "compartments." The size of each unit must be sufficient for practical management, but it may vary greatly depending on the management objectives.

Even-aged management is used widely. Many valuable commercial species grow best in these full-light conditions. Furthermore, even-aged management has many economic advantages. Site preparation and planting can be done economically over large areas, using machinery and fire. Artificial regeneration allows the foresters to control the quality of the trees they use and to select the best trees. As trees grow, they all have approximately the same size. This standardization of products helps in mechanizing harvest and simplifies processing later on at the sawmill or pulp mill. Logging costs per unit of timber removed are lower in a clear-cutting operation than in a selection harvest because mechanical harvesting is easier and the area that must be covered to extract a specific amount of timber is smaller. Finally, the fresh vegetation that succeeds a clear-cut is a favorite food for some wildlife, like deer.

Nevertheless, even-aged management has some disadvantages. Clear-cut land is ugly. This has caused considerable opposition to clear-cutting on public forests. This aesthetic problem is sometimes reduced by clear-cutting only small tracts of land and by leaving a screen of trees around the clear-cut areas, at least until the young trees cover the ground.

4.3 EXAMPLE: CONVERTING SOUTHERN HARDWOODS TO PINE

In this example we shall study a linear-programming model, originally proposed by Curtis (1962), to manage the very simple forest represented in Fig. 4.1(*a*). There are only two compartments on this forest, labeled 1 and 2. Compartment 1 has an area of 120 acres, compartment 2 has 180. The two compartments are currently covered by southern hardwoods of low quality. However, they are on distinct soils and timber grows better on compartment 2 than on compartment 1.

One objective of the owner of this property is to convert the entire area to a pine plantation during a period of 15 years. The forest created at the end of this period should be *regulated*, with a rotation age of 15 years. That is to say, one-third of the forest should be covered with trees 0 to 5 years old, a third with trees 6 to 10 years old, and another third with trees 11 to 15 years old. This would lead to a pattern of age classes as shown in Fig. 4.1(*b*). Note, however, that the age classes do not have to be contiguous.

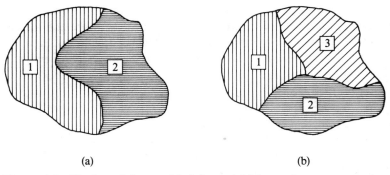

(a)   (b)

Figure 4.1   Hardwood forest with (*a*) two initial age classes converted to a regulated pine plantation with (*b*) three age classes.

Finally the owner desires to maximize the amount of wood that will be produced from this forest during the period of conversion to pine. The owner, however, will not cut any of the pine stands before they are 15 years old.

4.4 MODEL FORMULATION

Decision Variables

The harvest-scheduling problem consists in deciding *when*, *where*, and *how much* timber to cut in order to reach all management objectives. Since we use an even-aged silviculture, a natural decision variable should measure the area cut. More precisely, let $X_{i,j}$ be the area to be cut from initial compartment i, in period j, where i and j are integer subscripts. Here, i may take the value 1 or 2 since there are only two compartments in the initial forest. In order to keep the number of variables reasonably small, we must work with time units that are often longer than 1 year. Let us use a time unit of 5 years in this example. Therefore, j can take the value 1, 2, or 3 depending on whether a cut occurs during the first 5 years of the plan, the second 5 years, or the third.

Thus, all the possible harvests in compartment 1 are defined by the three decision variables $X_{1,1}, X_{1,2}, X_{1,3}$, while those possible on compartment 2 are $X_{2,1}, X_{2,2}, X_{2,3}$. Naturally, all the decision variables must be positive or zero.

Constraints

One set of constraints expresses the fact that, no matter what the choice of variables is, the entire forest must have been cut once during the management plan. This is necessary and sufficient to convert the entire land to southern pine. Therefore, for the first initial compartment we must have:

$$X_{1,1} + X_{1,2} + X_{1,3} = 120 \text{ acres}$$

and for the second:

$$X_{2,1} + X_{2,2} + X_{2,3} = 180 \text{ acres}$$

The second set of constraints expresses the requirement that the sequence of harvests be such that it leads to a regulated forest at the end of the 15-year plan. To achieve this, one must cut one-third of the forest every 5 years, and plant it to southern pine. In terms of the decision variables that we are using, this means that:

$$X_{1,1} + X_{2,1} = \frac{180 + 120}{3} = 100 \text{ acres}$$

This is the area cut during the first 5 years, which will be covered with trees 11 to 15 years old at the end of the conversion. Similarly, during the second period we must cut:

$$X_{1,2} + X_{2,2} = 100 \text{ acres}$$

and during the third period:

$$X_{1,3} + X_{2,3} = 100 \text{ acres}$$

Objective Function

One of the management objectives is to maximize the total *quantity* of hardwoods cut during the conversion. Therefore, the objective function must express the quantity cut in terms of the decision variables, $X_{i,j}$. Since these measure areas that were cut, we need data on the quantity available in each compartment, per unit area, throughout the 15 years of management. These data are shown in Table 4.1. The expected timber yield is given in tons, since the hardwoods are of poor quality, useful only to make pulp.

With these data, we can now express the objective function as a linear function of the decision variables. The expected total forest output during the 15-year management plan is:

$$Z = 16X_{1,1} + 23X_{1,2} + 33X_{1,3} + 24X_{2,1} + 32X_{2,2} + 45X_{2,3} \text{ tons}$$

where $16X_{1,1} + 23X_{1,2} + 33X_{1,3}$ is the expression of the tonnage of hardwood cut from the first compartment only and the remainder is that cut from the second compartment.

In similar fashion, one can calculate readily the tonnage produced during any one of the three periods, in terms of the decision variables. For example, the tonnage produced during the last 5 years of the plan is $33X_{1,3} + 45X_{2,3}$.

TABLE 4.1   PROJECTED YIELD BY COMPARTMENT AND 5-YEAR
MANAGEMENT PERIOD

Compartment		Tons per acre		
No.	Area (acres)	1st period	2nd period	3rd period
1	120	16	23	33
2	180	24	32	45

TABLE 4.2 LINEAR-PROGRAMMING TABLEAU FOR THE HARDWOODS-CONVERSION EXAMPLE

	$X_{1,1}$	$X_{1,2}$	$X_{1,3}$	$X_{2,1}$	$X_{2,2}$	$X_{2,3}$	
Z	16	23	33	24	32	45	
COM1	1	1	1				= 120
COM2				1	1	1	= 180
AGC1	1			1			= 100
AGC2		1			1		= 100
AGC3			1			1	= 100

In summary, the model that expresses the problem posed in this example has the following expression. Find $X_{1,1}$, $X_{1,2}$, $X_{1,3}$, $X_{2,1}$, $X_{2,2}$, $X_{2,3}$, all non-negative, such that:

$$\max Z = 16X_{1,1} + 23X_{1,2} + 33X_{1,3} + 24X_{2,1} + 32X_{2,2} + 45X_{2,3}$$

subject to

$$X_{1,1} + X_{1,2} + X_{1,3} = 120$$
$$X_{2,1} + X_{2,2} + X_{2,3} = 180$$
$$X_{1,1} + X_{2,1} = 100$$
$$X_{1,2} + X_{2,2} = 100$$
$$X_{1,3} + X_{2,3} = 100$$

A convenient way of displaying this model is shown in Table 4.2. This format gives all the information necessary to prepare the input for most computer programs. Each column has a name (that of the variables), and each row has also a name. In this manner, the position of each coefficient in the table is defined by the names of the column and row in which it is located.

4.5 SOLUTION

The solution of the model developed in the previous section is given Tables 4.3 and 4.4. The first table shows the sequence of harvests that would maximize the tonnage of wood cut in converting the initial compartments into a regulated pine forest.

The data in Table 4.3 express the area cut in every compartment and period. For example, 100 acres of the first compartment are cut during the first

TABLE 4.3 HARVEST PLAN THAT MAXIMIZES TONNAGE: AREA DATA

	Acres per period			
Compartment	1	2	3	Total acres
1	100	20	0	120
2	0	80	100	180
Total	100	100	100	300

TABLE 4.4   HARVEST PLAN THAT MAXIMIZES TONNAGE: TONNAGE DATA

Compartment	Tons per period			Total tons
	1	2	3	
1	1600	460	0	2060
2	0	2560	4500	7060
Total	1600	3020	4500	9120

5 years and the other 20 acres during the next 5 years. We would start cutting in compartment 2 only in the second period, removing 80 acres, and finishing the compartment in the last period.

The column totals show clearly that three blocks of 100 acres each are created every 5 years, thus leading to the regulated forest that is desired. Note that the three age classes that have been created cover land of different productivity. Therefore, regulation done in this way does not ensure that the periodic yield of the forest created at the end of the conversion will be constant. This may be unimportant to some owners. If it is important, the model should be changed to achieve this objective.

Table 4.4 shows the tonnage of wood harvested in each compartment of the forest, by period. The total volume produced by the forest is 9120 tons. This is the maximum that can be got. But it should be kept in mind that this may not be the only way of getting that amount. As the theorem of linear programming told us (see Sec. 3.3), the solution we get may just be one of several that would lead to the same value of the objective function.

4.6 MAXIMIZING PRESENT VALUE

The column totals in Table 4.4 show an increasing production from 1600 tons in the first 5 years to 3020 tons in the next 5, and 4500 tons in the last. This may be just what the owner wants, but someone who is selling wood for profit would prefer, other things being equal, to harvest more early and to invest the proceeds at a rate of return that is better than what is offered by the growth of the poor hardwoods.

The linear program we have used in the previous section can be used to determine the harvesting plan that will best meet these new requirements. To do this, the objective function must be changed. The coefficients of the decision variables should now express the *present value* of the timber cut on each acre of land and in each time period.

Since the timber is fairly homogeneous, the price should be the same everywhere. We will also ignore the possible changes in price over time. Consequently, the timber is arbitrarily assigned a value of $1 per ton.

The calculations will be done with a discount rate of 5 percent per year. The tonnage cut is accounted for at the middle of the 5-year period during which it has been done. For example, 1 acre cut from compartment 2 in period

TABLE 4.5 HARVEST PLAN THAT MAXIMIZES PRESENT
VALUE: TONNAGE DATA

Compartment	Tons per period			Total tons
	1	2	3	
1	0	2300	660	2960
2	2400	0	3600	6000
Total	2400	2300	4260	8960

3 yields the present value:

$$\frac{45}{(1 + 0.05)^{12.5}} = \$24.5 \text{ per acre}$$

This becomes the coefficient of $X_{2,3}$ in the objective function. The final
expression of the new objective function is then:

$$\max Z' = 14.2 X_{1,1} + 16.0 X_{1,2} + 17.9 X_{1,3}$$
$$+ 21.2 X_{2,1} + 22.2 X_{2,2} + 24.5 X_{2,3}.$$

The new optimal harvesting strategy, expressed in tonnage produced, is
shown in Table 4.5. The total volume produced by the forest is smaller than
when tonnage was maximized. However, more is produced in the first 5 years.
Also, the entire cut of the first 5 years is concentrated in the second compartment instead of the first.

4.7 A NOTE ON REDUNDANCIES

A careful examination of the solutions of the two linear programs in Tables
4.3 to 4.5 shows that there are always only four positive variables in the
optimum solution. Yet, there are five constraints in the linear program (see
Table 4.2).

In Sec. 3.3 we saw that the optimum solution found by the simplex
procedure, if it exists, is a basic feasible solution. We also observed that a
basic feasible solution has as many basic (positive) variables as there are
independent constraints. The key word here is *independent*. In fact, in the
hardwoods-conversion example, the five constraints are not independent. It
can be readily shown that any one of the constraints in Table 4.2 can be
obtained by algebraic manipulation of the other four.

For example, consider the constraint named AGC1 in Table 4.2. It can
be obtained in the following steps:

a. Add constraints COM1 and COM2, left and right, thus:

$$X_{1,1} + X_{1,2} + X_{1,3} + X_{2,1} + X_{2,2} + X_{2,3} = 300 \text{ acres}$$

b. Add constraints AGC2 and AGC3 in the same manner:

$$X_{1,2} + X_{1,3} + X_{2,2} + X_{2,3} = 200 \text{ acres}$$

Then, subtract the relationship obtained in **b** from that in **a**, left and right. This yields $X_{1,1} + X_{2,1} = 100$ acres; that is the constraint AGC1.

Verify that this can be done for any one of the constraints in this model. Any one results necessarily from the others; in other words, any one constraint is redundant and can be eliminated without changing the problem.

Redundancy is not very important in this case since it leads to the elimination of only one equation. However, in some situations hundreds of redundant equations can be present in a model. This increases unnecessarily the cost of solving a model. More importantly, it is useful to look for redundancies because this gives additional insight into the structure of the model. An example of this will be given in Chap. 6.

4.8 GENERAL FORMULATION

The model we have used to solve the small example of conversion of a southern hardwood forest to a regulated pine plantation can be generalized to handle as many initial compartments as necessary and as many time periods as desired.

In general, there are m initial compartments in the forest, and the management plan is established for p periods. Each decision variable $X_{i,j}$ measures the area cut from compartment i in period j. Therefore, the complete set of $m \times n$ decision variables is:

$$X_{1,1}, X_{1,2}, \ldots, X_{1,p}, X_{2,1}, \ldots, X_{m,1}, X_{m,2}, \ldots, X_{m,p} \text{ (all positive or zero)}$$

The area in each initial compartment is indicated by a_i. A first set of constraints states that the area cut from each compartment throughout the planning horizon must be equal to the area of that compartment, that is:

$$\sum_{j=1}^{p} X_{i,j} = a_i \qquad i = 1, \ldots, m$$

There are as many constraints of this kind as there are compartments.

A second set of constraints specifies the area that must be cut during each period, from the entire forest. Let this area be designated by y_j. Then:

$$\sum_{i=1}^{m} X_{i,j} = y_j \qquad j = 1, \ldots, p$$

There are as many constraints of this kind as there are periods in the plan. Any one of the constraints is redundant, due to the fact that:

$$\sum_{i=1}^{m} a_i = \sum_{j=1}^{p} y_j = A,$$

where A is the total area of the forest.

To write the general form of the objective function, let $c_{i,j}$ be the increase of the objective function due to cutting 1 acre of land from compartment i in period j, for example, tons of wood per acre or present value of the timber cut, per acre. Then, each harvest $X_{i,j}$ contributes the amount $c_{i,j}X_{i,j}$ to the objective function. The amount contributed by compartment i alone throughout the plan is:

$$\sum_{j=1}^{p} c_{i,j}X_{i,j}$$

and the amount contributed by the entire forest is:

$$Z = \sum_{i=1}^{m} \sum_{j=1}^{p} c_{i,j}X_{i,j}$$

In summary, the general form of the model is: Find $X_{i,j} \geq 0$ for $i = 1, \ldots, m$ and $j = 1, \ldots, p$ such that:

$$\max Z = \sum_{i=1}^{m} \sum_{j=1}^{p} c_{i,j}X_{i,j}$$

subject to:

$$\sum_{j=1}^{p} X_{i,j} = a_i \qquad i = 1, \ldots, m$$

$$\sum_{i=1}^{m} X_{i,j} = y_j \qquad j = 1, \ldots, p$$

In our example, all y_j's were equal to A/p, where A is the total area of the forest. This was done to obtain a regulated forest with rotation age p by the end of the plan.

4.9 CONCLUSIONS

This simple programming model for even-aged management is useful when one is able to decide in advance what area of the forest will be cut periodically, throughout the duration of the plan being drawn up. The optimum solution will then show the location and timing of harvests that lead to the highest production or to the highest present value.

For example, the model would be suitable in a situation where the dominant goal is to create a regulated forest in a specified amount of time. However, unless one is very firm about the regulation objective and on how to achieve it, this may not be the best way to manage a forest, especially if the goal is to maximize production or present value.

Another limitation of the model is that, once an area of a compartment is cut, the plantation that is created is not considered for harvest during the entire duration of the plan. This is adequate as long as the planning period is not too long, certainly not much longer than the desired rotation on the target forest. The models we will study in the next two chapters will help circumvent some of these limitations.

PROBLEMS

4.1. Consider the even-aged management model defined in Sec. 4.4. Would changing the compartment-acreage constraints from equalities to less-than-or-equal-to inequalities change the optimal solution to this model? Why? What about changing each period's conversion constraint from an equality to a greater-than-or-equal-to constraint? What about changing each period's conversion constraint from an equality to a less-than-or-equal-to constraint?

4.2. Would you expect the shadow prices for the same constraints in the models defined in Secs. 4.4 and 4.6 to be the same? If not, why should they differ? Verify your intuition by solving the two problems with a computer and comparing the values of these shadow prices.

4.3. Consider the even-aged management model defined in Sec. 4.4. Remove the first-period conversion constraint ($X_{1,1} + X_{2,1} = 100$), and solve the modified model with a computer to verify that this constraint is redundant. Perform this same test of redundancy for each of the other four constraints in the model.

4.4. Consider the even-aged management model defined in Sec. 4.6. Calculate new objective-function coefficients for this model, assuming a discount rate of 10 percent per year. Substitute these values into the objective function, and solve the modified model with a computer. How does the optimal harvesting plan change? Can you explain the reason for these changes?

4.5. The forester responsible for the management of 3038 acres of southern hardwoods wants to convert this land into a regulated pine plantation on a 20-year rotation. This may be accomplished over a 20-year planning horizon by harvesting and replanting one-quarter of the total forest area every 5 years. The initial forest can be divided into five relatively homogeneous compartments. The area in these compartments and the per-acre yield of hardwood pulpwood expected from each are shown below. Formulate a linear-programming model that the forester could use to determine which areas to harvest and replant in each 5-year period of the planning horizon to maximize pulpwood production.

PROJECTED PULPWOOD PRODUCTION (GREEN TONS PER ACRE)
PER COMPARTMENT PER PERIOD

Compartments	Area (acres)	Period			
		1	2	3	4
1	722	15.9	23.3	33.1	45.4
2	621	23.8	32.7	46.8	66.2
3	469	50.8	72.6	100.5	135.3
4	545	41.4	60.2	82.7	115.2
5	681	17.8	25.2	34.2	45.5

4.6. Solve the linear-programming model developed for Prob. 4.5 with a computer. Set up tables showing the total output during each 5-year period, and the area and the volume harvested from each compartment in each period.

4.7. Assuming a discount rate of 5 percent per year, and a pulpwood price of $20 per green ton, derive a new objective function for the linear-programming model developed for Prob. 4.5 that could be used to determine which areas to harvest and replant in each 5-year period of the planning horizon to maximize the present value of pulpwood production. (*Note*: Discount periodic pulpwood production values back to the present from the midpoint of each period, i.e., from 2.5, 7.5, 12.5, and 17.5 years.)

4.8. Solve the linear-programming model developed for Prob. 4.7 with a computer. Set up tables showing the total output during each 5-year period, and the area and the volume harvested from each compartment in each period. How does this harvest plan differ from that obtained in Prob. 4.6? What is the reason for the differences?

ANNOTATED REFERENCES

Curtis, F. H. 1962. Linear programming in the management of a forest property. *Journal of Forestry* 60(9):611–616. (The original source of the model described in this chapter, and one of the earliest applications of linear programming to forest management.)

Dykstra, D. P. 1984. *Mathematical programming for natural resource management.* McGraw-Hill, New York. 318 pp. (The Model I of Chap. 6, with regulatory constraints, is similar to the model of this chapter.)

Johnson, K. N., and H. L. Scheurman. 1977. Techniques for prescribing optimal timber harvest and investment under different objectives—Discussion and synthesis. *Forest Science* Monograph No. 18. 31 pp. (In their terminology, the model of this chapter is of the Model I type, because its variables preserve the identity of the initial harvesting units throughout the planning horizon.)

Leak, W. B. 1964. Estimating maximum allowable timber yields by linear programming. U.S. Forest Service Research Paper NE-17. Northeastern Forest and Range Experiment Station, Upper Darby. 9 pp. (Linear-programming formulation of the harvest scheduling problem similar to that used by Curtis.)

Chapter 5

Area and Volume Control Management with Linear Programming

5.1 INTRODUCTION

The model we shall study in this chapter was first developed by Loucks (1964); it is similar to Curtis' model studied in Chap. 4. The initial condition of the forest is represented in the same manner. There are several distinct compartments, each one is treated as a separate management unit. The decision variables are the same: they refer to the area cut from each compartment in different periods of the management plan.

One difference with this model lies in the way the regulation objective is handled. In the model of Curtis, this was done in a very rigid manner. For every time period, a specified fraction of the entire forest area was clear-cut. Here, instead, regulation is taken less literally, the regulatory constraints simply guide the total output of the forest. The regulatory constraints try to ensure that the amount of timber removed does not exceed the long-term potential output by any excessive amount. This is done by using the traditional management concepts of area and volume control.

Another difference in this model lies in the attention given to the periodic production of the forest throughout the management plan. In the model of Chap. 4, production could vary from period to period by any amount as long as production was maximized and regulation achieved. However, foresters often want to produce a quantity of timber that does not vary too much over time. For example, managers of national forests must, by law, make sure that the forest produces a nondeclining, even flow of timber. That is to say, the amount produced may increase over time, but it should not lessen. Foresters are allowed to depart from year to year from the planned even-flow level, due to special circumstances. But, decade after decade, even flow is still the rule.

5.2 PRELIMINARY DEFINITIONS

Before going into an example of the model, let us define the concepts of area and volume control, as we shall use them here. Before proceeding, we should stress that area and volume control mean slightly different things to different people. The definition given here is a somewhat flexible interpretation. We shall use a more rigid interpretation in the model of Chap. 14.

The concepts of area and volume control management are based on the model of the *regulated forest*. Let A be the area of a forest. This forest is regulated if it consists of r blocks of equal area, A/r, each one covered by a stand of trees in a single age class. Therefore, if the time unit is 1 year, the youngest age class consists of trees that are 0 to 1 year of age, the second oldest age class has trees 1 to 2 years old, and so on, to the oldest age class that consists of trees $r - 1$ to r years old.

Every year, the oldest age class is cut, starting with the oldest trees. For that reason, r is referred to as the *rotation age*. Let v_r be the volume per acre of timber in the oldest age class, say in cubic feet (ft^3). Then, the yearly production of the regulated forest is:

$$Q_r = \frac{A}{r} \times v_r$$
$$\text{(ft}^3/\text{y)} \quad \text{(a/y)} \quad \text{(ft}^3/\text{a)}$$

With this formula it is easy to determine the best rotation, or at least the rotation that maximizes the yearly production of timber. It is $r*$, the value of r for which v_r/r is greatest.

That is to say, the optimum rotation is equal to the age of a stand when its "mean annual increment" is greatest. We shall see in the next chapter how to calculate the rotation that maximizes the discounted value of revenues.

No matter what rotation age is used, the yearly production of the regulated forest can be maintained *perpetually*, and it remains *constant* as long as the productivity of the land, measured by v_r, does not change.

It is this image of a rotation, so similar to the movement of a clock, and the idea of a perpetual and constant output, akin to perpetual celestial motion, that may explain the fascination of pioneer foresters of the sixteenth and seventeenth centuries with the model of a regulated forest. Even now, the model is used constantly, almost automatically, by foresters.

We have already used briefly the concept of a regulated forest in the previous chapter, we shall use it in the next one, and it plays a key role in the methods of area and volume control. The purpose of these methods is to ensure that no more is cut from a particular forest during the time spanned by the management plan than what the forest could produce in the long run, if it were regulated.

Area-control management is based on the observation that, were a regulated forest of area A managed for y years, the area that would be cut in it would be $y(A/r)$ acres. Area-control management proceeds to suggest that, regardless of the status of the current forest, the area cut from it during a period of y years be at most $y(A/r)$.

Volume-control management applies the principle of area control to standing volume instead of area. It suggests that at most the fraction y/r of the original standing volume be cut from the existing forest during the y years for which the harvest schedule is being drawn up.

Both area-control and volume-control methods are largely rules of thumb. In no way are they optimal guides. It should be clear, for example, that area control makes little sense in a forest that has very little timber on it. In that respect, volume control has the advantage that it takes into consideration the condition of the growing stock, but it is still arbitrary. Nevertheless, both management principles are widely used. We shall see in the next sections how they can be integrated into a programming model.

5.3 EXAMPLE: OPTIMIZING THE YIELD OF A LOBLOLLY-PINE PLANTATION

Consider a loblolly-pine forest of 500 acres, with two age classes, one of trees 21 to 25 years old, covering an area of 200 acres and the other one of trees 41 to 45 years old.

The owner of the forest wants to maximize the volume that the forest will produce during the next 15 years. In addition, the amount of timber available should increase regularly by 10 percent every 5 years. The silviculture is even-aged management, with clear-cutting followed by planting. The initial plan is to use area-control management, but the consequences of volume control should also be investigated.

5.4 MODEL FORMULATION

Decision Variables

As in the model of Chap. 4, the decision variables that define the future harvest schedule most simply are the areas cut from each initial compartment in every period of the plan. To keep the number of variables small, we must choose a sufficiently long lapse of time for each period, lets say 5 years. In this example, this leads to the following decision variables: $X_{1,1}$, $X_{1,2}$, $X_{1,3}$, $X_{2,1}$, $X_{2,2}$, $X_{2,3}$, where the first subscript of each variable refers to the compartment where the cut occurs and the second subscript refers to the time period.

Objective Function

The objective function expresses the total volume of timber cut during the 15 years of the plan as a linear function of the decision variables. To write it, we

TABLE 5.1   EXPECTED VOLUME FOR A LOBLOLLY-PINE FOREST

Compartment	Volume (1000 ft^3 / a)		
	1st period	2nd period	3rd period
1	1.2	2.3	2.5
2	3.1	3.2	3.5

need the volume per acre that is expected from each compartment at different points in time in the future. These data are presented in Table 5.1. Using these data, we can now express the objective function as:

$$Z = 1.2X_{1,1} + 2.3X_{1,2} + 2.5X_{1,3} + 3.1X_{2,1}$$
$$+ 3.2X_{2,2} + 3.5X_{2,3} \; (1000 \; \text{ft}^3)$$

The object of the problem is to find the values of the decision variables that make this function as large as possible, subject to the constraints expressing the other management objectives and the amounts of resources that can be used.

There are three kinds of constraints in this model: first, constraints that refer to the limited land available; second, constraints expressing the desired pattern of production during the plan; finally, constraints subjecting the management alternatives to either area-control or volume-control management.

Land Availability Constraints

The area of land that is cut in each compartment cannot exceed the area available. As in the harvest scheduling model of Chap. 4, land that is planted during the management plan will not be cut before the end of the plan. However, in contrast with that model, the entire area of each compartment does not need to be cut. Thus, the land availability constraints take the form:

$$X_{1,1} + X_{1,2} + X_{1,3} \leq 200 \; \text{acres, for the first compartment,}$$

and

$$X_{2,1} + X_{2,2} + X_{2,3} \leq 300 \; \text{acres for the second compartment.}$$

Timber-Flow Constraints

These constraints express the fact that the amount of timber produced by the forest should increase regularly by at least 10 percent every 5 years. Let V_1, V_2, and V_3 be the amount of timber cut during the first, second, and third 5-year periods of the plan. Then, a possible pattern of production that satisfies the management objectives is:

$$V_2 = 1.10V_1 \quad \text{and} \quad V_3 = 1.10V_2$$

The expression of V_1, V_2, and V_3 in terms of the decision variables is:

$$V_1 = 1.2X_{1,1} + 3.1X_{2,1}$$
$$V_2 = 2.3X_{1,2} + 3.2X_{2,2}$$
$$V_3 = 2.5X_{1,3} + 3.5X_{2,3}$$

The final expression of the timber flow constraints is then:

$$2.3X_{1,2} + 3.2X_{2,2} = 1.1(1.2X_{1,1} + 3.1X_{2,1})$$

and

$$2.5X_{1,3} + 3.5X_{2,3} = 1.1(2.3X_{1,2} + 3.2X_{2,2})$$

or, more compactly:

$$2.3X_{1,2} + 3.2X_{2,2} - 1.3X_{1,1} - 3.4X_{2,1} = 0$$

and

$$2.5X_{1,3} + 3.5X_{2,3} - 2.5X_{1,2} - 3.5X_{2,2} = 0$$

Area-Control Constraint

If the forest is managed under the area-control system, only the fraction y/r of the entire forest area may be cut during the entire duration of the plan, where r is the rotation age and in our example, $y = 15$ years.

Since the objective of the owner is to maximize the volume of timber produced by this forest, a suitable value of the rotation is the age that maximizes the mean annual increment. For loblolly pine on site 70, this occurs at 30 years. The productivity is then about 83.3 $ft^3/a/y$.

Given this rotation age, the most that can be cut from the loblolly-pine forest in the example when area control is used is $500 \times (15/30) = 250$ acres. The expression of the area control constraint is then:

$$X_{1,1} + X_{1,2} + X_{1,3} + X_{2,1} + X_{2,2} + X_{2,3} \le 250 \text{ acres.}$$

Volume-Control Constraint

If, instead, we choose volume-control management, at most one-thirtieth of the standing volume can be cut during the average year of the plan, which is half of the volume in 15 years. However, Loucks suggests a correction for the fact that the standing volume of the forest will grow during the 15 years. For that reason, Loucks' volume-control formula uses the average expected volume in any 5-year period of the entire plan. That is:

$$[(1.2 \times 200 + 3.1 \times 300) + (2.3 \times 200 + 3.2 \times 300)$$
$$+ (2.5 \times 200 + 3.5 \times 300)]/3 = 1380 \quad (1000 \text{ ft}^3)$$

The maximum volume that can be cut during 15 years, under volume control is $(15/30)1380 = 690$ (1000 ft^3). Consequently, the final form of the volume-control constraint for this sample problem is:

$$1.2X_{1,1} + 2.3X_{1,2} + 2.5X_{1,3} + 3.1X_{2,1} + 3.2X_{2,2} + 3.5X_{2,3} \le 690$$

In summary, the linear-programming model for the management plan of the loblolly-pine plantation in the example is:

Find $X_{1,1}, X_{1,2}, \ldots, X_{2,3}$, all nonnegative, such that:

$$\max Z = 1.2X_{1,1} + 2.3X_{1,2} + 2.5X_{1,3} + 3.1X_{2,1} + 3.2X_{2,2} + 3.5X_{2,3}$$

subject to:

Land availability:

$$X_{1,1} + X_{1,2} + X_{1,3} \leq 200$$
$$X_{2,1} + X_{2,2} + X_{2,3} \leq 300$$

Timber flow:

$$2.3X_{1,2} + 3.2X_{2,2} - 1.3X_{1,1} - 3.4X_{2,1} = 0$$
$$2.5X_{1,3} + 3.5X_{2,3} - 2.5X_{1,2} - 3.5X_{2,2} = 0$$

Area control:

$$X_{1,1} + X_{1,2} + X_{1,3} + X_{2,1} + X_{2,2} + X_{2,3} \leq 250$$

or

Volume control:

$$1.2X_{1,1} + 2.3X_{1,2} + 2.5X_{1,3} + 3.1X_{2,1} + 3.2X_{2,2} + 3.5X_{2,3} \leq 690$$

The same model is presented in Table 5.2 in a form appropriate to prepare the input of a computer program. All the parameters of the model are entries in the table. Each column is defined by the name of a variable, each row or constraint by a four-character name. Each parameter in the linear program is then defined by the name of the row and of the column to which it belongs.

In Table 5.2, the blank line that separates the two constraints AREC and VOLC indicates that usually only one of them is selected. That is, the forest is either managed under area *or* volume control. In the next section we will examine the optimum solutions corresponding to these two management

TABLE 5.2 LINEAR-PROGRAMMING TABLEAU FOR AREA AND VOLUME CONTROL

	$X_{1,1}$	$X_{1,2}$	$X_{1,3}$	$X_{2,1}$	$X_{2,2}$	$X_{2,3}$	
Z	1.2	2.3	2.5	3.1	3.2	3.5	
COM1	1.0	1.0	1.0				≤ 200
COM2				1.0	1.0	1.0	≤ 300
FLO1	-1.3	2.3		-3.4	3.2		$= 0$
FLO2		-2.5	2.5		-3.5	3.5	$= 0$
AREC	1.0	1.0	1.0	1.0	1.0	1.0	≤ 250
VOLC	1.2	2.3	2.5	3.1	3.2	3.5	≤ 690

Note: The constraint AREC is used for area control management, VOLC for volume control.

strategies. Alternatively, the two constraints can both be left in the model but, in general, only one of them will be binding at the optimum.

5.5 SOLUTIONS

The solutions of the loblolly-pine example are reported in Table 5.3 for the case of area-control management and in Table 5.4 for volume control.

The data in the two tables show that the two management strategies do not lead to very different results. For example, under both systems the first compartment remains completely untouched. More land is cut under area control (250 acres instead of 212) and more total volume is also produced. In both cases, the quantity of timber cut every 5 years rises regularly by 10 percent, as required by the management objectives.

Nevertheless, it is unclear how good these control procedures really are. The usefulness of any regulatory system depends in part on the long-term objectives of the forest owner, and on the suitability of the forest that is left at the end of the plan to meet these objectives.

For example, Table 5.4 shows that if the owner of this forest opts for volume control, at the end of the 15 years she will have a forest that has 72 acres in the youngest age class (trees 0 to 5 years old), 72 acres in the second age class (trees 6 to 10 years old), and 68 acres of trees 11 to 15 years old. In addition, the 200 acres of compartment 1 will be covered by trees 36 to 40 years old and there will be $300 - 212 = 88$ acres of land left from compart-

TABLE 5.3 OPTIMUM HARVEST PLAN UNDER AREA
CONTROL MANAGEMENT

Compartment	Period			Total
	1	2	3	
1 Area cut (acres)	0	0	0	0
Volume (1000 ft^3)	0	0	0	0
2 Area cut (acres)	80	85	85	250
Volume (1000 ft^3)	248	272	297	817

TABLE 5.4 OPTIMUM HARVEST PLAN UNDER VOLUME
CONTROL MANAGEMENT

Compartment	Period			Total
	1	2	3	
1 Area cut (acres)	0	0	0	0
Volume (1000 ft^3)	0	0	0	0
2 Area (acres)	68	72	72	212
Volume (1000 ft^3)	209	229	251	690

Note: Figures may not add up exactly due to round off errors.

ment 2 covered with trees 56 to 60 years old, which is well beyond the rotation age of maximum mean annual increment (30 years).

The value of such a forest, including the land on which it grows, lies in its long-term ability to produce timber, but what it can produce is not easy to determine. For that purpose it would be useful to require that the forest be in some form of a steady-state regime when the end of the plan is reached. In the next chapter we will study a model that permits us to do this in a flexible way.

Meanwhile, the area and volume control formulas remain simple and, for that reason, useful rules to follow in laying out timber harvesting schedules. They do, at least in a rough manner, ensure that the long-term productive potential of the forest is not exceeded.

5.6 ALLOWING FOR DIFFERENT ROTATIONS

In the example used above, it was assumed that the two compartments differed only by the age of the stands they were carrying, but that the site quality was the same in both. This led to the choice of a same rotation to manage the entire forest (30 years, the age at which mean annual increment is maximum). However, if the sites, or the species grown on the two compartments, are so different that they justify different rotation ages, then the model must be modified.

Assume, for example, that 30 years is the appropriate rotation for the second compartment only, but that it should be 40 years on the first compartment because of its lower site quality. Then, there should be two area control constraints in the model, namely:

For compartment 1: $X_{1,1} + X_{1,2} + X_{1,3} \leq \left(\dfrac{15}{40}\right)200 = 75$ acres

For compartment 2: $X_{2,1} + X_{2,2} + X_{2,3} \leq \left(\dfrac{15}{30}\right)300 = 150$ acres

These two constraints would now replace the area control constraint AREC in the linear-programming tableau in Table 5.2.

Similarly, if volume control were applied, we would now have two constraints instead of the constraint VOLC, namely:

For compartment 1:

$$1.2X_{1,1} + 2.3X_{1,2} + 2.5X_{1,3} \leq \left(\frac{15}{40}\right)\left[200\frac{(1.2 + 2.3 + 2.5)}{3}\right]$$
$$\leq 150 \ (1000 \ ft^3)$$

For compartment 2:

$$3.1X_{2,1} + 3.2X_{2,2} + 3.5X_{2,3} \leq \left(\frac{15}{30}\right)\left[300\frac{(3.1 + 3.2 + 3.5)}{3}\right]$$
$$\leq 490 \ (1000 \ ft^3)$$

5.7 GENERAL FORMULATION

The model we have just used in the small example of the loblolly-pine forest can be generalized to deal with a forest that has many compartments and with a management plan as long as desired.

Using the same general notations as in Chap. 4, we may initially have m compartments. The plan is to be drawn for p periods. Then the set of decision variables is $X_{i,j}$, with $i = 1, \ldots, m$ and $j = 1, \ldots, p$. In all, there are $m \times p$ variables. Each one refers to the area cut from compartment i in period j.

The object of the problem is to find the values of the $X_{i,j}$'s such that the total amount of timber produced throughout the plan be maximum. The general form of the objective function is then:

$$\max Z = \sum_{i=1}^{m} \sum_{j=1}^{p} v_{i,j} X_{i,j}$$

where $v_{i,j}$ is the expected volume per acre in compartment i and period j. The summation over j expresses the volume produced by a specific compartment i throughout the plan, and the summation over i then expresses the volume produced by the entire forest. The objective function may be given another meaning by changing the coefficients $v_{i,j}$. For example, a manager may be interested in maximizing the discounted value of the timber produced. In that case, $v_{i,j}$ would be replaced by the expected discounted value resulting from one acre of land cut in compartment i during period j.

The land-availability constraints state that at most the area in each compartment may be cut during the plan:

$$\sum_{j=1}^{p} X_{i,j} \le a_i \qquad i = 1, \ldots, m$$

where a_i is the area of compartment i. There are m constraints of this kind, one for each compartment. In this model, an area that has been cut cannot be cut again before the end of the plan. Thus, the model is suitable only as long as the length of the plan is shorter than the rotation.

The timber-flow constraints express the relationship between the volume cut in one period and that cut in the next. Let f_j be the fraction by which the cut in j must exceed that in $j - 1$. Then, the general expression of the flow constraint is:

$$\sum_{i=1}^{m} v_{i,j} X_{i,j} - (1 + f_j) \sum_{i=1}^{m} v_{i,j-1} X_{i,j-1} = 0 \qquad j = 2, \ldots, p$$

There are $p - 1$ constraints of this kind.

Finally, if area control is used, the total area cut cannot exceed yA/r, where y is the length of the plan and r is the rotation, expressed in the same unit of time, and A is the entire area of the forest. In terms of the decision variables, this gives:

$$\sum_{i=1}^{m} \sum_{j=1}^{p} X_{i,j} \leq y \frac{A}{r}$$

If volume control is used instead, the volume cut cannot exceed the fraction y/r of the average expected growing stock. The expected growing stock in any period, j, is:

$$S_j = \sum_{i=1}^{m} v_{i,j} a_i$$

and the average growing stock, over the entire plan is:

$$S = \frac{1}{p} \sum_{j=1}^{p} S_j$$

so that the final expression of the volume control constraint is:

$$\sum_{i=1}^{m} \sum_{j=1}^{p} v_{i,j} X_{i,j} \leq \frac{y}{r} S$$

As noted in the example, there may be more than one area or volume constraint if the rotation age is not the same throughout the forest. In that case, there is one area or volume constraint for each compartment or group of compartments that is managed under the *same rotation* age. The expression of the constraints remains the same, except that the subscript i in the area and volume constraints refers only to compartments that are managed under the same rotation.

5.8 CONCLUSIONS

In this chapter we have formulated and applied a model of timber harvest scheduling in an even-aged forest that uses the old concepts of area and volume control, embedded within a linear program. Area and volume control are expressed as constraints limiting either the total area or the total volume cut during the duration or the plan. Additional constraints regulate the volume of timber produced over time. The linear program is used to maximize the volume produced, or its discounted value, within these constraints.

This model does not allow an area to be cut twice during the period of the plan, a limitation that applied also to the model of Chap. 4. This may not be a serious problem as long as the management plan is shorter than one rotation. A more serious criticism, perhaps, is that area and volume control are somewhat arbitrary rules of thumb. It is hard to determine the value of the forest left at the end of the plan under these policies. Furthermore, they may be limiting the cutting alternatives too much, eliminating possibilities that would increase the achievement of the management objectives. The model we shall study in the next chapter will eliminate some of these limitations.

PROBLEMS

5.1. A forest is composed of three even-aged compartments of ponderosa pine. The area of each compartment is shown below, along with projected per acre board foot lumber volume on each during the next three 5-year periods. With volume control, how much volume could be harvested over the next 15 years of a 65-year rotation, based on the average forest volume over all three periods? For a harvest scheduling model based on 5-year periods, how would you express this constraint? (Use $X_{i,j}$ to represent the number of acres harvested in compartment i in period j.)

PROJECTED LUMBER VOLUME PER ACRE (THOUSAND BOARD FEET)
FOR A PONDEROSA PINE FOREST

Compartment	Area (acres)	Period		
		1	2	3
1	2450	15	17	20
2	3760	20	27	34
3	8965	14	16	19

5.2. For the ponderosa pine forest described in Prob. 5.1, how many acres could be harvested under area control over the next 15 years of a 65-year rotation? For a harvest scheduling model based on 5-year periods, how would you express this constraint? (Use $X_{i,j}$ to represent the number of acres harvested in compartment i in period j.)

5.3. For the ponderosa pine forest described in Prob. 5.1, assume that compartment 2 is on a better site than compartments 1 and 3, so that the former should be managed on a 55-year rotation, and the latter on a 75-year rotation. With volume control, how much volume could be harvested over the next 15 years in compartment 1 alone? In compartments 2 and 3 together? For a harvest scheduling model based on 5-year periods, how would you express these two constraints? (Use $X_{i,j}$ to represent the number of acres harvested in compartment i in period j.)

5.4. For the ponderosa pine forest described in Prob. 5.1, again assume that compartment 2 is on a better site than compartments 1 and 3, so that the former should be managed on a 55-year rotation, and the latter on a 75-year rotation. With area control, how much volume could be harvested over the next 15 years in compartment 1 alone? In compartments 2 and 3 together? For a harvest-scheduling model based on 5-year periods, how would you express these two constraints? (Use $X_{i,j}$ to represent the number of acres harvested in compartment i in period j.)

5.5. In a harvest scheduling model for the ponderosa pine forest described in Prob. 5.1 with a 15-year planning horizon and 5-year periods, how would you constrain harvests to an equal periodic volume? How would you constrain the volume to increase by 25 percent per period? (Use $X_{i,j}$ to represent the number of acres harvested in compartment i in period j.)

5.6. In a harvest scheduling model for the ponderosa pine forest described in Prob. 5.1 with a 15-year planning horizon and 5-year periods, how would you constrain harvests to vary by no more than 10 percent, plus or minus, from the volume harvested in the previous period? (Use $X_{i,j}$ to represent the number of acres harvested in compartment i in period j. *Note:* This requires the use of two inequality constraints.)

5.7. The forester for a paper company in Wisconsin needs to develop a long-term harvesting plan for the company's 6000 acres of aspen forestland. This plan must cover a 20-year planning horizon, and should be broken down into five 4-year operating periods. The company's land has been divided into four compartments. The area in each compartment is shown below, along with the projected periodic per-acre volume of aspen pulpwood on each during the next five 4-year periods. Having been recently harvested, compartment 4 cannot be harvested again during the first two periods. Company policy dictates that this land must supply a constant periodic output of pulpwood, and that its production of pulpwood should be maximized, i.e., it should be managed on the rotation that maximizes mean annual increment. For all four compartments, this implies a 40-year rotation.

   Using area control, how many acres could be harvested in any 4-year period? Over the 20-year planning horizon?

   Using volume control, how much volume could be harvested in any 4-year period? Over the 20-year planning horizon?

PROJECTED PULPWOOD VOLUME PER ACRE (THOUSAND CUBIC FEET) FOR AN ASPEN FOREST

Compartment	Area (acres)	Period 1	2	3	4	5
1	1750	3.1	3.4	3.7	3.9	4.1
2	1610	4.4	4.5	4.4	4.9	4.2
3	1340	0.8	1.3	1.7	2.1	2.4
4	1300	—	—	2.5	2.9	3.2

5.8. Formulate an area-control harvest-scheduling model for Prob. 5.7 that could be used to determine the harvest schedule that would maximize total harvest over the planning horizon.

5.9. Solve the linear-programming model developed for Prob. 5.8 with a computer. Display the solution in tables showing the total output during each 4-year period and of the area and the volume harvested from each compartment in each period.

5.10. For the situation described in Prob. 5.7, formulate a volume-control harvest-scheduling model to determine the harvest schedule that would minimize the total area harvested over the planning horizon.

5.11. Solve the linear-programming model developed for Prob. 5.10 with a computer, and display the solution in tables showing the total output during each 4-year period, and the area and the volume harvested from each compartment in each period.

ANNOTATED REFERENCES

Clutter, J. L., J. C. Fortson, L. V. Pienaar, G. H. Brister, and R. L. Baily. 1983. *Timber management: A quantitative approach*. Wiley, New York. 333 pp. (The "XYZ Timber Co." problem in Sec. 10.2 is a harvest-scheduling problem similar to that of this chapter, but with harvest-volume constraints determined by contractual obligations instead of biological productivity.)

Davis, L. S., and K. N. Johnson. 1986. *Forest management*. McGraw-Hill, New York. 790 pp. (Chapter 14 covers volume control, area control, and other classical approaches to forest regulation. The Model I version of the "Daniel Picket Forest" problem in Chap. 15 is an area-control problem similar to the one in this chapter, but with several multiple-use constraints typical of public forest management.)

Dykstra, D. P. 1984. *Mathematical programming for natural resource management*. McGraw-Hill, New York. 318 pp. (The Model I in Chap. 6 with inventory and flow constraints, is similar to the one in this chapter.)

Johnson, K. N., and H. L. Scheurman. 1977. Techniques for prescribing optimal timber harvest and investment under different objectives—Discussion and synthesis. *Forest Science* Monograph No. 18. 31 pp. (In their classification, the model of this chapter, like that of Chap. 4, is of the Model I type, because it preserves the identity of the initial harvesting units throughout the planning horizon.)

Loucks, D. P. 1964. The development of an optimal program for sustained-yield management. *Journal of Forestry* 62(7):485–490. (This is the original formulation of the harvest-scheduling problem treated in this chapter.)

Navon, D. I. 1971. Timber RAM: A long-range planning method for commercial timber lands under multiple-use management. U.S. Forest Service Research Paper PSW-70. Pacific Southwest Forest and Range Experiment Station, Berkeley. 22 pp. (One of the first computer systems for building harvest-scheduling models of the kind discussed in this chapter. Designed for public forests, but applicable to industrial forests as well.)

Thompson, E. F., B. G. Halterman, T. J. Lyon, and R. L. Miller. 1973. Integrating timber and wildlife management planning. *Forestry Chronicle* 49(6):247–250. (Harvest-scheduling problem similar to the one in this chapter, but incorporating both area- and volume-control constraints to achieve multiple-use goals.)

Ware, G. O., and J. L. Clutter. 1971. A mathematical programming system for the management of industrial forests. *Forest Science* 17(4):428–445. (Another early computer system for building harvest-scheduling models of the kind discussed in this chapter. Designed for industrial forests.)

Chapter 6

A Dynamic Model of the Even-Aged Forest

6.1 INTRODUCTION

The models we studied in the two previous chapters did not allow a tract of land to be cut twice within the time of the management plan. Consequently, the objective function was influenced only by the cut from stands that existed at the beginning of the plan. New stands, arising from planting after cutting, did not affect the solution. Their potential productivity was ignored.

Nevertheless, the young stands that are created by a particular harvesting and reforestation schedule determine, to a large extent, the long-term productivity of a forest and its value. Therefore, the longer the planning horizon, the more important it is to take into account the influence of the regenerated forest on management criteria. The models we studied so far had fairly short planning horizons (15 to 50 years), but forest policy often deals with periods that span nearly a century. In these cases, a truly dynamic model is needed, one in which young stands can be harvested to produce timber and generate more young stands as many times as necessary to achieve management objectives during the planning period.

The purpose of this chapter is to study such a dynamic model, originally developed by Nautiyal and Pearse (1967). This model also describes the condition of the forest at the end of the plan in a way that is more flexible than that of Chap. 4 and more rigorous than the area or volume control approach of Chap. 5. We shall present some applications of this model. More applications will follow in Chap. 7.

6.2 EXAMPLE

Consider a small forest of short-leaf pine that consists of two distinct compartments. The land in both compartments is of the same quality (site index of 60 ft at age 50). Compartment 1 covers 100 acres and compartment 2 covers 200. The trees of compartment 1 are 1 to 10 years old, those on compartment 2 are 11 to 20 years.

The owner wants to keep this property for an indefinite length of time. Therefore, long-term consequences of anything that is done on the forest must be predicted. In this chapter, we shall assume that the owner's objective is simply to maximize the amount of timber produced. In the next chapter, we shall study the effect of economic objectives and different timber-flow policies.

6.3 A MODEL OF FOREST GROWTH

In this model, the forest is defined by the area in each age class. Age classes may be contiguous or dispersed throughout the forest. The only silvicultural procedures applied are clear-cutting of part or all of each age class, followed immediately by reforestation with trees of the same species.

The general decision variable in the model is designated by $X_{i,j}$ the area cut from age class j in period i. In contrast with the models studied so far, j does not refer to a specific compartment with a precise geographic location. For example, $X_{3,4}$ and $X_{1,4}$ refer to cuts in age class 4 in period 3 and 1, but the location of the cut is not specified.

In order to keep the number of variables small, a sufficiently long time unit must be used for age classes and cutting periods. In this example we use 10 years. Therefore, $X_{3,4}$ means the cut done in the third decade, that is 21 to 30 years after the beginning or the plan, on the area that has trees in age class 4, that is, trees 31 to 40 years old.

Using these variables and the initial conditions of the forest, it is possible to calculate the area in each age class at any future point in time. For the forest of Sec. 6.2 this is done as follows:

The state of the forest is observed at the beginning of each decade. At the beginning of the plan there are 100 acres of land in age class 1 and 200 acres in age class 2. During the first decade, $X_{1,1}$ acres are cut from age class 1 and $X_{1,2}$ acres from age class 2. The total area cut during the first decade is $X_{1,1} + X_{1,2}$. This constitutes age class 1 at the beginning of the second decade. By that time, what remains of age class 1, $100 - X_{1,1}$, has become age class 2 and what remains of age class 2, $200 - X_{1,2}$, has become age class 3.

This description of the cut-and-growth process can continue as long as desired. It is general in that harvest can occur at any point in time and in any age class. In Table 6.1 the calculations have been pursued to show the state of the forest at the beginning of the fourth decade, before any harvest. The results show clearly that the area in each age class at any point in time is a

TABLE 6.1 EXPRESSION OF THE STOCK AND CUT OF AN EVEN-AGED FOREST (ADAPTED FROM NAUTIYAL AND PEARSE, 1967)

Decade		1	2	3	4	5
				Age class		
1	stock	100	200			
	cut	$X_{1,1}$	$X_{1,2}$			
2	stock	$X_{1,1}+X_{1,2}$	$100-X_{1,1}$	$200-X_{1,2}$		
	cut	$X_{2,1}$	$X_{2,2}$	$X_{2,3}$		
3	stock	$X_{2,1}+X_{2,2}+X_{2,3}$	$X_{1,1}+X_{1,2}-X_{2,1}$	$100-X_{1,1}-X_{2,2}$	$200-X_{1,2}-X_{2,3}$	
	cut	$X_{3,1}$	$X_{3,2}$	$X_{3,3}$	$X_{3,4}$	
4	stock	$X_{3,1}+X_{3,2}+X_{3,3}+X_{3,4}$	$X_{2,1}+X_{2,2}+X_{2,3}-X_{3,1}$	$X_{1,1}+X_{1,2}-X_{2,1}-X_{3,2}$	$100-X_{1,1}-X_{2,2}-X_{3,3}$	$200-X_{1,2}-X_{2,3}-X_{3,4}$

linear function of the initial condition of the forest and of all the cuts that have been made up to that point.

For example, the area in age class 4 at the beginning of the third decade is $200 - X_{1,2} - X_{2,3}$. This is what is left of the timber initially in age class 2. The area in age class 2 at the beginning of the third decade is $X_{1,1} + X_{1,2} - X_{2,1}$; this is timber that was not in the initial forest but that results from reforestation since the beginning of the plan.

The process of obtaining all equations may seem laborious, but a very fast way of writing only the necessary equations will be provided in Sec. 6.5.

6.4 TERMINAL STATES

It is useful to specify the state in which the forest will be at the end of the plan in such a way that its value can be determined easily. The value of a forest depends in turn on what it can produce. Thus, we need a terminal forest state such that its output is well defined. The model of the regulated forest provides such a state. A forest that is regulated is such that the growing stock and the cut remain constant in perpetuity.

By specifying that the harvest schedule must lead to a regulated forest by the end of the plan, we ensure a pattern of production such that during the early years of the plan, production takes whatever value best meets the objectives of the owner. Because the plan we are seeking converts the initial forest into a regulated structure, we shall refer to the duration of the plan as the *conversion period*. Beyond this period, production is assumed to continue at a constant level, defined by the rotation age that has been selected for the regulated forest.

It should be emphasized that the terminal regulated forest will most likely never be reached. Nor should regulation be one of the major objectives of management. Regulation is simply a useful model to specify the terminal state of the forest. As time goes by, management conditions and objectives will certainly change, new harvest schedules will be drawn up, and the regulated state be postponed further.

Nevertheless, the terminal state of the forest should be consistent with the management objectives. For example, if the general objective is to maximize timber production, then the appropriate rotation age for the terminal regulated forest is the age at which mean annual increment is maximum. This ensures a steady state that maximizes the amount of timber produced year after year after conversion.

For short-leaf pine on site 60, mean annual increment culminates around age 30. With the time unit we are using, this corresponds to age class 3 and to a yield of approximately 5 thousand cubic feet per acre (Fig. 6.1). Consequently, if our short-leaf pine forest were regulated to maximize timber production it would consist of three age classes, each one covering an area of

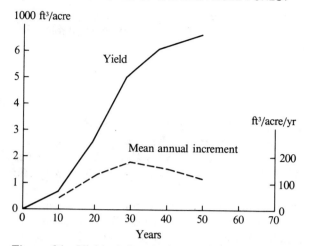

Figure 6.1 Yield of short-leaf pine on land of site index 60. (Data from Smalley and Bailey, 1974.)

$300/3 = 100$ acres. The production of that forest would be:

$$\begin{array}{ccccc} 100 & \times & 5 & = & 500 \\ \text{(a/10 y)} & & \text{(1000 ft}^3\text{/a)} & & \text{(1000 ft}^3\text{/10 y)} \end{array}$$

This is the forest we will use as the terminal state in the first specification of the model.

6.5 LINEAR-PROGRAMMING FORMULATION

Constraints

Using the last row of Table 6.1, it is straightforward to write the *terminal-state equations*. These equations give the area in each age class at the end of the conversion in terms of the decision variables. The fact that the forest should have 100 acres in age classes 1, 2, and 3 at the beginning of the fourth decade is expressed as:

$$X_{3,1} + X_{3,2} + X_{3,3} + X_{3,4} = 100 \quad \text{(age class 1)}$$
$$X_{2,1} + X_{2,2} + X_{2,3} - X_{3,1} = 100 \quad \text{(age class 2)}$$

and

$$X_{1,1} + X_{1,2} - X_{2,1} - X_{3,2} = 100 \quad \text{(age class 3)}$$

Furthermore, there should be nothing in age classes 4 and 5:

$$X_{1,1} + X_{2,2} - X_{3,3} = 100 \quad \text{(age class 4)}$$
$$X_{1,2} + X_{2,3} + X_{3,4} = 200 \quad \text{(age class 5)}$$

Of course, all $X_{i,j}$'s must be positive or zero. In addition, the area cut from a particular age class cannot exceed the area that is available. For example, for a solution to be meaningful, we must have:

$$X_{1,2} \leq 200$$

$$X_{2,3} \leq 200 - X_{1,2}, \text{ etc.}$$

But, in fact, all these constraints follow necessarily from the terminal-state equations that we have just written. For example, the equation relating to age class 5 in the terminal forest implies $X_{2,3} = 200 - X_{1,2} - X_{3,4}$. But since $X_{3,4} \geq 0$, it follows that $X3_{2,3} \leq 200 - X_{1,2}$. Finally, $X_{2,3} \leq 200 - X_{1,2}$ and $X_{2,3} \geq 0$ ensure that $X_{1,2} \leq 200$ acres.

This process can be repeated, starting with the expression of the area in each age class at the end of the conversion period. It shows that the area cut in different age classes and in different decades cannot be exceeded, given the terminal-state equations.

This is a good example of redundancy at work. The particular structure of the model implies that only 5 constraints are needed in this example instead of the 14 that would be used were no attention paid to redundancies. In fact, of the five terminal-state constraints, only four are needed. For example, the terminal equation for age class 5 can be obtained by adding equations for age classes 1, 2, and 3 and subtracting the equation for age class 4. But this is a minor saving. In the remainder of the discussion we will keep, for ease of understanding, all the terminal-state constraints.

Objective Function

Let us assume that the volume per acre in each age class of the forest is given by the yield function in Fig. 6.1. For example, regardless of the time when it occurs, 1 acre cut from age class 1 yields 500 ft^3 of timber, 1 acre cut from age class 2 yields 2500 ft^3, and so on. Thus, the volume cut from the entire forest during the 30 years of the conversion period is:

$$Z = 0.5X_{1,1} + 2.5X_{1,2}$$
$$+ 0.5X_{2,1} + 2.5X_{2,2} + 5.0X_{2,3}$$
$$+ 0.5X_{3,1} + 2.5X_{3,2} + 5.0X_{3,3} + 6.0X_{3,4}$$

where the first, second, and third lines express the volume (in 1000 ft^3) produced during the first, second, and third decade. Z is the appropriate objective function if the objective is to maximize the total volume produced.

The final expression of the model for the short-leaf pine forest is then: Find $X_{1,1} X_{1,2}, \ldots, X_{3,4}$, all positive or zero such that:

$$\max Z = 0.5X_{1,1} + 2.5X_{1,2} + 0.5X_{2,1} + 2.5X_{2,2} + 5.0X_{2,3} + 0.5X_{3,1}$$
$$+ 2.5X_{3,2} + 5.0X_{3,3} + 6.0X_{3,4}$$

TABLE 6.2 LINEAR-PROGRAMMING TABLEAU FOR A CONVERSION AND ROTATION OF 30 YEARS

	$X_{1,1}$	$X_{1,2}$	$X_{2,1}$	$X_{2,2}$	$X_{2,3}$	$X_{3,1}$	$X_{3,2}$	$X_{3,3}$	$X_{3,4}$	RHS
Z	0.5	2.5	0.5	2.5	5	0.5	2.5	5	6	
AGC1						1	1	1	1	= 100
AGC2			1	1	1	-1				= 100
AGC3	1	1	-1				-1			= 100
AGC4	1			1				1		= 100
AGC5		1			1				1	= 200

Subject to the terminal-state constraints:

$$X_{3,1} + X_{3,2} + X_{3,3} + X_{3,4} = 100 \quad \text{(age class 1)}$$
$$X_{2,1} + X_{2,2} + X_{2,3} - X_{3,1} = 100 \quad \text{(age class 2)}$$
$$X_{1,1} + X_{1,2} - X_{2,1} - X_{3,2} = 100 \quad \text{(age class 3)}$$
$$X_{1,1} + X_{2,2} + X_{3,3} = 100 \quad \text{(age class 4)}$$
$$X_{1,2} + X_{2,3} + X_{3,4} = 200 \quad \text{(age class 5)}$$

Tableau Form

It is easier to visualize the general structure of the model by writing it in tableau form, as in Table 6.2. There are five constraints in the model, as many as the possible age classes in the forest at the end of the conversion period. The constraints in Table 6.2 are separated in two groups by a blank line.

The first three constraints express the age classes that have been created from land that was cut and reforested since the beginning of the plan. For example, constraint AGC3 refers to the area in age class 3 at the beginning of the fourth decade. This is the area that was cut over during the first decade, $X_{1,1} + X_{1,2}$, minus what was cut in the second decade when the land was in age class 1, $X_{2,1}$, minus what was cut in the third decade when the land was in age class 2, $X_{3,2}$.

The last two constraints show instead what has happened to the age classes that were on the forest at the beginning of the plan. For example, the 100 acres initially in age class 1 must have been completely cut, otherwise there would be some land in age class 4 at the end of the conversion. The cut may have occurred in period 1, 2, or 3 as expressed by the variables $X_{1,1}$, $X_{2,2}$, and $X_{3,3}$.

Changing the Rotation

Changing the rotation age for the terminal regulated forest, other things remaining equal, is done simply by changing the right-hand-side (RHS) part of the linear programming tableau. For example if the desired rotation is $n = 2$ decades, then the two first age classes in the regulated forest should cover 150 acres each. The new RHS of the tableau should then be:

Row name	RHS
AGC1	150
AGC2	150
AGC3	0
AGC4	100
AGC5	200

If instead, the desired rotation is $n = 4$, then the new RHS would be:

Row name	RHS
AGC1	75
AGC2	75
AGC3	75
AGC4	25
AGC5	200

where the RHS of constraint AGC4 reflects the fact that in order to have 75 acres of land in age class 4 by the end of third decade one must cut 25 acres from the land that is initially in age class 1.

It is clear that, given this initial forest, it is not possible to convert it to a regulated forest of rotation higher than $n = 5$ decades in three decades.

Changing the Conversion Period

Let p be the chosen length of the conversion period, in decades. In our example, $p = 3$. Increasing the value of p requires adding variables and constraints to the linear-programming tableau. For example, let us assume that the conversion period for the short-leaf pine forest is set at 40 instead of 30 years. Then, the new linear-programming tableau, assuming the same objective and a rotation of 30 years, would look as shown in Table 6.3. The changes

TABLE 6.3 LINEAR-PROGRAMMING TABLEAU FOR A CONVERSION OF 40 YEARS AND A ROTATION OF 30 YEARS

	$X_{1,1}$	$X_{1,2}$	$X_{2,1}$	$X_{2,2}$	$X_{2,3}$	$X_{3,1}$	$X_{3,2}$	$X_{3,3}$	$X_{3,4}$	$X_{4,1}$	$X_{4,2}$	$X_{4,3}$	$X_{4,4}$	$X_{4,5}$	RHS
Z	0.5	2.5	0.5	2.5	5.0	0.5	2.5	5.0	6.0	0.5	2.5	5.0	6.0	6.5	
AGC1										1	1	1	1	1	= 100
AGC2					1	1	1	1	−1						= 100
AGC3			1	1	1	−1				−1					= 100
AGC4	1	1	−1				−1				−1				= 0
AGC5	1			1			1					1			= 100
AGC6		1			1			1					1		= 200

relative to the tableau for a conversion period of 30 years are:

1. Addition of variables $X_{4,1}$ to $X_{4,5}$, referring to harvests in the fourth decade
2. Addition of one constraint, AGC1, referring to the new age class 1 resulting from reforestation of land cut over during the fourth decade
3. Addition and changes of coefficients in the main matrix and the RHS to reflect the new harvest opportunities, and the presence of one additional age class at the end of the conversion.

The systematic pattern of the coefficients in the linear-programming tableau helps in making the changes necessary to lengthen or shorten the conversion period.

6.6 SOLUTIONS FOR VOLUME MAXIMIZATION

The solution of the management problem for the short-leaf pine forest, when the objective is to maximize timber production is shown in Table 6.4. The optimum solution consists in cutting 100 acres from age class 2 during the first decade of the plan. In this example, the best strategy is to regulate the forest very fast. Full regulation is achieved within 10 years.

In contrast, Table 6.5 shows the solution of the linear program when the terminal rotation is set at 40 years ($n = 4$). We already know that this rotation does not maximize the production of the regulated forest; the best rotation for that purpose is 30 years. It is interesting to observe that lengthening the terminal rotation also decreases the maximum that can be produced during the conversion period (987.5 thousand cubic feet instead of 1250). Full regulation is achieved only at the very end of the plan. After 40 years there are four age classes, each one of 75 acres.

TABLE 6.4 MANAGEMENT PLAN THAT MAXIMIZES TIMBER PRODUCTION WITH A ROTATION OF 30 YEARS

Decade		Acres per age class			Total cut (1000 ft^3)
		1	2	3	
1	stock	100	200		
	cut		100		250
2	stock	100	100	100	
	cut			100	500
3	stock	100	100	100	
	cut			100	500
4	stock	100	100	100	
					1250

TABLE 6.5   MANAGEMENT PLAN THAT MAXIMIZES TIMBER PRODUCTION
WITH A ROTATION OF 40 YEARS

Decade		Acres per age class				Total cut (1000 ft^3)
		1	2	3	4	
1	stock	100	200			
	cut		75			187.5
2	stock	75	100	125		
	cut			75		375.0
3	stock	75	75	100	50	
	cut			25	50	425.0
4	stock	75	75	75	75	
						987.5

6.7 GENERAL FORMULATION

The model developed in this chapter applies to the following general situation. Initially, we have a forest of total area A with m age classes. The area in each age class is a_j and each age class spans u years. The forest is managed for p periods, each one u years long. At the end of this conversion period we want a regulated forest with a rotation of nu years. During conversion we desire to maximize the volume produced.

The harvesting schedule is defined by the decision variables $X_{i,j}$, the area cut from age class j in period i. The number of age classes at any point in time i is $m + i - 1$ (verify this in Table 6.1). Let v_j be the volume per acre in age class j, at any point in time. Then, the expression of the objective function is:

$$Z = \sum_{i=1}^{p} \sum_{j=1}^{m+i-1} v_j X_{i,j}$$

At the end of the conversion period p, the forest must be regulated with a rotation of nu years. Given the goal of maximizing volume, a suitable rotation, n^* is that which maximizes the mean annual increment, v_n/nu. Regulation is defined by $m + p$ equations. For simplicity, we shall write these equations only for the usual case where the conversion is longer than the rotation ($p > n$). These equations can be separated in two groups:

1. *Age classes created from harvests during the conversion:*

$$\sum_{j=1}^{m+i-1} X_{i,j} - \sum_{k=1}^{p-i} X_{k+i,k} = 0 \qquad \text{for } i = 1, \ldots, p - n$$

$$= \frac{A}{n} \qquad \text{for } i = p - n + 1, \ldots, p - 1$$

$$\sum_{j=1}^{m+i-1} X_{i,j} = \frac{A}{n} \qquad \text{for } i = p$$

The first $p - n$ equations refer to areas that are older than the rotation, and thus must cover zero acres. The others refer to areas that constitute the age classes in the regulated forest.

2. *Areas cut from the initial age classes:*

$$\sum_{k=1}^{p} X_{k,\,k+i-1} = a_i \qquad \text{for } i = 1, \ldots, m$$

This set of equations refers to age classes that are older than the rotation at the end of the conversion, and which must have been entirely cut by that time.

Verify that the special cases described in Tables 6.2 and 6.3 fit within this general formulation. Of course, no one needs to remember these arcane formulas. All that is needed is to be able to build tables like 6.2 and 6.3 for any specific data set. As we have seen before, that is straightforward.

6.8 CONCLUSIONS

In this chapter we have developed a model of the even-aged forest that can describe fully the condition of the various age classes at any point in time, given initial conditions and the subsequent regime of harvests. The terminal state at the end of the plan was a regulated forest. It turned out that the equations expressing the terminal state were sufficient to ensure that, throughout the plan, no more was cut from every age class than what was available. These equations became the constraints of a linear program. The objective function we used so far expressed the total volume produced by the forest. In the next chapter we shall see how the model can also be used to design harvest schedules with economic objectives, subject to additional management constraints.

PROBLEMS

6.1. Section 6.3 in the text shows a method to represent the area in any age class in any decade for an even-aged forest. Table 6.1 illustrates this method for a forest that starts with 100 acres in age class 1, 200 acres in age class 2, and that grows for four decades.

Modify Table 6.1 to reflect an additional initial 50 acres in age class 3. (*Note:* This will require consideration of a sixth age class.)

6.2. Construct a table similar to Table 6.1 for a forest that starts with only 50 acres in age class 2, and 100 acres in age class 4. Extend the new table until the beginning of the fifth decade. (*Note:* There is no need for a variable $X_{1,1}$ or a variable $X_{1,3}$, or for terminal-state equations for stands initially in age classes 1 or 3.)

6.3. Write the terminal-state equations for the forest described in Prob. 6.1. Assume a terminal rotation of two decades and regulation by the beginning of the fourth decade. How would these equations be changed to reflect a terminal rotation of three decades?

Using the per-acre yields shown below, write the objective function for volume maximization that would correspond to this terminal state.

Age (years)	Per-acre yield (1000 ft^3)
10	0.3
20	1.5
30	4.0
40	5.0
50	5.5
60	5.8
70	5.9
80	6.0
90	6.0
100	5.8

6.4. Write the terminal-state equations for the forest described in Prob. 6.2, assuming a terminal rotation of two decades and regulation by the beginning of the fifth decade. How would these equations be modified to reflect a terminal rotation of three decades? Of four decades?

Using the per-acre yields shown above, write the objective function for volume maximization that would correspond to these terminal states.

6.5. Write the model for Prob. 6.3 in tableau form, showing the RHS's for terminal rotations of either two or three decades.

6.6. Write the model for Prob. 6.4 in tableau form, showing the RHS's for terminal rotations of two, three, and four decades.

6.7. Modify the tableau from Prob. 6.5 to reflect a lengthening of the conversion to four decades.

6.8. Modify the tableau from Prob. 6.6 to reflect a shortening of the conversion to three decades.

6.9. Solve both volume maximization problems for Prob. 6.3 with a computer. Summarize the harvest schedules in tables like Table 6.4. When is regulation achieved in each case?

6.10. Solve all three of the volume maximization problems from Prob. 6.4 with a computer. Summarize the harvest schedules in tables similar to Table 6.4. In what decade is regulation achieved in each case?

ANNOTATED REFERENCES

Clutter, J. L., J. C. Fortson, L. V. Pienaar, G. H. Brister, and R. L. Bailey. 1983. *Timber management: A quantitative approach*. Wiley, New York. 333 pp. (The Model II version of the "XYZ Timber Co." problem in Chap. 10 belongs (in Johnson and Scheurman's terminology) to the same category of models as the one in this chapter; it also adds other constraints typical of industrial forests.)

Davis, L. S., and K. N. Johnson. 1986. *Forest management.* McGraw-Hill, New York. 790 pp. (The Model II version of the "Daniel Picket Forest" problem in Chap. 15 belongs to the same class models as the one in this chapter; it has additional constraints typical of public forests.)

Dykstra, D. P. 1984. *Mathematical programming for natural resource management.* McGraw-Hill, New York. 318 pp. (Chapter 6 contains another example of a Model II, in Johnson and Scheurman's terminology.)

Hallanger, W. 1973. The linear programming structure of the problem. *In* Sustainable harvest analysis 1971 and 1972 (C. J. Chambers and R. N. Pierson, eds.) pp. 67–71. Washington Department of Natural Resources, Harvest Regulation Report No. 5. 97 pp. (Outlines a model structure similar to that used by Nautiyal and Pearse.)

Iverson, D. C., and R. M. Alston. 1986. The genesis of FORPLAN: A historical and analytical review of Forest Service planning models. U.S. Forest Service, General Technical Report INT-214. Intermountain Research Station, Ogden. 30 pp. (A review of the evolution of models from forms similar to those in Chaps. 4 and 5 of this book to those in Chaps. 6 and 7.)

Johnson, K. N., and H. L. Scheurman. 1977. Techniques for prescribing optimal timber harvest and investment under different objectives—Discussion and synthesis. *Forest Science* Monograph No. 18. 31 pp. (Categories harvest-scheduling models as either Model I or Model II, the former resembling the models used in Chaps. 4 and 5 of this book, and the latter those used in Chaps. 6 and 7. The main difference between them is that Model I preserves the identity of the initial harvesting units throughout the planning horizon, while Model II creates a new harvesting unit out of the acres regenerated in each period.)

Johnson, K. N., T. W. Stuart, and S. A. Crim. 1986. FORPLAN version 2: An overview. U.S. Forest Service, Land Management Planning Systems Section, Fort Collins. (Last version of a linear-programming system, widely used for forest management in the U.S. Forest Service. Can be used to build models of the type presented in Chaps. 4, 5, 6 and 7 of this book.)

Nautiyal, J. C., and P. H. Pearse. 1967. Optimizing the conversion to sustained yield—A programming solution. *Forest Science* 13(2):131–139. (Basis of the harvest-scheduling models used in Chaps. 6 and 7 of this book. The Model II of Johnson and Scheurman bears a strong resemblance to the model of Nautiyal and Pearse.)

Smalley, G. W., and R. L. Bailey. 1974. Yield tables and stand structure for short-leaf pine plantations in Tennessee, Alabama, and Georgia highlands. U.S. Forest Service, Research Paper SO-97. (Source of yield data used in this chapter.)

Chapter 7

Economic Objectives and Timber-Flow Policies for Even-Aged Forests

7.1 INTRODUCTION

In the preceding chapter we used Nautiyal and Pearse's model to forecast the growth of an even-aged forest over a very long time period. Given the initial state of the forest and a specific harvesting schedule, we could predict how the forest would look at any future date. The model also ensured that at the end of the management plan we would have a regulated forest with a specified rotation. We used that model to calculate harvest schedules that would maximize the total volume of timber produced by the forest.

The purpose of this chapter is to apply the model to answer the following questions:

Given a specific even-aged forest, what is the management plan that maximizes its economic value?

How do we choose the rotation of the terminal regulated forest?

How long should we take to convert the current forest to a regulated structure?

We shall also use the model to study policies controlling the flow of timber production from a forest. Is even flow the best policy? What are the alternatives? In what circumstances are they superior to even flow?

We shall continue to use as an example the short-leaf pine forest of Chap. 6. The initial conditions are the same: there are 100 acres in age class 1 and 200 acres in age class 2. The silviculture remains the same: immediate artificial regeneration after harvest. The yield function is that described in Fig. 6.1. The conversion period is kept initially at 30 years ($p = 3$). Therefore, the constraints that relate the areas cut in every decade from every age class are the same as those in Table 6.2. But the objective function will change to reflect the economic objective. The right-hand side coefficients will also have to be changed to correspond to the economic rotation.

7.2 ECONOMIC ROTATION FOR THE REGULATED FOREST

The rotation of the regulated forest that will be obtained after 30 years should be consistent with the goal of present-value maximization. This economic rotation can be approximated by calculating the rotation n (expressed in decades to agree with the time unit used in the remainder of the model) that maximizes the soil expectation value of a stand. A sensitivity analysis will be done later to see if another rotation would be best for our purpose. The *soil expectation value* is defined as follows:

Let v_n be the volume per acre of a stand cut at age n and q be the value of the timber per unit of volume, sold as standing trees. Then, the gross return obtained every n decades is:

$$qv_n = w_n$$

Let c be the cost of reforestation. Ignoring other minor costs, the net return per acre every time a harvest occurs is:

$$w_n - c$$

The present value of these returns recurring continually every n decades is:

$$\frac{w_n - c}{(1 + r)^{10n} - 1}$$

where r is the interest rate expressed as a fraction per year. From this we must subtract the cost of establishing the initial stand. This leads to the following expression of the soil expectation value per acre:

$$SEV = \frac{w_n - c}{(1 + r)^{10n} - 1} - c$$

where SEV = soil expectation value. This term refers to the value of the land used in this kind of forestry. It is the amount one would be willing to pay for that land to generate a rate of return r. A similar formula was developed first by Martin Faustmann (1849). It is used often to calculate the economic rotation for even-aged forests. Nevertheless, the formula applies strictly to a single stand that is cut and replanted every rotation, starting from bare land, not to a regulated forest. But in practice, it is a sufficiently good approximation of the rotation for a regulated forest.

The economic rotation for the forest of our example can now be readily computed. This is done by increasing gradually the value of n to find the one that maximizes the soil expectation value of a stand, SEV.

TABLE 7.1 DETERMINATION OF THE ECONOMIC ROTATION FOR AN EVEN-AGED SHORT-LEAF PINE STAND

(1)	(2)	(3)	(4)	(5)	(6)	(7)	(8)
1	10	0.5	250	200	1.26	252	202
2	20	2.5	1250	1200	0.45	540	490
3	30	5.0	2500	2450	0.21	514	464
4	40	6.0	3000	2950	0.11	325	275
5	50	6.5	3250	3200	0.06	192	142

$(1) = n$

$(2) = 10n$ (years)

$(3) = v_n$ (1000 ft^3/a)

$(4) = w_n = qv_n$ ($/a)

$(5) = w_n - c$ ($/a)

$(6) = 1/[(1 + r)^{10n} - 1]$

$(7) = (w_n - c)/[(1 + r)^{10n} - 1]$ ($/a)

$(8) = (w_n - c)/[(1 + r)^{10n} - 1] - c =$ SEV ($/a)

The results of the calculations are shown in Table 7.1. They assume an interest rate of 6 percent per year, a price q of $500 per thousand cubic feet of stumpage and a reforestation cost of $50 per acre. The economic rotation is $n^* = 2$ decades since for that rotation the SEV is maximum ($490 per acre). This means that the optimum regulated forest should contain two 10-year age classes. The oldest age class should be entirely cut every 10 years.

7.3 OBJECTIVE FUNCTION

The new objective function expresses the present value of the timber that is harvested during the conversion period, as a function of the decision variables. In our example, this is:

$$Z_{PV} = d_1(w_1 - c)X_{1,1} + d_1(w_2 - c)X_{1,2}$$
$$+ d_2(w_1 - c)X_{2,1} + d_2(w_2 - c)X_{2,2} + d_2(w_3 - c)X_{2,3}$$
$$+ d_3(w_1 - c)X_{3,1} + d_3(w_2 - c)X_{3,2} + d_3(w_3 - c)X_{3,3}$$
$$+ d_3(w_4 - c)X_{3,4}$$

where $w_1 - c$ is the return of cutting one acre from age class 1, net of reforestation cost, $w_2 - c$ is the return from age class 2, etc.

Each line represents the present value of the harvest during a decade. Each d_i is the discount factor expressing the present value of a dollar generated in the ith decade. For simplicity, each dollar is accounted for in the middle of the decade, that is:

$$d_i = \frac{1}{(1 + r)^{10i - 5}}$$

In our example, the interest rate is $r = 0.06$ per year. Therefore:

$$d_1 = \frac{1}{1.06^5} = 0.75$$

$$d_2 = \frac{1}{1.06^{15}} = 0.42$$

and

$$d_3 = \frac{1}{1.06^{25}} = 0.23$$

The expression of the objective function in the case of present value maximization is then, using the values of $w_i - c$ in Table 7.1:

$$Z_{PV} = 150X_{1,1} + 900X_{1,2}$$
$$+ 84X_{2,1} + 504X_{2,2} + 1029X_{2,3}$$
$$+ 46X_{3,1} + 276X_{3,2} + 564X_{3,3} + 679X_{3,4}$$

7.4 LINEAR PROGRAMMING SOLUTION AND FOREST VALUE

The final form of the linear programming tableau is shown in Table 7.2. This tableau differs from the one in Table 6.2 only by:

1. The coefficients of the objective function, which now express present value per acre instead of volume
2. The coefficients of the RHS which reflect a terminal rotation of 20 years instead of 30, in agreement with the results of Sec. 7.2.

The solution of this linear-programming model is presented in Table 7.3. The optimum harvesting schedule consists of cutting 150 acres from age class 2 during the first decade, cutting the entire 100 acres from age class 2 during the second decade, and 50 acres from age class 3, plus the all 150 acres in age class 2 during the third decade. Regulation is achieved just at the end of the 30 years when the forest consists of 150 acres each in age classes 1 and 2.

The present value of the timber that will be produced in that way during the conversion period is $278,300. In addition, the regulated forest will continue to produce, beyond the conversion, constant annual revenues equal to:

$$15 \times 1200 = 18,000$$
$$\text{(a/y)} \quad \text{(\$/a)} \quad \text{(\$/y)}$$

TABLE 7.2 LINEAR-PROGRAMMING TABLEAU TO MAXIMIZE PRESENT VALUE

	$X_{1,1}$	$X_{1,2}$	$X_{2,1}$	$X_{2,2}$	$X_{2,3}$	$X_{3,1}$	$X_{3,2}$	$X_{3,3}$	$X_{3,4}$	RHS
Z_{PV}	150	900	84	504	1029	46	276	564	679	
AGC1						1	1	1	1	= 150
AGC2			1	1	1	−1				= 150
AGC3	1	1	−1				−1			= 0
AGC4	1			1				1		= 100
AGC5		1			1				1	= 200

TABLE 7.3 MANAGEMENT PLAN THAT MAXIMIZES PRESENT VALUE

Period	Acres per age class			Volume ($1000 ft^3$)	Present value ($\$1000$)
	1	2	3		
1 stock	100	200			
cut		150		375	135.0
2 stock	150	100	50		
cut		100	50	500	101.9
3 stock	150	150			
cut		150			41.4
4 stock	150	150		375	
				$\overline{1250}$	$\overline{278.3}$

The present value of an annual perpetual income of $18,000 is, with an interest rate of 6 percent per year; $18,000/0.06 = \$300,000$; but since that recurring income will start 30 years hence only, its present value is $\$300,000/1.06^{30} = \$52,200$.

In summary, the total present value of the management program, over an infinite horizon is:

$$F = \$278,300 + \$52,200 = \$330,500$$

This present value of the net returns from the forest, over an infinite horizon, is the *value* of the initial forest, given the management regime that has been proposed. It is the maximum amount that a buyer would be willing to pay for the whole forest, including land and growing stock, and earn a real rate of return of 6 percent per year.

With the notations used above, the general expression of this forest value is:

$$F = Z_{PV}^* + \frac{(A/10n)(w_n - c)/r}{(1 + r)^{10p}}$$

where Z_{PV}^* is the maximum present value of returns in the linear program describing the conversion process, while the remainder of the expression is the present value of the returns that the regulated forest will produce after conversion.

It should be clear by now that the value of a forest depends essentially on how it will be managed. In the next section, we shall examine how the period of conversion and the terminal rotation influence forest value.

7.5 SENSITIVITY OF FOREST VALUE TO ROTATION AND CONVERSION PERIOD

The conversion period of 30 years that we have selected in the previous calculations is arbitrary, and, to a lesser extent, so is the terminal rotation. It is

TABLE 7.4 FOREST VALUE FOR DIFFERENT ROTATIONS AND
CONVERSION PERIODS

Conversion length (years)	Value ($1000) by rotation (years)			
	10	20	30	40
20	287	330	320	247
30	309	331	329	284
40	320	333	330	307

therefore worthwhile to investigate the effect of changing these two parameters on the value of the forest.

For a given conversion period, changing the rotation is extremely simple; it corresponds to a change in the RHS parameters of the linear-programming model. If instead the conversion period is changed, variables and constraints must be added or deleted to reflect the changes in harvesting possibilities (see Chap. 6).

Table 7.4 shows the present value of harvest schedules on the short-leaf pine forest of our example, when the rotation is changed from 10 to 40 years and the conversion period is either 20, 30, or 40 years. When $p = 3$, the linear-programming tableau is as in Table 7.2; the constants on the right-hand side will change depending on the rotation. When $p = 4$, the tableau is as in Table 6.3, with appropriate right-hand side coefficients, except for the objective function, which now expresses the present value of the returns during conversion, that is:

$$Z_{PV} = 150X_{1,1} + 900X_{1,2}$$
$$+ 84X_{2,1} + 504X_{2,2} + 1029X_{2,3}$$
$$+ 46X_{3,1} + 276X_{3,2} + 564X_{3,3} + 679X_{3,4}$$
$$+ 26X_{4,1} + 156X_{4,2} + 319X_{4,3} + 384X_{4,4} + 416X_{4,5}$$

The forest values reported in Table 7.4 show that:

1. Regardless of the length of the conversion period, the best rotation age is 20 years. Recall that this is also the rotation that maximizes the soil expectation value of a stand. However, the longer the conversion, the smaller the influence of the rotation on forest value.
2. For a given rotation, forest value increases as the conversion period lengthens. But the gain between 20 and 40 years is negligible when the best rotation is used.

These results have been verified for many different initial conditions, conversion periods, and rotations. To summarize: When the objective is to maximize the present value of returns, a good rotation for the terminal forest is that which maximizes the soil expectation value of a single stand.

In addition, it is generally better to work with a long conversion period. This is due to the fact that the terminal-state constraints limit the manager's options. Therefore, it is better to have these constraints as far in the future as possible. Nevertheless, if the economic rotation is used, the conversion period has little effect on forest value.

One must also keep in mind that the longer the conversion period, the larger the problem to be solved. Furthermore, what the model produces is just a temporary plan. A few years after implementation is started, conditions will have changed and a new plan will have to be drawn up. Therefore, there is little sense in working with a conversion period that is extremely long.

Another remark is pertinent; it has to do with the traditional controversy between the objectives of maximizing either volume produced or present value. In the last chapter, Table 6.4 showed a harvesting schedule that maximized the volume produced. The rotation was set at 30 years, the age of maximum mean annual increment, and the conversion period was set at 30 years. Using the same price, interest rate, and reforestation costs of this chapter, we find that this schedule leads to a forest value of $320,000. In contrast, Table 7.4 shows that the highest forest value obtainable, using the same conversion period of 30 years, is $331,000. This is only 3 percent higher. Given the errors of measurements, risk, and other factors, the difference is probably not significant in this case.

7.6 ALTERNATIVE TIMBER FLOW POLICIES

Up to this point, the only management objectives reflected by the planning models were the terminal state of the forest and the volume, or present value, of the timber produced. With no other constraint, linear-programming solutions may give erratic patterns of production over time. In many cases, the manager will want to keep the flow of timber that is harvested decade after decade within certain limits. In this section we expand the model developed so far to reflect these constraints. We shall then apply this model to investigate the consequences of different timber-flow policies.

Free-Flow Policy

In the previous examples, no constraint limited the fluctuations of production over time. It turned out that when the object was to maximize the volume of timber, the output increased gradually every decade (Tables 6.4 and 6.5 in Chap. 6). However, when present value was maximized, the output of the forest was less regular, 33 percent higher during the second decade than in the first and in the third (Table 7.3). In general, the pattern of production that is obtained depends on the initial condition of the forest and on the objective function.

Variations in output can be greater than those observed in our example, especially if the initial forest consists largely of overmature timber (old growth). Since that timber has high value per acre, the optimum solution is to cut as early and as much as possible. The only limit is set by the terminal state.

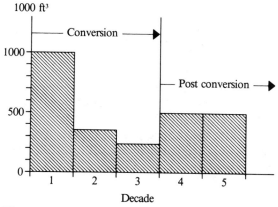

Figure 7.1 Irregular output on an old-growth forest when present value is maximized.

An example of this is shown in Fig. 7.1 The data for that figure are those of the short-leaf pine plantation used in the previous section, but the initial age classes were distributed in a different way, 50 acres in age classes 1 and 2, and 200 acres in age class 3. The conversion period and the rotation were set at 30 years. The corresponding linear program is shown in Table 7.5.

To maximize the present value of this forest, under a free-flow policy, one would produce 1 million cubic feet of timber during the first decade, 375,000 during the second, and only 250,000 during the third. At the end of the third decade, the forest would be regulated and produce 500,000 ft^3 per decade forever (Fig. 7.1). The corresponding forest value would be $542,000.

This kind of production would in fact be illegal in a national forest since it does not fulfill the *nondeclining even-flow* policy specified in the National Forest Management Act. A strict interpretation of this policy requires that the production of the forest be the same during each decade of the plan and that it be equal to the amount the forest will produce every decade beyond the conversion period. In our model, the following describes such a policy.

TABLE 7.5   LINEAR-PROGRAMMING TABLEAU TO MAXIMIZE PRESENT VALUE UNDER A FREE-FLOW POLICY AND A 30-YEAR ROTATION

	$X_{1,1}$	$X_{1,2}$	$X_{1,3}$	$X_{2,1}$	$X_{2,2}$	$X_{2,3}$	$X_{2,4}$	$X_{3,1}$	$X_{3,2}$	$X_{3,3}$	$X_{3,4}$	$X_{3,5}$	RHS
Z_{PV}	150	900	1831	84	504	1029	1231	46	276	564	679	746	
AGC1								1	1	1	1	1	= 100
AGC2				1	1	1	1	−1					= 100
AGC3	1	1	1	−1					−1				= 100
AGC4	1				1					1			= 50
AGC5		1				1					1		= 50
AGC6			1				1					1	= 200

Even-Flow Policy

Under a strict *even-flow* policy the forest must produce the same amount during each period of the plan as the terminal regulated forest. Let us continue with the forest used in building the model of Table 7.5. That is, the conversion period is 30 years and the rotation for the regulated forest is also 30 years. In order to find the harvesting schedule, if it exists, that produces an even flow of timber, one must add appropriate constraints to the linear program in Table 7.5. The constraints express the fact that the volume produced in each decade is equal to the volume that the terminal regulated forest will produce. The general expression of this volume is:

$$\frac{A}{n} v_n$$

where A is the total area of the forest, n the rotation in decades, and v_n the volume per acre at age n. The formula makes it clear that the periodic volume produced from a forest under strict even flow depends only on the land area, its productivity, and the rotation selected for the terminal forest. In our case, the volume produced every decade is equal to $(300/3) \times 5 = 500$ (1000 ft^3). Consequently, under even flow, the sequence of harvests during each decade must be such that:

Decade 1: $0.5X_{1,1} + 2.5X_{1,2} + 5.0X_{1,3}$ $= 500$
Decade 2: $0.5X_{2,1} + 2.5X_{2,2} + 5.0X_{2,3} + 6.0X_{2,4}$ $= 500$
Decade 3: $0.5X_{3,1} + 2.5X_{3,2} + 5.0X_{3,3} + 6.0X_{3,4} + 6.5X_{3,5} = 500$

This set of constraints added to those in Table 7.5 leads to the linear-programming model in Table 7.6. Solving it leads to a forest value under even flow of \$413,000, 24 percent less than under the free-flow policy.

The best rotation under even flow can in principle be determined by changing the right-hand sides of the constraints named AGC and FFF in Table 7.6. However, it is simple to determine the rotation that maximizes the

TABLE 7.6 LINEAR-PROGRAMMING TABLEAU TO MAXIMIZE PRESENT
VALUE UNDER AN EVEN-FLOW POLICY AND A 30-YEAR ROTATION

	$X_{1,1}$	$X_{1,2}$	$X_{1,3}$	$X_{2,1}$	$X_{2,2}$	$X_{2,3}$	$X_{2,4}$	$X_{3,1}$	$X_{3,2}$	$X_{3,3}$	$X_{3,4}$	$X_{3,5}$	RHS
Z_{PV}	150	900	1831	84	504	1029	1231	46	276	564	679	746	
AGC1								1	1	1	1	1	= 100
AGC2				1	1	1	1	−1					= 100
AGC3	1	1	1	−1					−1				= 100
AGC4	1				1					1			= 50
AGC5		1				1					1		= 50
AGC6			1				1					1	= 200
FFF1	0.5	2.5	5.0										= 500
FFF2				0.5	2.5	5.0	6.0						= 500
FFF3								0.5	2.5	5.0	6.0	6.5	= 500

present value of the *gross* returns. Under strict even flow, the forest produces every year the volume $(A/10n)v_n$, of which the value is $q(A/10n)v_n$, and the present value, over an infinite horizon, is:

$$\frac{q(A/10n)v_n}{r}$$

However, since q, A, and r are constant, the maximum present value of gross returns is obtained by choosing n that maximizes $v_n/10n$, the mean annual increment. Under even flow, economic and biological criteria almost meet. The only difference between economic and biological rotation may occur due to the reforestation costs during the conversion period. Nevertheless, the best rotation is likely to be closer to the point of maximum mean annual increment than to the one obtained from the Faustmann formula. For that reason we have set the rotation at 30 years in our example.

Again, the best rotation can, in principle, be found by changing the right-hand side of the constraints in Table 7.6. However, for some rotations, the conversion period must be lengthened considerably to get a *feasible solution*. Sometimes, there may be no solution at all that yields the desired even flow. This is the case if there is very little growing stock on the land at the beginning of the plan. In that situation, the even-flow level must be decreased to what the initial stock can support, by shortening the terminal rotation. But a strict even-flow policy makes little sense when there is little initial stock. A more reasonable alternative would be to ask that timber output increase steadily throughout the conversion period. The corresponding model is left to the reader as an exercise.

In any case, even if we have a rich initial forest, an even-flow policy is costly compared to what a free-flow policy would give. Nevertheless, there may be good reasons to use even flow. For example, one may want to slow down the liquidation of stands that are several hundred years old because they may acquire very high *aesthetic* value in the near future. Cutting a 500-year-old Douglas fir grove is, for all practical purpose, an irreversible process. Or, one may want to avoid dumping too much timber on the market, which would as a result depress prices. Remember that the model we use assumes that the unit price is the same, regardless of the quantity sold. This would be true only for a small forest in a large market. In Chap. 14 we shall examine a model that recognizes the possible effects of output on prices.

Nevertheless, strict even flow is a very extreme policy. Often, more flexible policies can be followed that would satisfy some of the concerns of the proponents of even flow, while improving the economic results. We shall give an example of such a compromise next.

Accelerated-Cut Policy

This policy is applicable to a forest in which there is a large amount of overmature timber that grows little in economic value. The forest used to build the model in Table 7.6 is in such a state because 200 acres are older than the economic rotation given by the SEV formula. We have seen that strict even flow leads to a plan that projects a present value 24 percent below what a free-flow policy would return.

Still, the concerns of even-flow proponents are well taken. The pattern of production under free flow follows a cycle of very high amplitude. Timber output during the first decade is much higher than the long-term output of the regulated forest. It then falls below it in the second and the third decades (Fig. 7.1). This instability of production on a large forest could lead to a period of boom followed by depression for the communities that depend on it for their livelihood. A more stable system is needed, some compromise between free-flow and strict even-flow policies. The accelerated-cut policy is such a compromise.

An *accelerated-cut* policy limits the pattern of timber production so that it never falls below the production of the terminal regulated forest. This allows plans to be made for activities that depend strictly on what the forest can yield in the long run. But, if any surplus is available, it can be used for profitable investments outside or within the forestry sector.

Whether a harvesting schedule that satisfies this concept exists can be determined readily with the model in Table 7.6. The only modification needed is to replace the equality signs in the flow constraint FFF1, FFF2, and FFF3 by greater-than-or-equal-to constraints. In that way, one is sure that the amount produced every decade will not be less than that of the regulated forest (500,000 ft^3). However, production may be higher if it increases present value.

The solution of the model in Table 7.6, modified to reflect the accelerated-cut policy, is summarized in Fig. 7.2. Production is some 150,000 ft^3 higher in the first decade than in the remainder of the 30-year plan, when output is exactly equal to what the regulated forest can produce. The forest value promised by this plan is $468,000. This is 14 percent less than what a free-flow policy would give but it avoids some of its problems. On the other hand, the present value of the accelerated-cut policy is 13 percent higher than that of the best strict even-flow policy.

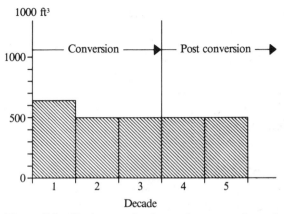

Figure 7.2 Timber production under an accelerated-cut policy.

7.7 GENERAL FORMULATION

The model uses the same representation of forest growth as that in Chap. 6. There are initially m initial age classes, the area in each class is a_i. Each age class spans u years. A harvesting schedule is to be drawn up for p periods, each one of u years. The schedule is defined by the variables $X_{i,j}$, the area cut from age class j in period i; i varies from 1 to p and for each value of i, j varies from 1 to $m + i - 1$.

At the end of the plan, or conversion period, the forest must be regulated. Regulation is defined by a set of equations. Each equation measures the area in each age class of the regulated forest, given a specified rotation. The general form of the equations was given in Chap. 6. But, as pointed out in that chapter, the easiest way to write these equations is to use a table like Table 7.2.

The objective function expresses the discounted value of all harvests during conversion:

$$Z_{PV} = \sum_{i=1}^{p} \sum_{j=1}^{m+i-1} d_i(w_j - c)X_{i,j}$$

where $d_i = 1/(1 + r)^{iu - u/2}$ is the discount factor for a yearly interest rate r and $w_j = qv_j$ is the value per unit area in age class j, for a timber price q and a volume per acre v_j. The value of the forest is equal to:

$$F = Z_{PV}^* + \frac{(A/nu)(w_n - c)/r}{(1 + r)^{pu}}$$

where Z_{PV}^* is the maximum of the objective function, A is the forest area, n is the rotation, and c is the reforestation cost. If a strict even-flow policy is imposed on the management program, the following constraints should be added to the model:

$$\sum_{j=1}^{m+i-1} v_j X_{i,j} = \frac{A}{n} v_n \qquad \text{for } i = 1, \ldots, p$$

If an accelerated cut policy is to be followed, the equality signs in the last constraints must be changed to $\geq$ signs.

7.8 CONCLUSIONS

The dynamic model of even-aged forest management developed in Chap. 6 has been expanded to investigate the economics of harvest scheduling in such a forest. The terminal value of the forest is simple to estimate if one assumes that a regulated forest is achieved by the end of the plan. Then, forest value (the value of the forest inclusive of land) is equal to the present value of what is produced during the conversion period plus the value of the production from the regulated forest.

It was shown that in the absence of any constraint on the flow of timber over time (free-flow policy), the rotation that maximizes forest value is that which maximizes the soil expectation value of a stand. The conversion period has little effect on forest value when that rotation is selected. The effect of the rotation on forest value decreases as the period of conversion increases.

Under a strict even-flow policy, the rotation that maximizes forest value tends to be closer to the age of maximum mean annual increment than to the age that maximizes the soil expectation value of a stand. The highest forest value under even flow may be much lower than under a free-flow policy in forests with large amounts of old timber.

The accelerated-cut policy is a compromise that ensures that timber production never falls below the long-term production of the forest. It allows high production in the early years of the plan, with a corresponding increase in forest value.

PROBLEMS

7.1. The rotation that maximized SEV for a short-leaf pine stand was determined in Table 7.1 for an interest rate of 6 percent per year. What rotation would maximize SEV if the guiding rate of interest were 3 percent per year? What kind of relationship does this imply between economic rotation and interest rate?

7.2. The objective function for maximizing the present value of a slash-pine plantation was derived in Sec. 7.3 with an interest rate of 6 percent. Recalculate the coefficients of this objective function with interest rates of 3 and 9 percent. Does the rate of interest have a significant impact on the relative value of harvesting in different decades? What effect will this have on optimal harvesting schedules? On the importance of harvests from regenerated or post-conversion stands to forest value?

7.3. Solve the harvest-scheduling model in Table 7.2 with a computer, using the two objective functions derived in Prob. 7.2. Compare the optimal harvest schedules for each with that in Table 7.3. How does the periodic harvest volume vary over time as a function of interest rates? Explain the pattern you observe.

7.4. Table 7.4 shows the present value of a slash-pine forest for terminal rotations of 10, 20, 30, and 40 years, and conversion periods of 20, 30, and 40 years. Break up each cell in this table into the value of harvests during the conversion and the value of harvests from the regulated forest after the conversion. (*Hint:* Compute the value of the harvests from the regulated forest as shown in Sec. 7.4, and subtract these values from those in Table 7.4 to obtain the value of the harvests during the conversion.)

How does the relative importance of the two components of forest value change as the conversion period increases? Explain this pattern. (Recall that the longer the conversion, the smaller the impact of the terminal rotation on forest value.)

Consider the effect of the terminal rotation on the value of harvests during conversion. Does it decline with the length of the conversion period?

7.5. A lumber company owning a 10,000-acre Douglas-fir forest in Oregon has charged you with developing its long-term harvest-scheduling plan. The company plans to hold onto the forest indefinitely, and therefore wants to manage it to maximize present value over an infinite time horizon. The harvestable volume per acre is directly related to stand age as shown below (it can be assumed to be constant for stands more than 180 years old). The forest's current growing stock, also shown below, has a significant old-growth component. Management currently consists of clearcutting followed immediately by aerial seeding. This management appears to maintain forest productivity close to its current level.

You plan to use a dynamic model to find the impact of alternative terminal rotation lengths and conversion periods on the forest's value. The model should use a time unit of 20 years, a constant stumpage price of $100 per thousand board feet (Mbft), and a conservative interest rate of 3 percent per year. Write out models in tableau form for maximizing the present value of harvests for conversions of 3 and 4 periods (sixty and eighty years) and terminal rotations of 2 and 3 periods (forty and sixty years). Solve these models using a computer.

Which combination of conversion length and terminal rotation maximizes forest value? (Note: Be sure to consider the value of harvests from the regulated forest.)

GROWING STOCK AND PER-ACRE YIELDS FOR A DOUGLAS-FIR FOREST

Age (years)	Age Class	Per-acre yield (Mbft)	Growing stock (Acres)
0–20	1	0.5	500
20–40	2	4.7	500
40–60	3	9.1	500
60–80	4	12.5	500
80–100	5	14.9	1000
100–120	6	16.6	1000
120–140	7	17.8	2000
140–160	8	18.8	4000
160–180	9	18.8	0

7.6. Calculate the volume harvested each 20-year period for the harvest schedule associated with the "optimal" combination of conversion length and terminal rotation found in Prob. 7.5. What pattern do you observe?

7.7. The management of the lumber company described in Prob. 7.5 is concerned about erratic period-to-period variations in the volume that would be harvested under a free-flow policy. Accordingly, they direct you to investigate even-flow and accelerated-cut policies. For an 80-year conversion and a 60-year terminal rotation, determine the constant 20-year output for an even-flow policy. What would the present value of the forest be under such a policy? What is the cost of the policy? What rotation would maximize forest value under an even-flow policy?

7.8. Write the even-flow constraints for the model from Prob. 7.5 for an 80-year conversion and a 60-year terminal rotation. Add these constraints to the model, and solve it with a computer to determine if such a policy is feasible.

7.9. Write the accelerated-cut constraints for the model of Prob. 7.5 for an 80-year conversion and a 60-year terminal rotation. Add these constraints to the model and solve it. What would be the value of the forest under such a policy?

7.10. Discuss the advantages and disadvantages of free-flow, even-flow, and accelerated-cut policies for the management of the forest described in Prob. 7.5.

7.11. Discuss the advantages and disadvantages of the dynamic forest models used in Chaps. 6 and 7 compared to those used in Chaps. 4 and 5.

ANNOTATED REFERENCES

Davis, L. S., and K. N. Johnson. 1986. *Forest management*. McGraw-Hill, New York. 790 pp. (Chapter 16 discusses the evaluation of alternative harvest schedules and harvest-flow constraints.)

Faustmann, M. 1849. On the determination of the value which forest land and immature stands possess for forestry. *In* Martin Faustmann and the evolution of discounted cash flow (M. Gane, ed). Commonwealth Forestry Institute Paper 42. Oxford. (Origin of the definition of soil expectation value used in this chapter.)

Fight, R. D., and D. L. Schweitzer. 1974. What if we calculate the allowable cut in cubic feet? *Journal of Forestry* 72(2):87–89. (Shows the importance of units of measurement in calculating harvest-flow constraints on public forests.)

Gould. E. M., Jr. 1960. Fifty years of management at the Harvard forest. Bulletin No. 29. Harvard Forest, Petersham, Mass. 30 pp. (A striking example of the economic gains resulting from an accelerated-cut policy).

Hann, D. W. and J. D. Brodie. 1980. Even-aged management: Basic managerial questions and available or potential techniques for answering them. U.S. Forest Service General Technical Report INT-83. Intermountain Forest and Range Experiment Station, Ogden. 29 pp. (Review of the different approaches that have been or could be used to schedule harvests for even-aged forests. Many references.)

Hrubes, R. J. 1976. National forest system working circles: A question of size and ownership composition. U.S. Forest Service General Technical Report PSW-16. Pacific Southwest Forest and Range Experiment Station, Berkeley. 8 pp. (How the geographic and organizational scope considered influences harvest flow constraints on public forests.)

Nautiyal, J. C., and P. H. Pearse. 1967. Optimizing the conversion to sustained yield—A programming solution. *Forest Science* 13(2):131–139. (This article was the first to outline the method of computing the interaction between conversion and rotation used in this chapter.)

Schweitzer, D. L., R. W. Sassaman, and C. H. Schallau. 1972. The allowable cut effect: Some physical and economic implications. *Journal of Forestry* 70(7):415–418. (Impact of forest age structure on harvest flow constraints. Possibility of increasing allowable harvests by combining old-growth and young-growth forests for planning purposes.)

Teeguarden, D. E. 1973. The allowable cut effect: A comment. *Journal of Forestry* 71(4):224–226. (Comment on Schweitzer, Sassaman, and Schallau's paper.)

Walker, J. L. 1977. Economic efficiency and the National Forest Management Act of 1976. *Journal of Forestry* 75(11):715–718. (An economic critique of the harvest flow constraints imposed on public forests.)

Chapter 8

Managing the Uneven-Aged Forest with Linear Programming

8.1 INTRODUCTION

In an *uneven-aged* or selection forest, many trees of different age and size coexist on small tracts of land. In contrast with an even-aged forest, distinct areas of homogeneous age classes cannot be distinguished. The ideal uneven-aged forest, where trees of all ages appear on the same acre, is however, rare. Often, trees may be grouped in patches of similar age, but the patches are too small to be managed like the even-aged compartments that we used in the previous chapters.

Large tracts are never clear-cut in the uneven-aged forest. Rather, one selects within stands single trees or group of trees. Consequently, unlike even-aged stands, uneven-aged stands have no beginning and no end. There are always trees on each acre of the uneven-aged forest, even immediately after harvest.

In a selection forest, regeneration is mostly natural. It comes from the stock of saplings in the understory emerging through the openings left by cutting the large trees. Therefore, this form of management works best with trees that are shade tolerant, for example, maples, hemlocks, cedars, spruces, and firs. Nevertheless, many forests of ponderosa pine in western United States are uneven-aged, despite the fact that the species needs light for good regeneration. In that case, instead of the pure form of selection cutting, trees are cut in small patches, leading to an overall structure that is essentially uneven-aged for management purposes.

Uneven-aged management leads to a forest with a more natural aspect than its even-aged counterpart. For that reason, it is very attractive for forests managed for multiple use, including recreation. For small, private woodlots, it is often the only form of cutting that is acceptable. In that case, a good-looking forest not only pleases the owner, but it often enhances the value of his property.

Unfortunately, uneven-aged management is usually believed to be inferior from a purely economic point of view. Of course, this is certainly not the case for a woodlot in which timber production is only a secondary object. But even for pure timber management, the case against uneven-aged management is not that clear. First of all, for some species, it is the only possible silviculture, if any regeneration is to be obtained at all. The starting of a new crop of good trees is the most costly operation in forestry. In uneven-aged management this cost is minimal.

On the other hand, the costs of harvesting, per unit of volume, are indeed generally greater in a selection forest. There are two reasons for this. First, more area must be covered to extract a given volume than by clear-cutting. This means higher costs for roading and movement of machinery and people. Second, the felling of trees and hauling of logs is a more delicate operation in a selection forest. Care must be taken not to damage the trees that are left, especially young saplings that will constitute the future crops. This is a labor-intensive process that can be done only by skilled workers and that is difficult to mechanize. For this reason, uneven-aged management is most appropriate for the production of large trees leading to expensive, high-quality timbers for which the cost of harvesting represents a small part of the value of the final product.

Perhaps because they are more complex than even-aged systems, selection cutting systems have not been studied as much. Relatively few models of selection forests exist, and little is known about the real economics of these forests for timber production. The object of this chapter is to study such a model, originally developed by Buongiorno and Michie (1980), and to use it to investigate problems of interest to forest managers. These problems include the length of the cutting cycle, i.e., the interval between successive cuttings on a given tract of land, and the intensity of the cut, i.e., the number and size of trees to be removed.

8.2 A GROWTH MODEL OF THE UNEVEN-AGED FOREST STAND

The model deals with an uneven-aged stand. A *stand* is an area small enough to be cut within a short period of time, say a year. Thus, a stand could be the entire woodlot of a farmer, or one-twentieth of a large industrial forest managed on a 20-year cutting cycle. The state of a stand is described by the diameter distribution of trees on the average acre. Usually, this distribution is determined from a few sample plots.

Table 8.1 shows the diameter distribution of a managed sugar-maple stand in the Lake States. To lighten notations, only three diameter classes have been used. In practice, six or seven classes are often necessary, but the

TABLE 8.1   DIAMETER DISTRIBUTION OF AN UNEVEN-AGED
SUGAR MAPLE STAND

Diameter class, i	Diameter range (inches)	Number of trees	Average diameter (inches)	Basal area of tree (ft^2)	Total basal area (ft^2 / a)
1	4.0–7.9	420	6.0	0.20	84
2	8.0–13.9	117	11.0	0.66	77
3	14.0 +	7	16.0	1.40	10
Total		544			171

principles remain the same. The table shows the typical inverse J shape of the diameter distribution in an uneven-aged stand, with many small trees and a few large ones.

In this model, the state of the stand at any point in time is represented by three variables: $y_{1,t}$, $y_{2,t}$, $y_{3,t}$, where $y_{i,t}$ is the number of live trees per acre in diameter class i at time t. A growth model is then a set of equations that gives the state of the stand at time $t + 1$, given its current state. Our model consists of three equations:

$$y_{1,t+1} = a_1 y_{1,t} + O_t$$
$$y_{2,t+1} = b_1 y_{1,t} + a_2 y_{2,t}$$
$$y_{3,t+1} = \qquad\qquad b_2 y_{2,t} + a_3 y_{3,t} \qquad\qquad (8.1)$$

where the variable O_t in the first equation is the *ingrowth*, the number of young trees that enter the first diameter class during the interval t to $t + 1$.

Each parameter a_i is the fraction of live trees in diameter class i at t that are still alive and in the same diameter class at $t + 1$. Each parameter b_i is the fraction of live trees in diameter class i at t that are alive, but in diameter class $i + 1$ at $t + 1$.

Consequently, the fraction of trees in age class i at t that are dead at $t + 1$ is $1 - a_i - b_i$, since a tree can only remain in the same class, grow into a higher class, or die. The time unit used is short enough that no tree can skip one diameter class.

Table 8.2 shows specific values of the parameters a_i and b_i that apply to the stand in Table 8.1. The parameters are based on observations from permanent plots that were remeasured several times. In Table 8.2, $a_1 = 0.80$

TABLE 8.2   FRACTION OF TREES STAYING IN THE SAME DIAMETER
CLASS, GROWING INTO A THE NEXT DIAMETER CLASS OR
DYING WITHIN 5 YEARS

Diameter class, i	Fraction staying, a_i	Fraction growing, b_i	Fraction dying, $1 - a_i - b_i$
1	0.80	0.04	0.16
2	0.90	0.02	0.08
3	0.90	0.00	0.10

and $b_1 = 0.04$ mean that on average 80 percent of the trees in the smallest diameter class will be in the same class 5 years later, while 4 percent of the trees will move to the larger class. The remaining 16 percent are expected to die.

With the parameters in Table 8.2, the growth model (8.1) becomes:

$$y_{1,t+1} = 0.80y_{1,t} \qquad\qquad\qquad + O_t$$
$$y_{2,t+1} = 0.04y_{1,t} + 0.90y_{2,t}$$
$$y_{3,t+1} = \qquad\qquad 0.02y_{2,t} + 0.90y_{3,t} \qquad\qquad (8.2)$$

To complete the model, we need an expression of the ingrowth, O_t. Biometric studies have shown that ingrowth is very erratic. Nevertheless, other things being equal, ingrowth tends to decrease with the basal area and to increase with the number of trees per unit area. For our sugar maple forest it was found that, on average:

$$\begin{array}{ccc} O_t & = 40 - 0.9B_t & + 0.3N_t \\ \text{(trees/acre/5 years)} & \left(\text{ft}^2/\text{acre}\right) & \text{(trees/acre)} \end{array}$$

where B_t and N_t are the basal area and number of trees, and the ingrowth is measured over a 5-year period. The relationship shows that, for two stands with the same number of trees per acre, ingrowth is smaller where the trees are larger, and thus the basal area per acre is higher. This is what we expect since in mature stands the thick canopy of the larger trees tends to suppress the growth of younger ones. On the other hand, for two stands of the same basal area per acre, the one with more trees per acre is a younger stand in which ingrowth is more active.

This expression of ingrowth can be changed readily into one involving $y_{1,t}$, $y_{2,t}$, and $y_{3,t}$ only, since:

$$N_t = y_{1,t} + y_{2,t} + y_{3,t}$$

and

$$B_t = 0.20y_{1,t} + 0.66y_{2,t} + 1.40y_{3,t}$$

where each coefficient is the basal area of the average tree in the corresponding diameter class (see Table 8.1). Thus:

$$O_t = 40 + 0.12y_{1,t} - 0.29y_{2,t} - 0.96y_{3,t}$$

Therefore, the final expression of the growth model is:

$$y_{1,t+1} = 0.92y_{1,t} - 0.29y_{2,t} - 0.96y_{3,t} + 40$$
$$y_{2,t+1} = 0.04y_{1,t} + 0.90y_{2,t}$$
$$y_{3,t+1} = \qquad\qquad 0.02y_{2,t} + 0.90y_{3,t} \qquad\qquad (8.3)$$

This basic growth model involves only variables describing the state of the stand at time t and $t + 1$. We shall use it in the next section to describe the growth of an undisturbed stand. Then, we shall use the model to determine the best cutting regime for different management objectives.

8.3 PREDICTING THE GROWTH OF AN UNMANAGED STAND

Stand Dynamics

Let $y_{1,0}$, $y_{2,0}$, and $y_{3,0}$ be the state of an uneven-aged stand at $t = 0$. We would like to predict its future state if it is not cut. To do this we can apply the basic growth relationship (8.3) iteratively. For example, to predict the undisturbed growth of the sugar maple forest displayed in Table 8.1 we set the initial conditions at:

$$y_{1,0} = 420 \qquad y_{2,0} = 117 \qquad y_{3,0} = 7 \text{ (trees per acre)}$$

Replacing these initial conditions in the growth equations gives the number of trees per acre after 5 years:

$$y_{1,1} = 0.92 \times 420 - 0.29 \times 117 - 0.96 \times 7 + 40 = 385.8$$
$$y_{2,1} = 0.04 \times 420 + 0.90 \times 117 \qquad\qquad = 122.1$$
$$y_{3,1} = \qquad\qquad 0.02 \times 117 + 0.90 \times 7 \qquad = 8.6$$

Substituting these values of $y_{1,1}$, $y_{2,1}$, and $y_{3,1}$ in the growth equations would in turn give us the state of the stand after 10 years, $y_{1,2}$, $y_{2,2}$, and $y_{3,2}$. We can proceed in that way for as long as we want. The recursive equations are easy to program in an electronic spreadsheet for microcomputers. Alternatively, one can write a more general simulation program, as discussed in Chap. 13. Regardless of the numerical solution used, the approach is general and can be applied to a model with as many diameter classes as necessary.

Figures 8.1 and 8.2 show predictions of basal area and number of trees per acre, starting with the stand in Table 8.1. That stand was logged heavily in the recent past. As a result, there were initially many trees in the smallest diameter class. If the forest were to grow undisturbed for 50 years, the number of trees in the smallest class would decline considerably. The number in the middle class would remain about constant, and that in the largest class would increase. The data for basal area, in Fig. 8.2, show the increasing importance of the largest diameter class in terms of occupation of the site. It is this dominance of the two largest diameter classes that leads to a subsequent decline in ingrowth and thus to a decline in the number of trees in the smallest diameter class.

Steady State

Figures 8.1 and 8.2 show the data for only 50 years. Pursuing the calculations much longer shows that the number of trees and basal areas oscillate with very

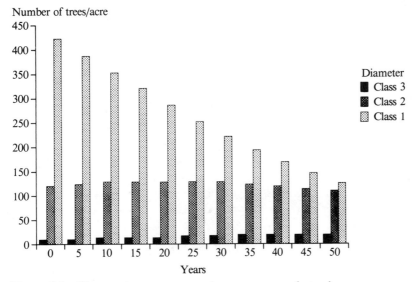

Figure 8.1 Changes in trees per acre in an unmanaged stand.

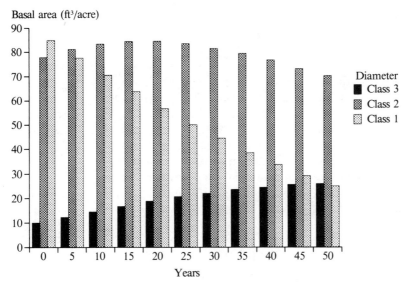

Figure 8.2 Changes in basal area per acre in an unmanaged stand.

long periods but decrease in amplitude, converging toward a steady state in which the stand remains unchanged forever.

There is a more direct way to determine the steady-state forest. By definition, *steady state* means that, regardless of the time when the stand is observed, it has always the same number of trees in each diameter class. That is:

$$y_{i,t+1} = y_{i,t} = y_i \qquad \text{for } i = 1, 2, 3, \text{ and for all } t$$

Substituting $y_{i,t+1}$ and $y_{i,t}$ by their unknown, steady-state value, y_i, in the growth model gives:

$$y_1 = 0.92y_1 - 0.29y_2 - 0.96y_3 + 40$$
$$y_2 = 0.04y_1 + 0.90y_2$$
$$y_3 = \qquad 0.02y_2 + 0.90y_3$$

This is a system of three equations in three unknowns that can be solved by substitution. The third equation yields $y_2 = 5y_3$; the second $y_1 = 2.5y_2$; which implies $y_1 = 12.5y_3$. This shows that, in the steady-state forest, there are 12.5 times as many trees in the smallest diameter class as in the largest, and 2.5 times as many as in the intermediate.

Replacing y_1 and y_2 in the first equation by their expression in terms of y_3 gives $y_3 = 11.7$, which in turn implies $y_2 = 58.5$ and $y_1 = 146.2$ trees per acre.

The steady-state distribution has the classical inverse J shape of uneven-aged stands. However, compared with the initial forest, it has fewer trees in the two smallest diameter classes and more in the largest. This is plausible, since the stand we started with is currently being managed and has its largest trees removed periodically.

8.4 GROWTH MODEL FOR A MANAGED STAND

We shall now adapt the model to predict the growth of a stand that is cut periodically. This will be done in two steps, first establishing the relationships that govern the growth of a managed uneven-aged stand and then determining the equations that define the steady state for such a stand.

Growth Equations

The harvest at a certain point in time t is described by the number of trees cut in each diameter class. In our example, this is $h_{1,t}$, $h_{2,t}$ and $h_{3,t}$, where $h_{i,t}$ is the number of trees cut from diameter class i at time t. The number of trees left after the cut in each diameter class i is thus $y_{i,t} - h_{i,t}$. These remaining trees develop according to the growth equations (8.3). Consequently, the growth of an uneven-aged stand that is cut periodically can be described by the following system of equations:

$$y_{1,t+1} = 0.92(y_{1,t} - h_{1,t}) - 0.29(y_{2,t} - h_{2,t}) - 0.96(y_{3,t} - h_{3,t}) + 40$$
$$y_{2,t+1} = 0.04(y_{1,t} - h_{1,t}) + 0.90(y_{2,t} - h_{2,t})$$
$$y_{3,t+1} = \qquad 0.02(y_{2,t} - h_{2,t}) + 0.90(y_{3,t} - h_{3,t})$$

$$(8.4)$$

This system of recursive equations describes the evolution of the stand under any sequence of harvests, regardless of their timing and level, as long as $h_{i,t} \leq y_{i,t}$. However, in this chapter we shall concentrate on harvest sequences that maintain the forest in a steady state (the classical sustained-yield management) and on cuts that occur at regular intervals. We shall use first a cutting cycle of 5 years, the time unit of the growth model, and show later how this can be changed.

Steady State for a Managed Stand

A managed uneven-aged stand is in a steady state if the amount cut from it is just equal to the amount by which the stand has grown since the last time that it was cut (Fig. 8.3).

This must be true for each diameter class. Let y_i be the number of trees in diameter class i before harvest and h_i be the number of trees cut in the steady state, then for any t:

$$y_{i,t+1} = y_{i,t} = y_i \quad \text{and} \quad h_{i,t+1} = h_{i,t} = h_i \quad \text{for } i = 1,2,3$$

which, substituted in the growth model (8.4), gives:

$$y_1 = 0.92(y_1 - h_1) - 0.29(y_2 - h_2) - 0.96(y_3 - h_3) + 40$$
$$y_2 = 0.04(y_1 - h_1) + 0.90(y_2 - h_2)$$
$$y_3 = \qquad\qquad 0.02(y_2 - h_2) + 0.90(y_3 - h_3) \qquad (8.5)$$

This is a system of three equations with six unknowns. The only meaningful solutions are those such that:

$$h_i \le y_i \quad \text{for } i = 1,2,3 \qquad (8.6)$$

because the number of trees cut from each class cannot exceed what is available. There is more than one solution to equations (8.5) and inequalities (8.6), that is, more than one combination of growing stock (y_1, y_2, y_3) and harvest (h_1, h_2, h_3) that maintain a steady state. Our goal is to find the solution that best meets specific objectives.

Number of trees/acre

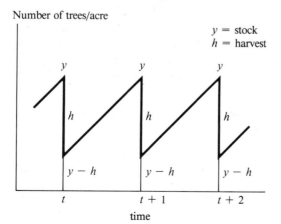

Figure 8.3   Steady state in a managed uneven-aged stand.

8.5 MAXIMIZING THE VOLUME PRODUCED

A classical goal of sustained-yield management is to maximize the volume produced per unit of time while maintaining the forest in a steady state. In our example this means that the stand is restored every 5 years to the state it was in 5 years earlier, and the volume cut every 5 years is constant. Table 8.3 shows the volume, in board feet (bft) of the average tree in each diameter class. The total volume cut from the forest every 5 years is:

$$Z_Q = 20 \quad h_1 + 100h_2 + 300h_3$$
$$\text{(bft)} \quad \text{(bft/tree) (trees)}$$

The object is to find the harvest h_1, h_2, h_3 that maximizes this function while satisfying the equations (8.5) and inequalities (8.6). Rearranging the variables in the usual linear-programming format gives the linear-programming tableau in Table 8.4. The optimum solution of this linear program is:

Growing trees per acre: $y_1^* = 500$, $y_2^* = 20$, $y_3^* = 0$

Trees cut per acre per 5 years: $h_1^* = 0$, $h_2^* = 20$, $h_3^* = 0$

Volume produced per acre per 5 years: $Z_Q^* = 2000$ bft

Thus, the optimum stand structure consists in having, just before harvest, 500 trees per acre in the smallest diameter class, 20 in the medium, and nothing in the largest. The optimum cutting rule is to remove every 5 years all the trees from the medium diameter class. This leads to a maximum constant production of 400 board feet per acre per year.

TABLE 8.3 VOLUME AND VALUE OF AVERAGE TREES BY DIAMETER CLASS

Diameter class, i	Volume, q_i (bft)	Value, v_i ($)
1	20	0.15
2	100	4.00
3	300	10.00

TABLE 8.4 LINEAR-PROGRAMMING TABLEAU TO MAXIMIZE VOLUME WITH A CUTTING CYCLE OF 5 YEARS

	y_1	y_2	y_3	h_1	h_2	h_3	
Cla1	0.08	0.29	0.96	0.92	−0.29	−0.96	= 40
Cla2	−0.04	0.10		0.04	0.90		= 0
Cla3		−0.02	0.10		0.02	0.90	= 0
Gec1	1			−1			≥ 0
Gec2		1			−1		≥ 0
Gec3			1			−1	≥ 0
Z_Q				20	100	300	

Using the growth model, verify that in 5 years, the stand is restored to its initial structure just before the harvest.

8.6 ECONOMIC HARVEST AND CUTTING CYCLE

The object here is to determine the structure of the steady-state forest and the corresponding harvest that maximizes the net present value of returns to the owner. We shall proceed in two steps: (1) finding the best stock and harvest for a given cutting cycle, and then (2) determining the effect of changing the cutting cycle.

Maximizing Present Value for a Given Cutting Cycle

For the sugar maple stand in our example, using the data in Table 8.3, the value of the harvest cut periodically in a steady state is:

$$V_H = 0.15h_1 + 4h_2 + 10h_3 \ (\$/a)$$

This value recurs every 5 years and can be sustained forever. Thus, the present value of all the harvests starting at time zero is, assuming an interest rate of 5 percent per year:

$$P_H = V_H + \frac{V_H}{1.05^5 - 1} = V_H \frac{1.05^5}{1.05^5 - 1},$$

which leads to:

$$P_H = 0.69h_1 + 18.5h_2 + 46.2h_3 \ (\$/a)$$

However, to receive this the owner must invest the initial growing stock, which has a value of:

$$V_S = 0.15y_1 + 4y_2 + 10y_3 \ (\$/a)$$

This is undoubtedly a cost since the money tied up in growing stock could be used in other ways. Consequently, what the owner needs to maximize is the present value of the harvests, net of the investment in growing stock, that is:

$$Z_{PV} = P_H - V_S$$
$$Z_{PV} = 0.69h_1 + 18.5h_2 + 46.2h_3 - 0.15y_1 - 4y_2 - 10y_3 \qquad (8.7)$$
$$(\$/a)$$

This is the new objective function. The constraints on the possible values of y_1, y_2, y_3 and h_1, h_2, h_3 remain the same as in Table 8.4; they ensure a sustained yield. The optimum solution for this program is:

Growing trees per acre: $y_1^* = 500, \ y_2^* = 20, \ y_3^* = 0$

Trees cut per acre per 5 years: $h_1^* = 0, \ h_2^* = 20, \ h_3^* = 0$

Present value: $Z_{PV}^* = 215 \ (\$/a)$

In this example, the cutting rule is the same as that which maximizes volume produced: cut all the middle-sized trees every 5 years. But this is not always so.

Changing the Cutting Cycle

To study the effect of variations in the length of the cutting cycle, we need a model to predict the growth of a stand over several units of time. We have seen how to do this by iteration in Sec. 8.3. But a more compact model can be obtained readily from the growth equations (8.3). These equations can be rewritten in matrix notation (see App. A for further explanations) as:

$$\mathbf{y}_{t+1} = \mathbf{Gy}_t + \mathbf{c} \tag{8.8}$$

where:

$$\mathbf{G} = \begin{bmatrix} 0.92 & -0.29 & -0.96 \\ 0.04 & 0.90 & 0 \\ 0 & 0.02 & 0.90 \end{bmatrix} \qquad \mathbf{c} = \begin{bmatrix} 40 \\ 0 \\ 0 \end{bmatrix} \qquad \mathbf{y}_t = \begin{bmatrix} y_{1,t} \\ y_{2,t} \\ y_{3,t} \end{bmatrix}$$

Starting in state $\mathbf{y}_t$ and applying this relationship twice we get:

$$\mathbf{y}_{t+2} = \mathbf{Gy}_{t+1} + \mathbf{c} = \mathbf{G}(\mathbf{Gy}_t + \mathbf{c}) + \mathbf{c} = \mathbf{G}^2\mathbf{y}_t + \mathbf{Gc} + \mathbf{c}$$

so that, the growth of the forest between t and $t + 2$ is given by the recursive equation:

$$\mathbf{y}_{t+2} = \mathbf{Ky}_t + \mathbf{u} \tag{8.9}$$

where $\mathbf{K} = \mathbf{G}^2$ and $\mathbf{u} = \mathbf{Gc} + \mathbf{c}$.

Equation (8.9) is analogous to (8.8). Therefore, everything we did with a cutting cycle of 5 years can be done with a cutting cycle of 10 by just replacing the coefficients of the matrix $\mathbf{G}$ by those of matrix $\mathbf{K}$ and the coefficients of vector $\mathbf{c}$ by those of vector $\mathbf{u}$.

The matrices $\mathbf{K}$ and $\mathbf{u}$ can be obtained from $\mathbf{G}$ and $\mathbf{c}$ for any cutting cycle that is a multiple of the time unit used in the growth model. To continue our example, let us use a cutting cycle of 10 years; then:

$$\mathbf{K} = \mathbf{G}^2 = \begin{bmatrix} 0.83 & -0.55 & -1.75 \\ 0.07 & 0.80 & -0.04 \\ 0 & 0.04 & 0.81 \end{bmatrix} \quad \text{and} \quad \mathbf{u} = \mathbf{Gc} + \mathbf{c} = \begin{bmatrix} 76.8 \\ 1.6 \\ 0 \end{bmatrix}$$

and the steady-state equations (8.5) become:

$$\begin{aligned} y_1 &= 0.83(y_1 - h_1) - 0.55(y_2 - h_2) - 1.75(y_3 - h_3) + 76.8 \\ y_2 &= 0.07(y_1 - h_1) + 0.80(y_2 - h_2) - 0.04(y_3 - h_3) + 1.6 \\ y_3 &= 0.04(y_2 - h_2) + 0.81(y_3 - h_3) \end{aligned}$$

where $h_i \leq y_i$ for $i = 1, 2, 3$. These equations are the constraints in the new linear program (Table 8.5).

Given the objective to maximize present value, the only change in the objective function (8.7) is that the time interval in the discount formula

TABLE 8.5   LINEAR-PROGRAMMING TABLEAU TO MAXIMIZE PRESENT
VALUE WITH A CUTTING CYCLE OF 10 YEARS

	y_1	y_2	y_3	h_1	h_2	h_3	
Cla1	0.17	0.55	1.75	0.83	−0.55	−1.75	= 76.8
Cla2	−0.07	0.20	0.04	0.07	0.80	−0.04	= 1.6
Cla3		−0.04	0.19		0.04	0.81	= 0
Gec1	1			−1			≥ 0
Gec2		1			−1		≥ 0
Gec3			1			−1	≥ 0
Z_{PV}	−0.15	−4.0	−10.0	0.39	10.4	25.9	

increases from 5 to 10 years, leading to:

$$P_H = V_H \frac{1.05^{10}}{1.05^{10} - 1} = \frac{(0.15h_1 + 4h_2 + 10h_3)1.05^{10}}{1.05^{10} - 1}$$
$$= 0.39h_1 + 10.4h_2 + 25.9h_3$$

so that the expression of the new objective function is:

$$Z_{PV} = P_H - V_S$$
$$= 0.39h_1 + 10.4h_2 + 25.9h_3 - 0.15y_1 - 4y_2 - 10y_3$$

The complete linear-programming tableau for a 10-year cutting cycle appears in Table 8.5. The optimum solution of this linear program is:

Growing trees per acre: $y_1^* = 452$, $y_2^* = 33$, $y_3^* = 0$
Trees cut per acre per 10 years: $h_1^* = 0$, $h_2^* = 33$, $h_3^* = 0$
Present value: $Z_{PV}^* = 145$ ($/a)

Thus, the rule is to cut all the trees in the intermediate diameter class every 10 years. This is the same as for a cutting cycle of 5 years, but the effects are different. About twice as many trees are cut under the longer cutting cycle and slightly less timber is produced in that way, 330 bft/a/y instead of 400.

Furthermore, the net present value yielded by the 10-year cutting cycle is $70 per acre less than than for a 5-year cycle. However, as we shall see next, the presence of other costs may make the longer cutting cycle more profitable.

Effect of Fixed Costs on the Economic Cutting Cycle

In the assumptions made so far, the owner was selling his trees on the stump and incurred no cost in preparing the sale of timber, seeking willing buyers, preparing the bids, and overseeing the harvest. But this may not be very realistic; in most circumstances, the owner will have such costs.

To pursue our example, $40 per acre to prepare and supervise a sale. Furthermore, let us assume this cost shall remain constant in the future. Then, the net present value under a cutting cycle of 5 years is:

$$215 - 40\left(\frac{1.05^5}{1.05^5 - 1}\right) = \$30 \text{ per acre}$$

while with a 10-year cutting cycle it is:

$$145 - 40\left(\frac{1.05^{10}}{1.05^{10} - 1}\right) = \$41 \text{ per acre}$$

In this case, the longer cutting cycle would be best.

8.7 GENERAL FORMULATION

The example we have followed throughout this chapter is just one particular case of a general model of uneven-aged management that has the following form. For conciseness, matrix notation is used throughout.

Model of Stand Growth

An uneven-aged stand is represented by the vector y_t of order n, in which each entry is the average number of trees per acre in a particular diameter class at time t. The number of trees cut from the stand at time t is designated by the column vector h_t, of order n. The growth of the forest is described by the recursive equation:

$$y_{t+1} = G(y_t - h_t) + c \tag{8.10}$$

where G is a matrix of coefficients of order $n \times n$ and c is a vector of constant parameters. These coefficients are derived from two sets of data: (1) the fraction of trees that move from one diameter class to another during a single time period, and (2) an equation that relates ingrowth positively to the number of trees per acre and negatively to basal area.

The growth of an initial forest y_0 can be predicted for as long as necessary by using equation (8.10) recursively:

$$y_1 = G(y_0 - h_0) + c$$
$$y_2 = G(y_1 - h_1) + c$$
$$\vdots$$

In this chapter we concentrated on sustained-yield regimes, that is, those that maintain the forest in a perpetual steady state. For the forest to be in a steady state, the harvest h and growing stock y must be such that:

$$y_{t+1} = y_t = y \quad \text{and} \quad h_t = h \quad \text{for all } t$$

Substituting in the basic growth equation shows that sustained-yield harvests and growing stock must satisfy the system of equations:

$$y = G(y - h) + c \quad \text{or} \quad y - G(y - h) = c$$

and, in addition, the harvest cannot exceed the stock: $y - h \geq 0$.

If the forest is not cut at all, then $\mathbf{h} = 0$ and the steady-state stand is such that $\mathbf{y} = \mathbf{Gy} + \mathbf{c}$.

Maximization of Volume

Let the volume of the average tree in each diameter class be designated by the row vector $\mathbf{q}$, of dimension n. Then, the volume cut from the steady-state forest is $Z_Q = \mathbf{qh}$. The optimum harvest and residual stock under sustained yield is obtained by solving the following linear program:

$$\max Z_Q = \mathbf{qh}$$

subject to:

$$\mathbf{y} - \mathbf{G}(\mathbf{y} - \mathbf{h}) = \mathbf{c}$$
$$\mathbf{y} - \mathbf{h} \geq 0 \tag{8.11}$$

Maximization of Present Value

Let the value of the average tree in each diameter class be designated by the row vector $\mathbf{v}$, of dimension n. Then, the value of the harvest from the steady-state forest is $\mathbf{vh}$.

The present value of all harvests, over an infinite horizon is:

$$P_H = \mathbf{vh} \frac{(1 + r)^T}{(1 + r)^T - 1}$$

where r is the interest rate per year and T is the length of the cutting cycle in years. The value of the investment in growing stock needed to provide these returns is $\mathbf{vy}$. Therefore, the net present value of the returns is:

$$Z_{PV} = \mathbf{vh} \frac{(1 + r)^T}{(1 + r)^T - 1} - \mathbf{vy}$$

The optimum harvest $\mathbf{h}$ and residual growing stock $\mathbf{y}$ under sustained yield are then obtained by solving a linear program with the objective function Z_{PV} and the same constraints as in (8.11).

Changing the Cutting Cycle

In the constraints of (8.11), the matrices $\mathbf{G}$ and $\mathbf{c}$ must be consistent with the length of the cutting cycle. $\mathbf{G}$ and $\mathbf{c}$ can be computed readily for any cutting cycle that is a multiple of the time unit in the basic growth model. As shown in Sec. 8.6 the growth of a stand during m time units is given by:

$$\mathbf{y}_{t+m} = \mathbf{Ky}_t + \mathbf{u}$$

where

$$\mathbf{K} = \mathbf{G}^m \quad \text{and} \quad \mathbf{u} = \sum_{i=0}^{m-1} \mathbf{G}^i \mathbf{c}$$

so that changing the cutting cycle from 1 to n time units is equivalent to replacing the matrices **G** and **c** in the constraints of (8.11) by **K** and **u**.

Similarly, the coefficients of the objective function Z_{PV} must be consistent with the cutting cycle. Then, one linear program is solved for each cutting cycle. The cutting cycle that leads to the highest present value is best, from an economic point of view.

Effect of Fixed Costs

To determine the economic cutting cycle, one must subtract from the present value, Z_{PV}, the present value of the fixed costs (per acre) that are not reflected in the price vector **v**. These costs may vary with the management regime; they tend to lengthen the economic cutting cycle.

8.8 CONCLUSIONS

In this chapter we first studied a growth model of an uneven-aged stand consisting of a set of recursive equations. The model can be used to predict the evolution of an uneven-aged stand under varied management regimes.

We then used the growth model to predict the harvest and growing stock that kept a stand in a steady state. The next step was to use a linear program to determine the cutting rules that maximized either the total volume produced per unit of time, or the present value of returns, for a given cutting cycle. We then showed how to vary the cutting cycle.

Actual stands are not in a steady state, nor should they be. Like the regulated forest used in even-aged management, the steady state of an uneven-aged stand is useful as a distant and changing goal that is never achieved. The economic growing stock and cutting cycle for the steady state are as useful as the economic rotation for the even-aged regulated forest. They give us a target.

Given the particular condition of a stand, the steady-state cutting rules may not be optimal, although they will eventually convert the stand into the optimal steady state, as we shall see in Chap. 13. Their definite advantage is that they are simple rules that can be readily implemented in the field.

PROBLEMS

8.1. For a sugar-maple stand, the fractions of trees remaining in the same diameter class or growing into a larger class in five years are shown in the following table. Assuming that the definition of the diameter classes is the same as that used in the text, do these fractions show a faster or slower growing stand than the one described by Table 8.2? What fraction of the trees in each diameter class dies every 5 years?

FIVE-YEAR GROWTH PARAMETERS FOR A
SUGAR MAPLE STAND

Diameter class	Fraction remaining in same class	Fraction growing into next class
1	0.79	0.02
2	0.88	0.01
3	0.85	0.00

8.2. Consider the following ingrowth equations:

1. $O_t = 40 - 0.9BA_t + 0.3N_t$

2. $O_t = 35 - BA_t + 0.1N_t$

where all terms are defined as in Sec. 8.2 in the text. For a stand of 540 ft^2/acre of basal area and 110 trees/acre, which equation implies more ingrowth? Assume the basal area remains at 540 ft^2/acre but the number of trees per acre changes, how does the ingrowth change for the two equations? Assume the number of trees remains at 110 trees/acre but the basal area changes, how does the ingrowth change for the two equations?

8.3. The set of equations (8.1) in the text describes the state of an uneven-aged stand at time $t + 1$ in terms of ingrowth, and the state of the stand at time t. Modify these growth equations to include a fourth diameter class.

8.4. The owner of a woodlot of northern oaks has asked for your advice regarding its management. He favors uneven-aged silviculture because his home is in the center of the lot and he wants to minimize the visual effect of cut trees.

   This owner has obtained some growth data for northern oak stands on similar sites, shown below, from his Extension agent. You will use these data to provide the owner with a set of equations to predict the growth of the oaks.

   To do this, substitute the growth data shown below and the ingrowth equation $O_t = 35 - BA_t + 0.1N_t$ into the growth equations developed in Problem 8.3. Write the resulting set of equations in a form similar to equations (8.3) in the text.

   Which do you think would be more difficult to actually determine, the ingrowth equation or the fractions characterizing the growth of larger trees? Why?

FIVE-YEAR GROWTH PARAMETERS FOR AN OAK STAND

Diameter class	Fraction remaining in same class	Fraction growing into next class	Basal area of individual tree (ft^3)
1	0.78	0.03	0.20
2	0.87	0.02	0.66
3	0.89	0.01	1.40
4	0.90	0.00	2.50

8.5. Write the steady-state equations for an undisturbed stand using the growth equations developed in Problem 8.4. The results should be similar to those of Sec. 8.3 in the text. Using these equations, calculate the steady-state number of trees, by diameter class for an undisturbed stand. Plot the number of trees against diameter class. Does this plot have the inverse J shape associated with uneven-aged forests?

8.6. Consider the growth model for northern oak developed in Problem 8.4. Replace the ingrowth equation by $O_t = 40 - 0.9BA_t + 0.3N_t$. With the resulting model, compute the new number of trees per acre in a steady state, for an undisturbed stand. How do the results differ from those found in Problem 8.5? Why?

8.7. Consider two possible initial states for a stand of northern oaks,

1. $y_{1,0} = 200$, $y_{2,0} = 30$, $y_{3,0} = 0$, $y_{4,0} = 0$, and

2. $y_{1,0} = 20$, $y_{2,0} = 10$, $y_{3,0} = 5$, $y_{4,0} = 1$.

State **1** describes a stand that has been heavily cut over, state **2** a stand in which many of the trees in the smallest diameter class have died from deer browsing.

Use the growth model developed in Problem 8.4 to forecast the number of trees in each diameter class after 5, 10, 15, 20, and 25 years of undisturbed growth from each initial state. Can you detect any convergence towards the steady state identified in Problem 8.5?

8.8. Modify the growth equations developed in Problem 8.4 to reflect the growth of a stand cut every 5 years. What equations should be satisfied by the harvest and the stock in a steady state, i.e., to provide a constant periodic harvest? What constraints must the variables representing the stock and the harvest satisfy for a meaningful solution?

8.9. Using the growth equations for a managed stand developed in Problem 8.8, develop a linear program to determine the steady-state harvest that would maximize the volume produced per unit of time. Use the data in the following table to write the objective function.

VOLUME AND VALUE BY DIAMETER CLASS FOR AN OAK STAND

Diameter class	Initial stand (trees)	Volume / tree (bft)	Value / bft ($)	Value / tree ($)
1	110	10	0.01	0.10
2	26	90	0.05	4.50
3	5	325	0.35	113.75
4	1	300	0.45	135.00

8.10. Using the growth equations for a managed stand obtained in Problem 8.8, develop a linear program to determine the steady-state harvest that would maximize present value. Assume the stand is cut every 5 years and that the time horizon is infinite. Use the data in the preceding table and an interest rate of 6 percent per year to write the objective function. How does the harvest that maximizes present value differ from the one that maximizes volume found in Problem 8.9? What is the present value of the management regime that maximizes volume?

8.11. Modify the growth equations for a managed stand obtained in Problem 8.8 to reflect a 10-year cutting cycle. Still assuming an interest rate of 6 percent and the data in Problem 8.9, use linear programming to determine the steady-state harvest that maximizes present value. Assuming that the objective of the owner is purely economic, what is the best cutting cycle?

8.12. Assume the owner does his own work and that it costs him about $10 per acre to prepare and supervise a timber sale, regardless of how much timber is cut. How would this affect the relative value of cutting cycles of 5 or 10 years? Assume now that the owner hires a forestry consultant to do the work for him, at $50 per acre, how would this affect the relative value of the two cutting cycles?

ANNOTATED REFERENCES

Adams, D. M., and A. R. Ek. 1974. Optimizing the management of uneven-aged forest stands. *Canadian Journal of Forest Research* 4(3):274–287. (One of the first programming analyses of uneven-aged management. Uses nonlinear models.)

Boothby, R. D., and J. Buongiorno. 1985. UNEVEN: A computer model of uneven-aged forest management. CALS Research Report R3285, University of Wisconsin, Madison. 62pp. (Computer software implementing the concepts discussed in this chapter.)

Bosch, C. A. 1971. Redwoods: A population model. *Science* 172(3981):345–349. (Application of a model similar to that used in this chapter to model the growth and harvesting of California redwoods.)

Buongiorno, J., and B. R. Michie. 1980. A matrix model of uneven-aged forest management. *Forest Science* 26(4):609–625. (Source of the methods presented in this chapter.)

Chang, S. J. 1981. Determination of the optimal growing stock and cutting cycle for uneven-aged stand. *Forest Science* 27(4):739–744. (Uses marginal analysis instead of mathematical programming.)

Duerr, W. A., and W. E. Bond. 1952. Optimum stocking of a selection forest. *Journal of Forestry*. 50(1):12–16. (One of the pioneering economic analyses of uneven-aged forest management.)

Haight, R. G., J. D. Brodie, and D. M. Adams. 1985. Optimizing the sequence of diameter distributions and selection harvests for uneven-aged stand management. *Forest Science* 31(2):451–462. (Shows that the cutting rule that is best in the steady state may have to be changed depending on the initial condition of the stand.)

Hann, D. W., and B. B. Bare. 1979. Uneven-aged forest management: State of the art (or science?). U.S. Forest Service General Technical Report INT-50. Intermountain Forest and Range Experiment Station, Ogden. 18 pp. (Review of the philosophy and history of uneven-aged management, of the problems associated with developing and using quantitative models of uneven-aged stands.)

Leak, W. B., and J. H. Gottsacker. 1985. New approaches to uneven-aged management in New England. *Northern Journal of Applied Forestry* 2(1):28–31. (Concepts, measures and models must be kept simple in practical uneven-aged management.)

Leak, W. B., and R. E. Graber. 1976. Seedling input, death, and growth in uneven-aged northern hardwoods. *Canadian Journal of Forest Research* 6(3):368–374. (Biometric data for stands in New Hampshire.)

Martin, G. L. 1982. Investment efficient stocking guides for all-aged northern hardwoods forests. CALS Research Report R3129. University of Wisconsin, Madison. 12 pp. (Tables of economic growing stock and harvest in function of interest rate, cutting cycle and site quality. Computed with the model of Adams and Ek.)

Nautiyal, J. C. 1981. Stumpage price function for hardwoods in the Niagara district of Ontario. *Canadian Journal of Forest Research* 12(2):210–214. (Documents how the price of timber changes in function of tree diameter.)

Rorres, C. 1978. A linear programming approach to the optimal sustainable harvesting of a forest. *Journal of Environmental Management* 6(3):245–254. (Further theoretical development of the model proposed by Usher.)

Smith, D. M. 1986. *The practice of silviculture*. Wiley, New York. 527 pp. (Chapter 15 covers the principles of uneven-aged stand structure and harvesting.)

Usher, M. B. 1966. A matrix approach to the management of renewable resources, with special reference to selection forests. *Journal of Applied Ecology* 3(2):355–367. (Application of a model similar to that used in this chapter to a scots pine forest.)

Chapter 9

Multiple Objectives Management with Goal Programming

9.1 INTRODUCTION

In all the applications of linear programming studied in the preceding chapters, we assumed that there was a single overriding management goal, such as maximizing the discounted value of net revenues. This objective was represented by the objective function. There could be other objectives, for example, maintaining an even flow of timber, but these were reflected by constraints, not by the objective function.

This way of handling multiple management objectives may not be satisfactory, for several reasons. Representing goals by standard linear-programming constraints is very rigid. For example, managers that follow even-flow policies have some flexibility in the amount of timber they produce year after year. The amounts do not have to be exactly constant; rather, they should be "nearly" constant. Constraints that impose strict constancy are not only unrealistic, they may easily lead to infeasible problems. In large problems with many constraints, finding the constraint that caused the infeasibility is difficult.

Representing some goals by constraints means, in effect, giving them priority over the goal reflected by the objective function, since the objective function is optimized within the feasible region defined by the constraints. Deciding which goal should be in the objective function and which ones should be represented by constraints is often arbitrary.

Goal programming attempts to correct these limitations of linear programming while retaining its useful basic structure and numerical solution. Goal programming provides a way of striving toward all objectives simultaneously, treating all goals in the same manner while giving different weights to the various goals, if necessary.

9.2 EXAMPLE: PULP PRODUCTION AND POLLUTION REVISITED

To introduce the basic concepts of goal programming we will use the example of the Maine pulp mill given in Sec. 2.3. The board of directors of the cooperative owning the pulp mill had decided that it wanted to produce mechanical and chemical pulp to maintain at least 300 workers and to generate \$40,000 of gross revenue per day, while minimizing the amount of pollution caused by the mill. This multiple-objective problem was formulated as a standard linear-programming model, as follows: Find X_1 and X_2, amounts of daily production of mechanical and chemical pulp, such that:

$$\min Z = X_1 + 1.5X_2 \quad \text{(daily pollution, BOD units)}$$

subject to

$$
\begin{aligned}
X_1 + \quad X_2 &\geq 300 &&\text{(workers employed)} \\
100X_1 + 200X_2 &\geq 40{,}000 &&\text{(daily revenues)} \\
X_1 \quad\quad &\leq 300 &&\text{(mechanical pulping capacity)} \\
X_2 &\leq 200 &&\text{(chemical pulping capacity)} \\
X_1, X_2 &\geq 0
\end{aligned}
$$

This model is useful, but it has some drawbacks. First, it treats the pollution goal in a way that is entirely different from employment and revenues. Unless there is a compelling reason for pollution to figure in the objective function, it could as well be represented by a constraint, while employment or revenue could be the objective function (to maximize). Remember, however, that there can be only one objective function.

Second, the level of goals may be unrealistic. If employment or/and revenue goals are too high, the problem may have no feasible solution. This would be easily corrected in this small example, but might cause much trouble in solving a large problem. These problems can be reduced by using the following goal-programming techniques.

9.3 GOAL-PROGRAMMING CONSTRAINTS

In goal programming all or some of the management goals are expressed by *goal constraints*. Consider the employment goal expressed by the first constraint in the linear program above. In goal programming, that constraint is written:

$$X_1 + X_2 + L^- - L^+ = 300$$

where L^- and L^+ are *goal variables*, both greater than or equal to zero (like other linear programming variables), such that: L^- is the amount by which employment falls short of the goal of 300 workers, and L^+ is the amount by which employment exceeds the goal. Depending on the values of L^- and L^+, three cases may occur:

$L^- = 0$ and $L^+ > 0$, in which case $X_1 + X_2 = 300 + L^+$, that is, $X_1 + X_2 > 300$, and the employment goal is exceeded

$L^- = 0$ and $L^+ = 0$, in which case $X_1 + X_2 = 300$ and the employment goal is just met

$L^- > 0$ and $L^+ = 0$, in which case $X_1 + X_2 = 300 - L^-$, i.e., $X_1 + X_2 < 300$, and the employment goal is not met

It is clear that with this system, no infeasibility can result from the employment goal since, even if the goal is set unrealistically high, L^- will fill the gap between $X_1 + X_2$ and the goal. On the other hand, employment may exceed the goal because of the variable L^+.

In a similar manner, we can write a goal constraint for the revenues goal:

$$100X_1 + 200X_2 + R^- - R^+ = 40,000$$

where R^- is the amount by which revenues fall short of $40,000 and R^+ is the amount by which revenues exceed $40,000. Both variables are nonnegative.

To handle the third goal in the same way as the two others, a level must be set for the pollution goal, say 400 units of BOD per day. Then, the corresponding goal constraint is:

$$X_1 + 1.5X_2 + P^- - P^+ = 400$$

where P^- is the number of units of BOD below the goal level and P^+ is the number in excess.

The other constraints remain the same as in the linear program of Sec. 9.2: they set the limits on the capacity of production of the plant. In summary, the constraints in the goal program are:

$$
\begin{aligned}
X_1 \quad + X_2 + L^- - L^+ &= 300 \\
100X_1 + 200X_2 + R^- - R^+ &= 40,000 \\
X_1 + 1.5X_2 + P^- - P^+ &= 400 \\
X_1 \qquad\qquad\qquad &\le 300 \\
X_2 \qquad\qquad &\le 200
\end{aligned}
\tag{9.1}
$$

where all variables are non negative.

The next step, by far the most difficult in goal programming, is to specify the objective function.

9.4 GOAL-PROGRAMMING OBJECTIVE FUNCTION

The objective function of a goal-programming problem contains all or part of the goal variables. The general purpose of the objective function is to make the total deviation from all goals as small as possible. However, simply minimizing the sum of all deviations, that is, in our example, writing the objective function as:

$$\min Z = L^- + L^+ + R^- + R^+ + P^- + P^+$$

would not make much sense since the goal variables have completely different units. What we minimize then, is the weighted sum of the deviations from all the goal, namely:

$$\min Z = w_l^- L^- + w_l^+ L^+ + w_r^- R^- + w_r^+ R^+ + w_p^- P^- + w_p^+ P^+$$

where $w_l^-, \ldots, w_p^+$ are constant *weights* having two purposes: (1) to make all weighted deviations commensurate and (2) to express the relative importance of each goal. For example, w_l^- and w_p^+ must be such that $w_l^- L^-$ and $w_p^+ P^+$ are in the same units. Also, the relative magnitude of w_l^- and w_p^+ shows how important it is to fall short of the employment objective by one person, relative to exceeding the pollution objective by 1 unit of BOD per day.

Clearly, assigning appropriate weights to each one of the goal variables is not a simple task. It involves considerable judgment as well as trial and error. Very often, a first solution is computed, based on a first set of goals and weights. Then, if the solution is not satisfactory, the goal levels and/or the weights are changed and a new solution is computed. These iterations continue until a satisfactory solution is obtained. At that point, the weights should be good indicators of the relative importance of each goal to the decision makers.

To simplify the choice of weights it is best to reduce the objective function to the simplest expression consistent with the problem at hand. Often, only a few variables are needed. In our example, one concern of the cooperative is to fall short of the employment goal. Therefore, only L^- needs to be in the objective function; any positive value of L^+ is welcome. Another concern is to underachieve the revenue objective, meaning that R^- must be kept small and should therefore be in the objective function, while R^+ does not need to be there. Finally, pollution must be kept low; therefore, P^+ must be in the objective function, but P^- can be omitted. In summary, the relevant expression of the objective function for our example is:

$$\min Z = w_l^- L^- + w_r^- R^- + w_p^+ P^+$$

The difficult task of assigning values to the weights can be simplified somewhat by working with *relative deviations* from the goals. Rewrite the objective function as:

$$\min Z = w_l^- \frac{L^-}{300} + w_r^- \frac{R^-}{40,000} + w_p^+ \frac{P^+}{400}$$

where the relative values of the weights w_l^-, w_r^- and w_p^- now express the relative importance of deviating by one percentage point from the respective goals. For example, assume that the cooperative feels that it is indifferent between a 1 percent deviation from any of the three goals. This is equivalent to setting all weights equal to 1. The expression of the objective function is then:

$$\min Z = \frac{1}{300} L^- + \frac{1}{40,000} R^- + \frac{1}{400} P^+$$

where Z is dimensionless. In this equation, the coefficients are very small, especially that of R^-. This may lead to serious round-off problems in calculating a solution. To avoid this, we multiply all the coefficients by the same large number, say 10,000, which, of course, does not affect the solution. The new value of the objective function is then:

$$\min Z = 33.3L^- + 0.25R^- + 25P^+ \tag{9.2}$$

A greater concern for employment than for the other two goals could be translated by setting $w_l^- = 2$ and $w_r^- = w_p^+ = 1$, leading to the objective function:

$$\min Z = 66.6L^- + 0.25R^- + 25P^+$$

Working with relative deviations from goals has the advantage of eliminating the different units of measurement. However, it should be kept in mind that this scheme has a precise meaning in terms of the relative value of the goals. For example, let us determine the relative value of employment and revenues implied by objective function (9.2). To do this, note that the change in the objective function is related to the change in each one of the goal variables by the equation:

$$dZ = 33.3dL^- + 0.25dR^- + 25dP^+$$

where the prefix d indicates a change in the corresponding variable. For a given level of the pollution variable, that is, for $dP^+ = 0$, the changes in employment and revenues that keep the objective function unchanged satisfy the equation:

$$0 = 33.3dL^- + 0.25dR^-$$

that is,

$$\frac{dR^-}{dL^-} = -133 \text{ (dollars per day per worker)}$$

Thus, the implication of objective function (9.2) is that the members of the cooperative are willing to see revenues decline by \$133 per day if employment increases by one worker.

9.5 GOAL-PROGRAMMING SOLUTIONS

The structure of the goal-programming problem expressed by the constraints (9.1) and the objective function (9.2) is that of an ordinary linear program that can be solved by the simplex method. The corresponding tableau, ready for computer solution, is presented in Table 9.1. The optimum solution of this problem is:

$$X_1^* = 200 \text{ tons of mechanical pulp per day}$$
$$X_2^* = 100 \text{ tons of chemical pulp per day}$$
$$P^-{}^* = 50 \text{ units of BOD per day}$$

TABLE 9.1 LINEAR-PROGRAMMING TABLEAU FOR THE GOAL-PROGRAMMING VERSION OF THE PULPMILL PROBLEM

	X_1	X_2	L^-	L^+	R^-	R^+	P^-	P^+	RHS	RHS'
LABO	1	1	1	−1					= 300	600
REVE	100	200			1	−1			= 40,000	60,000
POLL	1	1.5					1	−1	= 400	300
CAP1	1								= 300	300
CAP2		1							= 200	200
Z			33.3		0.25			25		
Z'			16.7		0.17			33.3		

Note: Z' and RHS' are alternative objective functions and right-hand sides.

All other variables are zero. That is, two of the goals are met exactly and the third one is exceeded, pollution being lower than the set goal. In a situation like this, where all goals are achieved, one may suspect that the original goals were too conservative. In essence, the system we are working with seems capable to do better than what we asked. The last solution seems *inefficient*.

Aware of this, the managers of the pulping cooperative decide to increase all goal levels boldly. They double the employment goal to 600 workers, increase the revenue goal by 50 percent to $60,000 per day, and reduce the pollution goal by 25 percent to 300 units of BOD per day. The new right-hand side of the linear-programming tableau is shown in Table 9.1 under the title RHS'. The new objective function is, using relative deviations from goals:

$$\min Z' = w_l^- \frac{L^-}{600} + w_r^- \frac{R^-}{60,000} + w_p^+ \frac{P^+}{300}$$

Assuming we still give same import to the relative deviations from each goal, so that the weights are unity, we get, after multiplying all coefficients by 10,000:

$$\min Z' = 16.7L^- + 0.17R^- + 33.3P^+$$

The solution of this new linear-programming problem is:

$X_1^* = 300$ tons of mechanical pulp per day

$X_2^* = 150$ tons of chemical pulp per day

$L^{-*} = 150$ workers

$P^{+*} = 225$ units of BOD per day

Therefore, in this second trial we fall short of the employment goal and pollute more than we would like to. On the other hand, the revenues goal is met exactly.

It may well be that the cooperative does not like this solution either. In that case, it can proceed through another iteration, changing weights in the objective function, or the level of goals, or both. It can also try to force a solution to satisfy certain restrictions. For example, assume that someone is adamant about the employment goal of 600 workers. This is equivalent to $L^- = 0$, which can be imposed simply by eliminating L^- from Table 9.1. In that case, the first constraint in the table is equivalent to $X_1 + X_2 - L^+ = 600$; that is, $X_1 + X_2 \geq 600$. However, this is a regular linear-programming constraint, which may lead to infeasibilities. In fact, in this particular example, it is not possible to reach that employment level. X_1 can be at most 300 tons per day and X_2 can be at most 200 tons per day, implying a maximum employment of 500 workers.

In general, elimination of any of the goal variables restricts the feasible region and may, therefore, lead to *infeasibilities*. Instead, no infeasibility may arise from any one of the constraints in which both goal variables are present, since they fill the gap between what can be achieved and the set goal level.

9.6 OBJECTIVE FUNCTIONS WITH ORDINAL WEIGHTS

Up to now, the weights used in the objective function were cardinal numbers, measuring the relative value of each goal. There is another way of expressing the objective function in goal programming that uses ordinal instead of cardinal weights.

The procedure assumes that all the decision maker is able to do is to *order* the goals by rank of decreasing importance, without specifying how much more important one goal is relative to the other.

In our example, assume that the pulping cooperative has decided that employment has top priority, pollution second priority, and revenues come last. The goal levels are those specified under RHS' in Table 9.1. As before, the cooperative managers are concerned about underachieving the employment and revenue goals and about exceeding the pollution goal. Consequently, the relevant objective function is:

$$\min Z = w_l^- L^- + w_r^- R^- + w_p^+ P^+$$

Goal programming with *ordinal weights* assumes that $w_l^- \gg w_p^+ \gg w_r^-$, that is, the employment goal has a very large, in fact infinite, weight relative to the weight of the pollution goal, which itself has infinite weight relative to the weight of the revenue goal.

The consequences of this weighting scheme are that all resources available must be used first to approach as close as possible to the employment goal. Then, the remaining resources, if any, must be used to approach as close as possible to the pollution goal. What is left is used to approach the revenue goal.

There are special algorithms to implement this concept. They solve a sequence of linear programs. In our example, the first linear program is:

$$\min Z = L^-$$

subject to the constraints in Table 9.1. The optimum solution of this problem is:

$$X_1^* = 300 \text{ tons per day}$$
$$X_2^* = 200 \text{ tons per day}$$
$$L^{-*} = 100 \text{ workers}$$
$$P^{+*} = 300 \text{ units of BOD per day}$$
$$R^{+*} = \$10,000 \text{ per day}$$

The second linear program is

$$\min Z = P^+$$

subject to the constraints in Table 9.1 and to $L^- = 100$ workers.

The solution of this second linear program is the same as the first one. Thus, the pollution cannot be decreased. In this example, giving top priority to employment has in effect determined revenues and pollution.

Ordinal ranking of goals is appealing because it seems, superficially at least, to do away with the difficult problem of determining the relative weights of the various goals. Nevertheless, it is questionable whether it leads to solutions that reflect the true values of the decision makers. In forestry, as in all human endeavors, few goals are absolute. The statement that "goal A has priority over goal B" is more a figure of speech than a precise guideline. It rarely means, as the algorithm presented above implies, that goal A must be satisfied to the maximum possible extent before goal B is considered at all. Most values are relative, and goal programming with cardinal weights is more likely to reflect these values. This leaves us with the problem of determining the relative weights. It is a difficult task, but one can hardly escape it.

9.7 A SECOND EXAMPLE: TIMBER HARVEST SCHEDULING

Goal programming procedures can be very useful in adding flexibility to timber-harvest scheduling models. As an example of how this can be done, we will use the dynamic model of even-aged management studied in Chaps. 6 and 7. That model showed how a forest in a particular initial state could be converted into a regulated forest of specified rotation, within a particular time period. This conversion was done while maximizing either the quantity of timber produced or its present value.

In Sect. 7.6, the model was applied to study different timber-flow policies. One of them was a free-flow policy, whereby production could take any value that maximized the objective. Another policy was strict even flow, in which the amount of timber produced was to remain constant and equal to the production of the regulated forest. The third option was called an accelerated-cut policy, such that production could exceed that of the regulated forest, but never fall below it.

In Sec. 7.6 we saw that it is often difficult to obtain solutions that correspond to a strict even flow. The existence of a solution depends on the initial state of the forest, the rotation for the ending regulated forest and the length of the conversion period.

Nevertheless, as noted at the beginning of this chapter, even flow is rarely a strict requirement. Thus, even if even flow cannot be achieved exactly, it should be useful to know what sequence of harvests gives a production that is *as close as possible* to even flow. Goal programming can be used for that purpose.

To see how this is done, let us use one of the examples in Chap. 6, specifically, the short-leaf pine forest that had initially two age classes, 100 acres aged 1 to 10 years and 200 acres aged 11 to 20 years. The yield function for that forest was given in Fig. 6.1. If the rotation age on the regulated forest is 30 years and the time unit is 10 years, there will be three age classes at the end of the plan, each one covering 100 acres. The system of constraints that the sequence of harvests must satisfy to achieve regulation in 30 years was shown in Table 6.2. There, the objective was to maximize the quantity of timber produced.

The regulated forest that results from this management scheme would produce every 10 years:

$$100 \quad \times \quad 5 \quad = \quad 500$$
$$\text{(acres/10 years)} \quad \text{(1000 ft}^3/\text{acre)} \quad \text{(1000 ft}^3/\text{10 years)}$$

It turns out that the problem specified in the linear program in Table 6.2 has no solution if strict even flow is imposed, that is, if the volume produced every decade must be exactly equal to 500,000 ft^3. Verify this by adding the following constraints to Table 6.2 and solving the new linear program:

$$0.5X_{1,1} + 2.5X_{1,2} \qquad\qquad\qquad = 500$$
$$0.5X_{2,1} + 2.5X_{2,2} + 5X_{2,3} \qquad\quad = 500$$
$$0.5X_{3,1} + 2.5X_{3,2} + 5X_{3,3} + 6X_{3,4} = 500$$

where each constraint expresses the volume produced in one decade.

However, goal programming can be used to design a harvest schedule that approaches even flow as closely as possible, given the constraints. This is done with the following goal variables:

F_1^- = the quantity by which production falls short of the 500,000 ft^3 goal in the first decade

F_1^+ = the quantity by which production exceeds the 500,000 ft^3 goal in the first decade

$F_2^-, F_2^+, F_3^-, F_3^+$ are defined in a similar manner for the second and third decades

Then, rewrite the even-flow constraints as:

$$0.5X_{1,1} + 2.5X_{1,2} \qquad\qquad\qquad + F_1^- - F_1^+ = 500$$
$$0.5X_{2,1} + 2.5X_{2,2} + 5X_{2,3} \qquad\quad + F_2^- - F_2^+ = 500$$
$$0.5X_{3,1} + 2.5X_{3,2} + 5X_{3,3} + 6X_{3,4} + F_3^- - F_3^+ = 500 \qquad (9.3)$$

These constraints cannot lead to infeasibilities since the F variables fill the

TABLE 9.2 GOAL-PROGRAMMING TABLEAU TO REGULATE AN EVEN-AGED FOREST WHILE MINIMIZING THE DEVIATIONS FROM EVEN FLOW

	$X_{1,1}$	$X_{1,2}$	$X_{2,1}$	$X_{2,2}$	$X_{2,3}$	$X_{3,1}$	$X_{3,2}$	$X_{3,3}$	$X_{3,4}$	F_1^-	F_1^+	F_2^-	F_2^+	F_3^-	F_3^+	
AGC1						1	1	1	1							= 100
AGC2			1	1	1	−1										= 100
AGC3	1	1	−1				−1									= 100
AGC4	1			1				1								= 100
AGC5		1			1				1							= 200
FFF1	0.5	2.5								1	−1					= 500
FFF2			0.5	2.5	5.0							1	−1			= 500
FFF3						0.5	2.5	5.0	6.0					1	−1	= 500
Z										1	1	1	1	1	1	

gap between the volume that can actually be produced and that which is desired. The objective function then expresses the total deviation from the desired even-flow level. This total deviation must be kept as small as possible, that is:

$$\min Z = F_1^- + F_1^+ + F_2^- + F_2^+ + F_3^- + F_3^+ \qquad (9.4)$$

In this particular case, the goal variables need not be weighted since they are all in the same unit (1000 ft^3 per decade). However, weights could be used if one were more concerned about underachieving the production goal than overachieving it, or more concerned about deviations in the early part of the plan than later on.

The complete goal-programming tableau, consisting of the constraints in Table 6.2, of constraints (9.3), and of the objective function (9.4), appears in Table 9.2. The solution of that problem is:

$$X_{1,2}^* = X_{2,3}^* = X_{3,3}^* = 100 \text{ acres}$$
$$F_1^{-*} = Z^* = 250,000 \text{ ft}^3$$

This solution leads to the production shown in Fig. 9.1. During the first 10 years, production is half what the forest will produce after it is regulated. This is the closest we can come to a perfectly even production.

Nevertheless, one may wonder if a solution exists that would keep production in every decade at, or above 500,000 ft^3. This can be found by eliminating F_1^-, F_2^-, and F_3^- from the model in Table 9.2. It turns out that in this case no feasible solution exists, although a different initial forest could have such a solution (see Sec. 7.6).

Another question a forest manager may ask is whether it is possible to spread the large deviation in the first decade over the entire duration of the plan. In our model, this could be done by adding the following constraints to those in Table 9.2:

$$F_1^- - F_2^- = 0 \quad \text{and} \quad F_2^- - F_3^- = 0$$

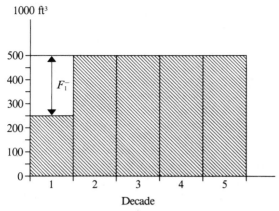

Figure 9.1   Timber production plan that minimizes deviations from even flow.

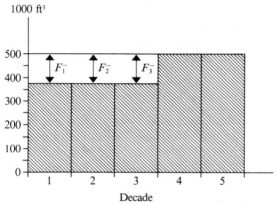

Figure 9.2   Timber production plan that minimizes constant deviations from even flow.

meaning that the deviation with respect to the desired timber output must be constant throughout the 30 years of the plan. This new problem does have a solution, namely:

$$X_{1,2}^* = 150 \text{ acres}$$
$$X_{2,2}^* = X_{3,2}^* = X_{3,3}^* = 50 \text{ acres}$$
$$F_1^{-*} = F_2^{-*} = F_3^{-*} = 125,000 \text{ ft}^3$$
$$Z^* = 375,000 \text{ ft}^3$$

The corresponding production is presented in Fig. 9.2. Note that the minimum total deviation from even flow (375,000 ft^3) is much higher than the one obtained without the last constraints (250,000 ft^3).

9.8 GENERAL FORMULATION

As we have seen in the previous examples, goal programming is just a particular formulation of the general linear-programming problem. If cardinal weights are used in the objective function, the solution is obtained by applying the simplex method once. If ordinal weights are used instead, the simplex method must be applied several times.

Constraints

A goal programming model has at least some constraints, called goal constraints, that contain goal variables. These variables measure the deviation between management goals and actual achievements. The general formulation of goal constraints is:

$$\sum_{j=1}^{n} a_{ij}X_j + D_i^- - D_i^+ = g_i \qquad \text{for } i = 1,\ldots,G \qquad (9.5)$$

where: X_j is the jth activity (decision) variable

$a_{i,j}$ is the (constant) contribution to goal i made by each unit of activity j

g_i is a constant measuring the target for goal i, and G is the total number of goals represented by goal-programming constraints.

D_i^- is a goal variable that measures the amount by which the contribution of all activities to goal i falls short of the goal level,

D_i^+ is the amount by which that contribution exceeds the goal level. All activities X_j and all goal variables, D_i^- and D_i^+ are greater than or equal to zero.

As long as both D_i^- and D_i^+ are present in a goal constraint, no infeasibility may arise due to that constraint. The goal variables always fill the gap between the goal and what can actually be achieved.

Other constraints may be present, of the usual linear-programming variety, that is:

$$\sum_{j=1}^{n} a_{i,j}X_j \gtrless b_i \qquad \text{for } i = G + 1,\ldots,m \qquad (9.6)$$

Objective Function

The general objective of goal programming is to minimize the sum of the weighted deviations from all goals. Thus, the general form of the objective function is:

$$\min Z = \sum_{i=1}^{G} \left(w_i^- D_i^- + w_i^+ D_i^+ \right) \qquad (9.7)$$

where w_i^- and w_i^+ are the constant weights given to each unit of deviation D_i^- and D_i^+, respectively.

These weights fulfill two purposes. They reduce all deviations from goals to a common unit of measurement and they reflect the relative value of each goal. Deviations that concern the decision maker most should receive larger weights, relative to the others. Deviations that are of no concern or that are favored may be omitted from the objective function altogether.

If some deviations from particular goals are unacceptable, the corresponding goal variable may be omitted from the appropriate goal constraint. For example, if goal g_i must not be exceeded, then D_i^+ may be omitted, thus forcing D_i^+ to be zero. But this procedure may lead to an infeasibility since the constraint is then equivalent to:

$$\sum_{j=1}^{n} a_{i,j} X_j \leq , = , \text{ or } \geq g_i$$

The choice of weights in the objective function (9.7) is made easier by considering the relative, rather than the absolute, deviations with respect to goals. The new expression of the objective function is then:

$$\min Z = \sum_{i=1}^{G} \frac{w_i^- D_i^- + w_i^+ D_i^+}{g_i}$$

where each weight w_i now applies to a relative deviation from goal i.

Ordinal Weighting of Goals

This procedure consists in ranking all goals in descending order, from top to least priority. Then, all resources are used to approach as close as possible to the goal that has top priority. Any resource left is then used to approach the second goal as much as possible. This is continued until the last goal is reached.

In terms of the general objective function (9.7) this system is equivalent to giving to the goal at the top of the list a weight that is infinitely large relative to the second, giving the second goal infinite weight with respect to the third, and so on, down to the bottom of the list.

The actual calculations proceed as follows: Assume that goal 1 has top priority, goal 2 second priority, and so on. Assume further that the decision maker is concerned about underachieving goal 1 and overreaching goal 2. Then, the first goal programming problem solved is:

$$\min Z = D_1^-$$

subject to constraints (9.5) and (9.6).

Let D_1^-* be the optimum value of D_1^-; this is as close as one can get to goal 1. Then a second goal programming problem is solved:

$$\min Z = D_2^+$$

subject to constraints (9.5), (9.6) and $D_1^- = D_1^-*$, where the last constraint ensures that resources are allocated to goal 2 only after goal 1 is satisfied to the maximum possible extent.

The procedure continues until all goals have been considered. Computer programs are available to go through these calculations automatically once goals have been ranked. The general formulation of the objective function

(9.7) admits a mixture of ordinal and cardinal weights. In particular, some goals may have the same priority (ranking), but different cardinal weights.

In using ordinal ranking of goals, one must keep in mind that it implies, in fact, giving infinite value to a goal relative to another. Few decisions in forest management involve such drastic choices. More often, there is a trade off between goals. Cardinal weights do represent these trade offs. Even if exact cardinal weights are never available, useful sets of weights can be got by trial and error.

9.9 CONCLUSIONS: GOAL VERSUS LINEAR PROGRAMMING

In management problems with multiple objectives, goal programming has two advantages relative to ordinary linear programming. First, all goals are represented in the same manner by goal constraints and variables. All goal variables appear in the objective function. This objective function minimizes the "cost" of deviating from all goals. Second, as long as all goal variables are present, goals can be set at any level without leading to infeasibilities. In practice, this is a considerable advantage with respect to linear programming. It means that it is easier to determine goal levels that are feasible and efficient using goal programming.

On the other hand, goal programming requires the determination of the relative value of the various goals. This is an extremely difficult task, for which no rigorous solution currently exists. Instead, the dual solution of linear programming gives us a powerful measure of the trade off between the goal in the objective function and those expressed by constraints. To gain the most out of this feature one should always try to express the objective function in a unit that is understood readily by most people.

For example, assume that a management plan for a national forest is expressed by a linear programming model. The objective function measures the value of the timber that the forest produces in a given year. Assume that recreation activity is expressed by a constraint saying that R visitor days of recreation must be provided. Then, the shadow price for the recreation constraint measures the marginal cost of one unit of recreation, in dollars per visitor day, in terms of timber revenue foregone. This is a very useful measure because it is expressed in a unit that most people can grasp. If the shadow price seems too low or too high, the recreation goal may be adjusted until a cost of recreation acceptable to all parties involved is obtained.

PROBLEMS

9.1. The manager of a National Forest in the Pacific Northwest is pondering how to harvest a particular tract of forest. He must consider both the economic and the environmental effects of his choice.

The forest tract of interest is composed of three compartments: A of 608 acres, B of 173 acres, and C of 32 acres. Two logging techniques may be used: tractor logging or hi-lead logging. Compartment B, however, is too steep for tractor logging, and the terrain in compartment C is too gentle to justify hi-lead logging. It is also possible not to log some areas at all. Estimates of the effects of each logging technique on timber production, stream sedimentation, increase in fire danger, costs, and revenues are shown in the following table.

EFFECTS OF ALTERNATIVE LOGGING TECHNIQUES

| | Compartment | | | | | | |
| | A | | | B | | C | |
Impacts	Tractor	Hi-lead	No logging	Hi-lead	No logging	Tractor	No logging
Timber (Mbft)	0.57	0.57		0.34		0.57	
Sediment (yd³)	7.84	7.74		13.30		17.20	
Fire danger (Index)	64.70	33.10	2.52	82.80	4.20	47.20	3.36
Management cost ($)	5.24	5.17		5.17		5.24	
Gross revenues ($)	64.50	74.90		44.40		64.50	

Note: All data are per acre.

Formulate a linear programming model that the manager could use to determine how to maximize gross revenues subject to the following constraints:

1. timber output of at least 450 thousand board feet (Mbft)
2. sedimentation not to exceed 7300 cubic yards (yd³)
3. fire danger index not to exceed 33900, and
4. management costs not to exceed $4500.

Try to solve this linear program with a computer. Is there a feasible solution?

9.2. Having determined that there is no feasible solution to the model developed in Problem 9.1, reformulate it as a goal-programming model, using the four constraints as goals. Add a fifth goal of earning $55,000 in gross revenues. The objective of the model should be to minimize the sum of the undesirable relative deviations from the goals. What is the best harvesting plan for the forest according to this model? What deviations would this entail from each goal? (Note: Multiply relative deviations by 10,000 to facilitate computations.)

9.3. Assume the manager of the forest described in Problem 9.1 has decided that the most important goal in that particular area of the forest is timber production, the second goal is fire control, and that all other goals are less important.

Formulate a goal-programming model to find the harvesting plan that would minimize the deviation from the timber output goal, ignoring all others. Solve this model with a computer. What is the best harvesting plan? What deviations would this entail from each goal?

9.4. Formulate a goal-programming model to decide how to harvest the forest to minimize the fire danger, while producing as much timber as in Problem 9.3. Solve this model with a computer. What is the best harvesting plan? What deviations would this entail from each goal?

9.5. In Problems 7.5 to 7.10 you developed models to determine the best harvesting plan for a Douglas-fir forest under various timber flow policies. In Problem 7.8 you discovered that, for the forest of interest, there was no way to achieve even-flow given a conversion period of 80 years and a rotation of 60.

Reformulate that problem as a goal-programming model with the objective of minimizing the sum of the positive and negative deviations from even-flow during the conversion period. Use equal weights for all deviations.

Solve this problem with a computer. What is the best harvesting plan?

Plot the volume cut and deviations from even-flow over time. What is the present value of this harvesting program? How does it compare with the present value of the accelerated-cut policy found in Problem 7.9?

9.6. Suppose that the owners of the forest used in Problem 9.5 decided that negative deviations from even-flow were unacceptable, and that positive deviations in each decade should be constant. Modify the goal programming model developed in Problem 9.5 to reflect this.

Solve this new problem with a computer. What is the best harvesting plan? Plot the harvests and deviations from even-flow over time. What is the present value of this harvesting program? What would the present value of the forest be under such a management? How does it compare with the present value of the accelerated-cut policy found in Problem 7.9, and with the present value found in Problem 9.5?

9.7. The foresters of a public forest in Arizona are developing a multiple-use plan for a 10,000-acre block of the forest. Half of this area is in high-site ponderosa-pine land, and the other half in low-site land. The plan must take into account the preferences of ranchers, loggers, recreationists, and environmentalists. Further, the plan should allocate all 10,000 acres to one of three kinds of management: (M1) wilderness, (M2) intensive timber management, or (M3) conversion to grassland. The yields per acre per year of high- and low-site land under each kind of management are shown in the following table.

YIELDS BY SITE AND KIND OF MANAGEMENT FOR
A PONDEROSA PINE FOREST

| | Yield per acre per year | | | | | |
| | High Site | | | Low Site | | |
Output	M1	M2	M3	M1	M2	M3
Timber (Mbft)	0	0.6	0	0	0.22	0
Forage (aum)	0	0.7		0	1.3	2.6
Water (a × ft)	0.33	0.35	0.73	0.25	0.26	0.30
Sediment (yd^3)	0.010	0.015	0.03	0.015	0.025	0.03
Dispersed Recreation (rvd)	0	0.5	0	0	0.5	0
Wilderness Recreation (rvd)	2.0	0	0	2.0	0	0

Note: All data are per acre and per year.

Formulate this planning problem as a linear program with the objective of maximizing timber yield subject to the following constraints:

1. forage output of at least 10,000 animal-unit months (aum),
2. water output of at least 4000 acre feet (a × ft),
3. sediment output no greater than 215 cubic yards (yd^3),
4. dispersed recreation output of at least 500 recreation visitor days (rvd),

and

5. wilderness recreation output of at least 4000 rvd.

Solve this problem with a computer. What is the best way of managing the low- and high-site lands?

9.8. Reformulate the forest planning problem developed in Problem 9.7 as a goal programming model, using the five constraints as goals. Add a sixth goal of harvesting at least 600 Mbft of timber. The objective function is now to minimize the sum of the undesirable relative deviations from the goals. What is the best way of managing the low- and high-site lands? What deviations does this entail from each goal?

ANNOTATED REFERENCES

Bare, B. B., and B. F. Anholt. 1976. Selecting forest residue treatment alternatives using goal programming. U.S. Forest Service General Technical Report PNW-43. Pacific Northwest Forest and Range Experiment Station, Portland. 26 pp. (Deciding how to dispose of logging residues given a number of economic, physical, and environmental goals.)

Bell, E. F. 1975. Problems with goal programming on a national forest planning unit. *In* Systems Analysis and Forest Resource Management, proceedings of a workshop sponsored by Systems Analysis Working Group, S.A.F., U.S. Forest Service Southeastern Forest Experiment Station, and the School of Forest Resources, University of Georgia, Athens, pp. 119–126. Society of American Foresters, Bethesda. 457 pp. (The basis for Problems 9.1 to 9.4 in this chapter.)

Bottoms, K. E., and E. T. Bartlett. 1975. Resource allocation through goal programming. *Journal of Range Management* 28(6):442–447. (Multiple-use management of a state forest with environmental and production goals.)

Dane, C. W., N. C. Meador, and J. B. White. 1977. Goal programming in land-use planning. *Journal of Forestry* 75(6):325–329. (Application to national forest planning. Stresses the use of goal programming for tradeoff analysis.)

Dress, P. E. 1975. Forest land use planning—An applications environment for goal programming. *In* Systems Analysis and Forest Resource Management, proceedings of a workshop sponsored by Systems Analysis Working Group, S.A.F., U.S. Forest Service Southeastern Forest Experiment Station, and the School of Forest Resources, University of Georgia, Athens, pp. 37–47. Society of American Foresters, Bethesda. 457 pp. (Discussion of the difficulties and limitations of goal programming for forest planning.)

Dyer, A. A., J. G. Hof, J. W. Kelly, S. A. Crim, and G. S. Alward. 1979. Implications of goal programming in forest resource allocation. *Forest Science* 25(4):535–543.

(Comparison of linear programming and goal programming models for forest planning. Discusses some of shortcomings of goal programming.)

Dykstra, D. P. 1984. *Mathematical programming for natural resource management.* McGraw-Hill, New York. 318 pp. (Chapter 8 covers goal programming.)

Field, D. B. 1973. Goal programming for forest management. *Forest Science* 19(2):125–135. (Outlines several possible applications of goal programming in forestry. Detailed example application to small woodland management.)

Field, R. C., P. E. Dress, and J. C. Fortson. 1980. Complementary linear and goal programming procedures for timber harvest scheduling. *Forest Science* 26(1):121–133. (Use of goal programming concepts in harvest scheduling models to get valuable sensitivity information without undue restriction of the alternatives considered.)

Hotvedt, J. E. 1983. Application of linear goal programming to forest harvest scheduling. *Southern Journal of Agricultural Economics* 15(1):103–108. (Industrial forest management with multiple financial goals.)

Mitchell, B. R., and B. B. Bare. 1981. A separable goal programming approach to optimizing multivariate sampling designs for forest inventory. *Forest Science* 27(1):147–162. (Optimizing inventory sampling among different forest strata.)

Porterfield, R. L. 1976. A goal programming model to guide and evaluate tree improvement programs. *Forest Science* 22(4):417–430. (Choosing selection strategies that will best improve multiple tree characteristics.)

Romesburg, H. C. 1974. Scheduling models for wilderness recreation. *Journal of Environmental Management* 2(2):159–177. (Application of several operations research techniques, including goal programming, to the problem of scheduling recreational use of wilderness areas.)

Rustagi, K. P. 1976. Forest management planning for timber production: A goal programming approach. Bulletin No. 89. Yale University School of Forestry and Environmental Studies, New Haven. 80 pp. (Outlines a two-stage (long and short range) goal programming approach to harvest scheduling and reforestation problems.)

Schuler, A. T., H. H. Webster, and J. C. Meadows. 1977. Goal programming in forest management. *Journal of Forestry* 75(6):320–324. (Application to multiple-use management of a national forest with recreation, hunting, timber, and grazing goals.)

Steuer, R. E. 1986. Multiple criteria optimization: Theory, computation, and application. Wiley, New York. 546 pp. (Comprehensive reference on goal programming and other multiple-objective problem solving techniques. Moderately difficult reading.)

Chapter 10

Forestry Programming Models with Integer Variables

10.1 INTRODUCTION

The forestry applications of linear and goal programming addressed in the previous chapters all had continuous variables. For example, in harvest-scheduling models, the areas cut in different age classes could take any fractional value. However, there are many decisions that deal with items that cannot be divided. For example, a whole person must be assigned to a particular task, not just part of it. In bidding on a particular timber sale, one must decide whether to bid for the entire sale or not at all; it is not possible to bid for just part of it. In building a network of forest roads, the roads must usually link specific points; thus, a road section must be built completely or not started at all.

Situations like these that involve *integer* variables are common in forest management. Fortunately, there are several methods to solve integer-programming problems. In the next section we shall first see briefly how these methods differ from standard linear programming. We shall then study in detail some applications of integer programming to problems of forest planning.

10.2 SHORTCOMINGS OF THE SIMPLEX METHOD WITH INTEGER VARIABLES

Surprisingly, perhaps, programming problems with integer variables are more difficult to solve than continuous linear-programming problems. For this reason, it is tempting to just solve an integer-programming problem by the simplex method, that is, assume that the variables are continuous and then round off the solution. This approach does lead sometimes to solutions that are sufficiently close to the optimum for all practical purposes. It is especially useful when there are many similar alternatives to choose from. However, serious mistakes may be made in this way because the rounded solution may not be feasible and, even if it is feasible, it may be far from optimal. The following example will show how this can occur.

The Consultant's Problem

A consulting forester has the opportunity of undertaking five different projects. Three of the projects are located in Georgia and two in Michigan. Each one of the Georgia projects would need 1 person-year of work to do and return $10,000. Each one of the Michigan projects would need 10 person-years and return $50,000. The consulting forester has a staff of 20 persons. Which projects should he take on in order to maximize total returns?

Model Formulation

This simple problem is clearly of the integer type because it is not possible to take on part of a project. Specifically, let X_g be the number of projects in Georgia which the consultant undertakes. Then, the possible values of X_g are $X_g = 0, 1, 2,$ or 3. Similarly, let X_m be the number of projects selected in Michigan. Then, $X_m = 0, 1,$ or 2.

With these decision variables, the problem of the consulting forester can be expressed as follows: Find X_g and X_m, both positive integers, such that:

$$\max Z = X_g + 5X_m \quad (\$10,000)$$

subject to:

$$X_g \qquad\qquad \leq 3 \quad \text{(projects)}$$
$$X_m \leq 2 \quad \text{(projects)}$$
$$X_g + 10X_m \leq 20 \quad \text{(person-years)}$$

Graphic Solution

Because this problem has just two decision variables it can be solved graphically. The necessary steps to do this are shown in Fig. 10.1. As in linear programming, the vertical axis, the horizontal axis, the line $X_g = 3$, and the line $X_g + 10X_m = 20$ define the boundaries of the feasible region. The latter goes through the points D of coordinates ($X_g = 0$, $X_m = 2$), and A of coordinates ($X_g = 3$, $X_m = 1.7$).

However, in contrast with linear programming, the feasible region is not the entire area within these boundaries. Only the grid of points highlighted by the black dots in Fig. 10.1 represent feasible solutions. At these points, all the constraints are satisfied, including the requirement that X_g and X_m be integers.

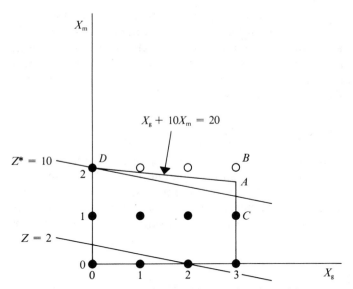

Figure 10.1 Graphic solution of the consultant's problem.

The optimum solution is then represented by the black dot in Fig. 10.1 at which the value of the objective function is maximum. To find it, we draw the graph of the objective function for an arbitrary value of Z, say $Z = 2 = X_g + 5X_m$. This line goes through the points of coordinates ($X_g = 2$, $X_m = 0$) and ($X_g = 0$, $X_m = 0.4$).

The value of the objective function increases regularly as the line representing the objective function gets farther from the origin. The value of the objective function is maximum when the line goes through point D. This point corresponds to the optimum solution:

$$X_g^* = 0, \qquad X_m^* = 2 \qquad \text{and} \qquad Z^* = 10 \qquad (10.1)$$

Problems Arising from Rounded Solutions

If, instead, the consultant's problem had been solved by ordinary linear programming, the optimum solution would have corresponded to point A. But, clearly, that solution is not appropriate because it is not an integer solution, it would suggest undertaking 1.7 projects in Michigan, which is not possible.

Assume that we recognize this and, therefore, round the optimum solution of the ordinary linear program to the nearest integer. This would then lead to the solution corresponding to point B. Now, this is an integer solution, but it is not feasible because point B does not satisfy the workforce constraint.

Suppose that we see this and decide to round the linear-programming solution to the nearest integer feasible solution. This solution would correspond to point C in Fig. 10.1. But the value of the objective function at that point is only $Z = 3 + 5(1) = 8$. This is $20,000 less than the true optimal solution (10.1) found by solving the integer-programming problem correctly.

This example shows the importance of finding exact solutions of programming problems with integer variables. Unfortunately, general integer programs are very difficult to solve, especially when there are many variables. Integer problems that deal with *boolean* variables, that is, variables that can take only the value 0 or 1, are easier to solve. They also have numerous areas of application. In the remainder of this chapter we will deal exclusively with models that use integer variables of this kind.

10.3 CONNECTING LOCATIONS AT MINIMUM COST

To start, it is worth observing that some problems with (0, 1) variables have such simple solutions that they do not require integer-programming algorithms to solve them. In fact, they can very often be solved by hand. An example of such a problem is that of the *minimum-spanning tree*. It arises every time we want to connect a set of locations so that the total "cost" or "length" of the connections is minimum.

Logging Okoume

A valuable species of tree cut in the tropical forest of West Africa is okoume (*Aucoumea klaineana*). The trees are typically found in clusters, amid vast areas of unexploited forest. Suppose that a logging company has obtained a concession for the exploitation of okoume in a virgin area. The forest survey has produced a map of the location of okoume stands (Fig. 10.2). Each circle shows the location of a stand of okoume. A forest engineer has started planning a possible road network that would connect the stands to the Taiwani River. There, the logs would be tied into rafts and floated down to the sea where they would be picked up by cargo boats. Not all the roads that have been drawn on the map are necessary. On the other hand, only those drawn on

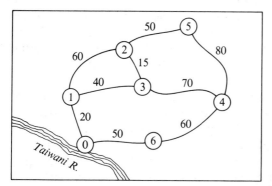

Figure 10.2 Possible roads for the exploitation of okoume stands.

the map may be considered. The object is to find the shortest road network that connects all of the okoume groves to the Taiwani.

Manual Solution

This is a typical minimum-spanning-tree problem. The solution requires only pencil and paper, and some attention. The shortest road network that connects all locations can be found by applying the following algorithm:

1. Select any location arbitrarily and connect it to the closest location.
2. Identify the unconnected location that is closest to a connected location and then connect the two. Repeat until all locations are connected.

Any tie can be broken arbitrarily and still lead to an optimum solution. A tie shows that there is more than one optimum solution. Let us apply this algorithm to the road network in Fig. 10.2.

Start arbitrarily at location 5. The closest location is 2. Thus, connect locations 2 and 5.

The closest unconnected location to locations 2 or 5 is 3, which is closest to 2. Thus, connect 2 and 3.

The closest unconnected location to locations 5, 2, or 3 is 1, which is closest to 3. Thus, connect 3 and 1.

The closest unconnected location to locations 5, 2, 3, or 1 is 0, which is closest to 1. Thus, connect 1 and 0.

The closest unconnected location to locations 5, 2, 3, 1, or 0 is 6, which is closest to 0. Thus, connect 0 and 6.

The closest unconnected location to locations 5, 2, 3, 1, 0, or 6 is location 4, which is closest to 6. Thus connect 4 and 6.

Stop: all locations have been connected.

The optimum road network found in this way is shown in Fig. 10.3. The total length of the network is 235 miles. Because there were no ties, no other system of same length would connect all okoume stands to the Taiwani River. It is interesting that the solution is unaffected by the choice of the initial location. Verify this by applying the algorithm with an initial location other than 5.

Naturally, the same solution would apply regardless of the measure of "distance" between locations. For example, the physical distance could be replaced by the estimated cost of building a particular road. Then, the objective would be to minimize the cost of connecting all stands. In fact, if cost estimates are available, they are preferable to mere distance. For an equal distance, the cost of a road will be much higher if a work of art, such as a bridge, is needed.

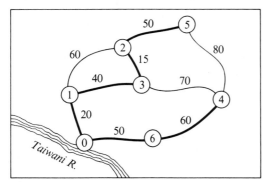

Figure 10.3   Shortest road network for the exploitation of okoume stands.

10.4 ASSIGNING FORESTERS TO TASKS

Another useful model with (0, 1) variables that has a simple solution is the so-called *assignment model*. The model is useful every time a set of people, machines, or objects must be assigned to a set of tasks or locations in order to optimize an objective that depends on the assignment made.

Problem Definition

As an example, assume that you are a forest supervisor who has just hired three new graduate foresters. You have examined the application material of these people carefully and you have done all the interviews yourself. From this you believe that, although these people are all good, some will perform better at particular tasks than others.

It turns out that there are really four job areas that urgently need additional staff: timber sales management, public relations, fire fighting, and inventory. But, for lack of money you were only able to hire three foresters. How should you assign each forester to a particular task in order to maximize the productivity of all three people?

Data

To answer that question, you need some measure of productivity. Clearly, not much is available besides your subjective judgment. You may try to quantify that judgment by giving a score of 0 to 10 to each combination of person and task. Thus if you expect that a particular individual will excel at a certain job, you will give that combination a score of 10. If you expect that the assignment will be a disaster, you will give it a score of 0. Any value between 0 and 10 is acceptable, and so are ties.

Table 10.1 shows the scores for all possible assignments of foresters to tasks. For example, Peter is expected to do very well in public relations (score of 9), but poorly in inventory work (score of 3).

TABLE 10.1 EXPECTED PERFORMANCE OF FORESTERS
ASSIGNED TO TASKS

	Task			
Foresters	1 timber sales	2 public relations	3 fires	4 inventory
1 Peter	5	9	8	3
2 Paul	7	6	4	6
3 Mary	6	9	5	8

Programming Formulation

Your problem is to assign foresters to tasks in such a way that the total score, your measure of overall performance, is maximum. This problem can be expressed as an integer-programming problem as follows:

Let X_{ij} be equal to 1 if forester i is assigned to task j, and to 0 otherwise. The subscript i varies from 1 to 3 and j varies from 1 to 4, as shown in Table 10.1. Then, all possible assignments of Peter can be expressed by the following equation:

$$X_{1,1} + X_{1,2} + X_{1,3} + X_{1,4} = 1 \qquad (10.2)$$

Given that each variable may take the value only of 0 or 1 and that they must all add up to 1, only one variable may take the value 1 and at least one variable must do so. Thus, Eq. (10.2) does express the fact that Peter should be assigned to a task, and to only one of them.

In the same manner, the equation that describes the possible assignments of the two other foresters are:

$$X_{2,1} + X_{2,2} + X_{2,3} + X_{2,4} = 1 \qquad \text{for Paul}$$
$$X_{3,1} + X_{3,2} + X_{3,3} + X_{3,4} = 1 \qquad \text{for Mary} \qquad (10.3)$$

We must now express the fact that each task may receive a forester. Note that because there are more tasks than foresters, the possibility that a task will not be assigned anybody must be recognized. For example, the constraint that shows how foresters may be assigned to timber sales administration is:

$$X_{1,1} + X_{2,1} + X_{3,1} \le 1 \qquad (10.4)$$

The less-than-or-equal-to operator is used because it is possible that nobody will be assigned to timber sales administration, in which case all three variables will be zero. The right-hand side of Eq. (10.4) indicates that at most one of the variables may be 1. The corresponding constraints for the three other tasks are:

$$X_{1,2} + X_{2,2} + X_{3,2} \le 1 \qquad \text{for public relations}$$
$$X_{1,3} + X_{2,3} + X_{3,3} \le 1 \qquad \text{for fire fighting}$$
$$X_{1,4} + X_{2,4} + X_{3,4} \le 1 \qquad \text{for inventory work} \qquad (10.5)$$

TABLE 10.2 LINEAR-PROGRAMMING TABLEAU FOR THE ASSIGNMENT OF FORESTERS TO TASKS

	$X_{1,1}$	$X_{1,2}$	$X_{1,3}$	$X_{1,4}$	$X_{2,1}$	$X_{2,2}$	$X_{2,3}$	$X_{2,4}$	$X_{3,1}$	$X_{3,2}$	$X_{3,3}$	$X_{3,4}$	
Z	5	9	8	3	7	6	4	6	6	9	5	8	
PETE	1	1	1	1									$= 1$
PAUL					1	1	1	1					$= 1$
MARY									1	1	1	1	$= 1$
ADMI	1				1				1				≤ 1
PUBL		1				1				1			≤ 1
FIRE			1				1				1		≤ 1
INVE				1				1				1	≤ 1

Finally, the objective function is written as follows:
Let $p_{i,j}$ be the measure of the expected performance of forester i if he or she is assigned to task j. For example, Table 10.1 shows that $p_{2,3} = 4$. Then, the contribution to overall performance of a particular assignment is $p_{i,j}X_{i,j}$ and the contribution of all possible assignments is the sum of $p_{i,j} X_{i,j}$ over all possible combinations of i and j. Thus, in our particular example, the expression of the objective function is:

$$Z = 5X_{1,1} + 9X_{1,2} + 8X_{1,3} + 3X_{1,4} + 7X_{2,1} + 6X_{2,2} + 4X_{2,3} + 6X_{2,4}$$
$$+ 6X_{3,1} + 9X_{3,2} + 5X_{3,3} + 8X_{3,4} \tag{10.6}$$

Solution

Equations (10.2) to (10.6) constitute an ordinary linear program, except that each variable is limited to the integer values 0 or 1. This linear program is presented in Table 10.2 to emphasize its particular structure: two 1's appear in each column and the right-hand side of every equation is 1. It turns out that the optimum solution of an assignment problem is always such that variables are either 0 or 1, regardless of whether this is imposed explicitly in the formulation. Thus, the standard simplex method of linear programming may be applied to the program in Table 10.2. Doing so leads to the following optimum solution: $X_{1,3}^* = X_{2,1}^* = X_{3,2}^* = 1$, and all other variables equal zero. The corresponding value of the objective function is 24 points.

The shadow prices are 8 for Paul and Mary and 6 for Peter, suggesting that if another person is to be hired, it would be better for the overall performance of the group that he or she have the characteristics of Paul or Mary rather than those of Peter. However, if one more forester is hired, the assignments to tasks may have to be changed.

10.5 TRANSPORTATION PLANNING FOR MULTIPLE-USE PROJECTS

Although the minimum-spanning-tree and the assignment models have numerous applications, they are not very flexible. Problems must have a very specific

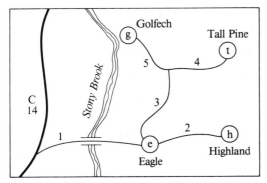

Figure 10.4   Road network for multiple-use forest development.

structure to yield appropriate integer solutions with those simple methods. The solution of more general problems requires specialized integer algorithms and computer programs. To illustrate the application of such problems, we will study a problem similar to one solved by Kirby (1975). It deals with the development of a road network to serve a set of forestry projects with multiple objectives.

Problem Definition and Data

The general setting is illustrated in Fig. 10.4. The figure shows a road network serving four forestry projects named Eagle, Highland, Tall Pine, and Golfech. The roads have not yet been built; the map represents only the possible ways the projects could be connected to the existing county road, C14.

Not all four projects need to be done; thus, the simple spanning-tree procedure cannot be used. On the other hand, the projects that are done must be connected to the county road. The cost of building each road section depends on its length, the topography, and any necessary work of art. For example, road section number 1 is especially expensive because it includes a bridge across Stony Brook. The civil engineers attached to the project have estimated the costs of each road section (Table 10.3). These costs are the cumulative discounted cost of building and maintaining the roads over the entire life of the the project.

The following objectives have been set for the entire system:

1. Each project has camping facilities. All camps taken together must be able to accommodate 2000 visitor-days per year.
2. The timber production from all projects should be at least 17 million cubic feet per year.
3. These goals must be met efficiently. That is, we seek the set of projects, and the related road system that meet the timber and recreation goals at least cost.

TABLE 10.3 COST OF BUILDING EACH ROAD SECTION

Section	1	2	3	4	5
Cost (10^6 $)	0.8	0.4	0.3	0.2	0.4

TABLE 10.4 TIMBER AND RECREATION EXPECTED FROM VARIOUS PROJECTS, AND RELATED COSTS

Results	Project			
	Eagle, e	Highland, h	Tall Pine, t	Golfech, g
Visitor-days (1000/y)	1	1	2	3
Timber (10^6 ft^3)	6	8	13	10
Cost (10^6 $)	0.7	0.1	0.5	0.8

On completion, each project is expected to produce the amounts of timber and recreation shown in Table 10.4. The expected cost of each project is also shown there. Again, this is the discounted value of expected costs over the entire life of the project. Thus, project costs in Table 10.3 are comparable with road costs in Table 10.2.

Model Variables

As for any mathematical programming problem, formulating the model requires specification of the variables, constraints, and objective function. In this case all decision variables take either the value 0 or 1, since a project is either done or not, and a road section is either build or not built. Specifically, let Y_1, Y_2, Y_3, Y_4, and Y_5 designate the decision to build or not a particular road section. For example $Y_1 = 1$ means that road section 1 is built, otherwise $Y_1 = 0$.

Similarly, let X_e, X_h, X_t, X_g refer to the decision to do or not a particular project. For example, project h (Highland) is done if $X_h = 1$; it is not done if $X_h = 0$.

Thus, in this formulation the problem is a pure integer programming problem with only boolean variables. This is one of the easier integer-programming problems to solve.

Objective Function

The objective function is very similar to those we have used in ordinary linear programs. The general expression of the cost of building the roads, in terms of the decision variables is:

$$0.8Y_1 + 0.4Y_2 + 0.3Y_3 + 0.2Y_4 + 0.4Y_5$$

while the cost of doing the projects is:

$$0.7X_e + 0.1X_h + 0.5X_t + 0.8X_g$$

so that the expression of the objective function, the total cost, is:

$$Z = 0.8Y_1 + 0.4Y_2 + 0.3Y_3 + 0.2Y_4 + 0.4Y_5$$
$$+ 0.7X_e + 0.1X_h + 0.5X_t + 0.8X_g \qquad (10.7)$$

Constraints

Some of the constraints are similar to the familiar constraints of ordinary linear programming. For example, the timber production goal is readily expressed as:

$$6X_e + 8X_h + 13X_t + 10X_g \geq 17 \qquad \text{(million cubic feet per year)} \qquad (10.8)$$

Note that the contribution of a particular project to this goal is either its total potential output, shown in Table 10.4, or nothing. For example, $X_t = 1$ implies that project Tall Pine is done and produces 13 million cubic feet of timber a year. $X_t = 0$ implies no production. Similarly, the recreation goal is expressed by the following constraint:

$$1X_e + 1X_h + 2X_t + 3X_g \geq 2 \qquad \text{(thousand visitor-days per year)} \qquad (10.9)$$

The road building options present a more interesting problem, one that is eminently suited to integer (0, 1) variables.

Consider first in Fig. 10.4 the road sections that lead to a project, say section 1. It must be built if project Eagle is done (it must also be built if either road section 3 or section 2 is built, a possibility that shall be considered later). This can be expressed by the following constraint:

$$X_e \leq Y_1$$

For this constraint to be satisfied, Y_1 must indeed take the value 1 (section 1 must be built) if X_e is equal to 1 (project Eagle is done). On the other hand, if $X_e = 0$ (project Eagle is not done), then the value of Y_1 that minimizes cost is $Y_1 = 0$ (section 1 is not built). In summary, the following constraints together with the objective function ensure that a road section is built only if the project to which it leads is done:

$$X_e \leq Y_1$$
$$X_h \leq Y_2$$
$$X_t \leq Y_4$$
$$X_g \leq Y_5 \qquad (10.10)$$

Some road sections may have to be built, not because they lead to a project themselves, but because they collect traffic from other roads. Consider for example road section 1. We have recognized that it must be built if project Eagle is done. But section 1 must be built also if either section 3 or 2 is built, even if project Eagle is not done. This possibility is reflected by the following constraint:

$$Y_2 + Y_3 \leq 2Y_1$$

This ensures that if either Y_2 or Y_3 or both are equal to 1 (i.e., either section 2 or 3 or both are built) then, Y_1 must be equal to 1 (section 1 is built). It is necessary to multiply Y_1 by 2 to allow for the fact that both Y_2 and Y_3 may be equal to 1. Any number larger than or equal to 2 will do, but numerical solutions work best with numbers that are close to 1 in absolute value. A similar constraint is needed to model the branching of road section 3 into sections 4 and 5. In summary, the constraints that ensure that a collector road is built if branches are built are:

$$Y_2 + Y_3 \leq 2Y_1 \quad \text{and} \quad Y_4 + Y_5 \leq 2Y_3 \tag{10.11}$$

Solution

The objective function (10.7) and the system of constraints (10.8) to (10.11) are represented in tableau form in Table 10.5. Each row has been given a mnemonic name. For example PROE refers to the constraint defining the relationship between project e and the road segment that leads directly into it. J345 refers to the constraint that defines the branching of road section 3 into 4 and 5. This form is useful for preparing input of computer programs that solve integer-programming problems. The form of the input is very similar to that used for ordinary linear programming. The more sophisticated mathematical programming systems have both linear- and integer-programming options. The user must simply indicate the integer variables and the largest value that they may take (upper bound). In our case all variables are integers and their upper bound is one.

TABLE 10.5 INTEGER-PROGRAMMING TABLEAU FOR MULTIPLE-USE ROADING, PROBLEM

	Y_1	Y_2	Y_3	Y_4	Y_5	X_e	X_h	X_t	X_g	
Z	0.8	0.4	0.3	0.2	0.4	0.7	0.1	0.5	0.8	
TIM						6	8	13	10	≥ 17
REC						1	1	2	3	≥ 2
PROE	-1					1				≤ 0
PROH		-1					1			≤ 0
PROT				-1				1		≤ 0
PROG					-1				1	≤ 0
J123	-2	1	1							≤ 0
J345			-2	1	1					≤ 0

Note: All variables are equal to 0 or 1.

The optimum solution for the problem shown in Table 10.5 is:

$$Y_1^* = Y_2^* = Y_3^* = Y_4^* = 1$$
$$X_h^* = X_t^* = 1$$

All other variables $= 0$

$Z^* = 2.3$ million dollars

21 Million cubic feet of timber per year will be produced

There will be accommodations for 3000 visitor-days per year.

In summary, the timber production objective and the recreation objective can be achieved at least cost by doing only two projects: Highland and Tall Pine. These projects should be connected to country road C14 by building road sections 1, 2, 3, and 4.

10.6 MODELS WITH INTEGER AND CONTINUOUS VARIABLES

Although up to now we have worked with models that have only either continuous variables or integer $(0, 1)$ variables, one encounters many forestry applications where both types of variables are needed.

Transportation Planning Revisited

As an example, reconsider the model of the previous section and assume that one does not have to complete the projects shown in Fig. 10.4. Thus, the decision variables X_e, X_h, X_t, and X_g are not integer $(0, 1)$ variables, but continuous variables that may take any value between 0 and 1. For example, $X_e = 0.8$ means that 80 percent of project Eagle is done.

Let us assume further that the output and the cost of each project are directly proportional to the level of completion of the project. For example, using the data in Table 10.4, if $X_e = 0.8$ then the Eagle project is expected to:

Support $0.8 \times 1000 = 800$ visitor-days per year

Produce $0.8 \times 6 = 4.8$ millions of cubic feet of timber per year

Cost $0.8 \times 0.7 = \$0.56$ million

Finally, assume that the objectives remain the same. Then, the formulation of the problem is exactly as in Table 10.5, except that only the decision variables referring to roads, Y_1 to Y_5, are integer, while the decision variables X_e to X_g are continuous and constrained to lie between 0 and 1. This is a typical mixed-integer-programming problem. Computer programs are available to solve it. The optimum solution of our new model is:

$$Y_1^* = Y_2^* = Y_3^* = Y_4^* = 1$$
$$Y_h^* = 1$$
$$Y_t^* = 0.69$$

All other variables $= 0$

$Z^* = \$2.1$ million

17 Million cubic feet of timber per year will be produced

Facilities will be provided for 2380 visitor-days per year

Thus, the projects selected and the road network remain the same as in the integer-programming version, but only 70 percent of project Tall Pine needs to be done in order to meet the timber and recreation objectives.

Start-up Costs

A useful application of mixed-integer programming is to model discontinuous functions. As an example, consider the cost of project Golfech. In the previous section, we have assumed that costs were directly proportional to the level of completion of the project, X_g. This would not be a satisfactory representation of costs if in fact the costs of starting the project were very large. In that case, a good cost function could look like the line OAB in Fig. 10.5. If the project is started, $0.3 million are needed for the basic infrastructure. Thereafter, costs increase linearly in direct proportion to the level of completion of the project. Thus, the cost function of project Golfech is:

$$C = 0.3 + 0.5X_g \quad \text{if the project is started}$$
$$C = 0 \quad\quad\quad\quad \text{otherwise}$$

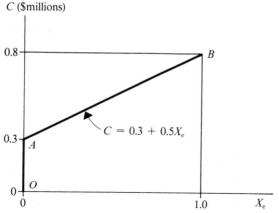

Figure 10.5   Cost function for a project with large start-up costs.

Note that we cannot simply add $0.3 + 0.5X_g$ to the objective function because the \$0.3 million are spent only if the project is started. This problem can be solved by introducing a boolean variable, S_g, that takes the value 1 if project Golfech is started, 0 otherwise. The new objective function is:

$$\min Z = 0.8Y_1 + \cdots + 0.5X_t + 0.3S_g + 0.5X_g$$

to which we impose the additional constraint:

$$X_g \leq S_g \tag{10.12}$$

Now, since S_g can take only the value 0 or 1, it must switch to 1 when X_g takes a positive value (i.e., when project Golfech is started). This in turn causes the objective function to increase by \$0.3 million, the start-up cost. On the other hand, if X_g is 0 (i.e., project Golfech is not started), the minimization of the objective function leads S_g to be equal to 0, as desired.

10.7 CONCLUSIONS

The techniques described in this chapter are useful to model and solve very practical forest management problems that involve integer variables. Nevertheless, some should be used cautiously. General programming problems with integer variables are difficult to solve, even with powerful computers. Problems with (0, 1) variables only are the easiest. In some cases, hand computations or ordinary linear programming will suffice, as illustrated by the minimum-spanning-tree and assignment models. Large mixed-integer-programming problems can be hard to solve, even with a modest number of integer (0, 1) variables. Therefore, in large models, the possibility of working with ordinary linear programming and rounding the final solution should not be neglected, as long as the problems mentioned at the beginning of the chapter are kept in mind. The simplex method and its variants are still the most powerful mathematical programming algorithms for solving problems with multiple constraints. They should be used whenever possible.

PROBLEMS

10.1. The paper division of a large forest products company wants to expand its facilities in Oregon, Georgia, or both. It wants to build one pulpmill and one newsprint mill. In the state selected for the pulpmill, it will also consider building a papermill; however, the division is allowed to spend at most \$900 millions. The division's estimates of the net present value of the expected revenues for each mill and location are shown below, together with the required initial capital.

Mill	Net present value ($ millions)	Capital requirement ($ millions)
Oregon pulpmill	25	500
Georgia pulpmill	22	450
Oregon papermill	12	260
Georgia papermill	10	270
Oregon newsprint mill	14	150
Georgia newsprint mill	14	170

The company's objective is to maximize the expected net present value of revenues from the new mills.

Formulate this problem as an integer program and solve it to find the best combination of mills. [Hint: Use one boolean variable to represent the decision to build or not to build a mill at a particular location. Then, write the objective function and the following constraints: (1) capital is limited, (2) only one pulpmill and one newsprint mill can be built, (3) only one papermill can be built, (4) a pulpmill must be built in a state before a papermill can be built there.]

10.2. A private developer wants to build a park for recreational vehicles with nine parking sites. These sites are represented in the figure below by numbered circles. Each site must be hooked up to a utilities system, and only the connections shown in the figure are possible. The length of each connection is given in hundred feet.

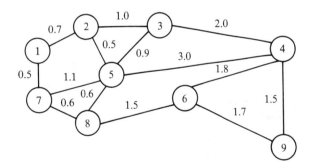

Assume construction costs are directly proportional to network length. Find the network that connects all sites at least cost.

10.3. Suppose that parking sites 2 and 3 in the park described in Problem 10.2 are separated from the others by a stream. While normal construction costs for the proposed utilities network will be $2000 per hundred feet, they will be twice as high between sites 1 and 2, 2 and 5, 5 and 3, and 3 and 4. Determine the cheapest network to serve all the sites.

10.4. A fire boss is fighting a forest fire with people and three machines: a small dozer, a large dozer, and a brush cutter. The fire is spreading on four fronts. Because of differences in vegetation and terrain, the efficiency of the machines is different on each front. The fire boss' estimates of the rates at which each machine can cut a fireline on each front are:

Machine	Front			
	1	2	3	4
Small dozer (ft/hr)	100	75	50	25
Large dozer (ft/hr)	150	100	80	0
Brush cutter (ft/hr)	55	70	45	40

Formulate and solve a model to assign each machine to a front to maximize the length of fireline cut by the three machines. (Assume that no more than one machine can be assigned to a front.)

10.5. A logging contractor operates three logging crews, and holds logging contracts for five timber sales. Terrain and stand characteristics vary between sales. One of the crews is equiped for cable logging on steep slopes, and the other two for conventional logging. Of the last two crews, one has a more experienced foreman and tends to be more productive. The contractor's estimates of daily harvesting rates per crew on each timber sale are, in thousands of board feet per day:

Crew	Timber Sale				
	1	2	3	4	5
Cable logging crew	75	40	65	35	20
Conventional crew with experienced foreman	20	60	15	55	30
Conventional crew with inexperienced foreman	15	55	10	55	25

The contractor's main objective is to maximize the daily rate of harvesting of the three crews. Formulate and solve a programming model to determine which timber sale the contractor should assign to each crew. Which sale should be left alone for the time being?

Problems 10.6 to 10.8 are adapted from Kirby (1975).

10.6. The director of a state forest is planning to harvest timber in a roadless part of the forest. Hunting will also be provided. In the figure below, A, B, C, D, E, and

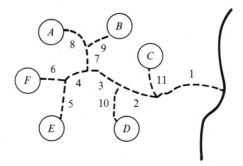

F, represent six areas under consideration. The dashed lines joining these areas are road sections, as yet not built. The existing road that these sections would tie into is shown as a solid line.

The cost of building each road segment, including the present value of future maintenance costs is:

Road section	1	2	3	4	5	6	7	8	9	10	11
Cost ($1000)	23	12	10	9	13	7	5	8	8	10	6

The anticipated annual production of timber, the number of hunter-days that each area can support, and the net present value (excluding roading costs) of the timber that shall be cut from each area are:

Forest area	A	B	C	D	E	F
Hunter-days (100 / year)	2	3	1	1	2	3
Timber (10^6 ft^3 / year)	6	9	13	10	8	3
Present value ($1000)	7	13	14	13	11	10

The director's objectives for the entire development are: (1) to minimize road construction costs, (2) to provide at least 400 hunter-days per year, (3) to cut at least 30 million cubic feet of timber per year, and (4) to generate at least enough revenue to cover the cost of roads.

Assume that each area under consideration must be completely developed, or not developed at all. Construct an integer programming model to determine the road sections that should be built and the forest areas that should be developed. Solve this model with a computer. What would be the annual timber production, the number of hunter-days, and the total net present value if this solution were adopted?

10.7. Consider the state forest described in Problem 10.6. To please environmentalists, the director wants to study the possibility of developing only part of the areas under consideration. Local timber operators object vigorously, claiming that this will result in less timber production.

Reformulate the model developed in Problem 10.6 to consider this issue. Assume that outputs, revenues, and costs are directly proportional to the extent each area is developed. For example, if one-third of area A is developed, the amount of timber produced shall be $6/3 = 2$ million cubic feet per year.

Solve this model and compare the solution to that of Problem 10.6. Would either road construction costs or annual timber harvest decrease?

10.8. For the forest development project described in Problem 10.6, road section 1 will have to bear traffic to and from all of the areas. Thus, it may be necessary to build this section to a higher standard than others. The carrying capacity of road 1 under three different standards, and the corresponding costs are:

Road standard	Low	Medium	High
Capacity (1000 tons / year)	40	50	70
Cost ($1000)	10	14	16

The traffic that would result from each forest area if it were fully developed is:

Area	A	B	C	D	E	F
Traffic (1000 tons / year)	8	4	14	13	10	7

Modify the model developed in Problem 10.6 (where both road sections and timber sales were treated as all-or-nothing decisions) to find the best standard for road section 1, assuming the same objective and constraints. [Hint: Replace the variable corresponding to road section 1 by three boolean variables constrained to sum to less-than-or-equal-to one. Add a constraint insuring that road 1 is sufficiently strong.]

Do the areas and roads selected differ from those found in Problem 10.6? What happens to roading costs? Why?

ANNOTATED REFERENCES

Bare, B. B., and E. L. Norman. 1969. An evaluation of integer programming in forest production scheduling problems. Research Bulletin No. 847. Agricultural Experiment Station, Purdue University, Lafayette. 7 pp. (Early evaluation of integer harvest scheduling models.)

Buongiorno, J., N. H. H. Svanqvist, and P. Wiroatmodjo. 1981. Forestry sector development planning: A model for Indonesia. *Agricultural Systems* 7:113–135. (Uses boolean variables to find the best location of a port for timber exports.)

Dunn, R. A. and K. D. Ramsing. 1981. *Management science: A practical approach to decisionmaking*. Macmillan, New York. 527 pp. (Chapter 7 introduces integer models using an application to the production of laminated wood beams.)

Dykstra, D. P. 1984. *Mathematical programming for natural resource management*. McGraw-Hill, New York. 318 pp. (Chapter 9 discusses resource-related applications of models with integer variables.)

Hillier, F. S, and G. J. Lieberman. 1986. *Introduction to operations research*. Holden-Day, Oakland. 888 pp. (Chapter 13 is a general introduction to integer and mixed-integer models.)

Jones, J. G., and E. G. Schuster. 1985. An application of discrete optimization for developing economically efficient multiple-use projects. U.S. Forest Service General Technical Report INT-178. Intermountain Forest Experiment Station, Ogden. 16 pp. (Mixed-integer model to evaluate multiple-use forestry options. The model is demonstrated using a timber production-elk habitat example.)

Jones, J. G., J. F. C. Hyde, III, and M. L. Meacham. 1986. Four analytical approaches for integrating land management and transportation planning on forest lands. U.S. Forest Service Research Paper INT-361. Intermountain Research Station, Ogden. 33 pp. (Mixed-integer approaches to planning harvesting, road construction, and other forest activities on a National Forest.)

Kirby, M. 1975. Land use planning, transportation planning, and integer programming. *In* Systems Analysis and Forest Resource management proceedings of a workshop sponsored by Systems Analysis Working Group, S.A.F., U.S. Forest Service Southeastern Forest Experiment Station, and the School of Forest Resources, University of Georgia Athens, Aug 11–13, pp. 271–284. Society of American Foresters, Bethesda. 457 pp. (Basis of roading model in Section 10.5 and in Problem 10.6.)

Kirby, M. 1978. Large-scale budget applications of mathematical programming in the Forest Service. *In* Operational management Planning Methods: Proceedings, Meeting of Steering Systems Project Group, International Union of Forestry Research Organizations, Bucharest, Romania, June 18–24, pp. 60–67. U.S. Forest Service General Technical Report PSW-32. Pacific Southwest Forest and Range Experiment Station, Berkeley. 117 pp. (Integer model used by the U.S. Forest Service to prepare budget requests in terms of a set of projects. In this case, a linear programming solution provided an acceptable approximation to the true integer solution.)

Randall, R. M. 1972. An operations research approach to Douglas-fir thinning. U.S. Forest Service Research Paper PNW-148. Pacific Northwest Forest and Range Experiment Station, Portland. 23 pp. (Integer model for planning commercial thinning operations.)

Taha, H. A. 1982. *Operations research: An introduction*. Macmillan, New York. 848 pp. (Chapter 8 is a general introduction to integer and mixed-integer programming models.)

Weintraub, A., and D. Navon. 1976. A forest management planning model integrating silvicultural and transportation activities. *Management Science* 22(12):1299–1309. (Mixed-integer model for long-range planning of timber harvest, road construction and maintenance, and transportation of logs on a forest.)

Chapter 11

Managing Time, Distances, and Flows with Networks

11.1 INTRODUCTION

A network model consists of a set of nodes connected by branches. Nodes may represent campgrounds, road intersections, water reservoirs, or points in time. In general, nodes can be thought of as points where some kind of flow begins, ends, or is transferred. Branches can be viewed as channels for flows between nodes. Some examples of networks are listed in Table 11.1. A surprisingly large number of forest systems can be represented by network models.

We already saw an application of networks in Chap. 10. There we observed that a simple method, the minimum-spanning-tree algorithm, could be used to determine the shortest road network that connected forest stands. This solution replaced an otherwise complicated integer-programming problem. The purpose of this chapter is to study some other important applications of network models.

We shall begin with what is perhaps the most important application of networks: the management of time in projects that involve many activities that depend on one another. The methods used to do this are called PERT or CPM. We shall apply them to fire management. We shall then apply network models to the management of park trails, first to find the shortest route, and then to determine the carrying capacity of the trails.

11.2 PROJECT SCHEDULING WITH PERT / CPM

Forestry projects, such as the preparation of a timber sale, the construction of a recreation area, or the development of a management plan, involve many

TABLE 11.1   EXAMPLES OF NETWORKS IN FORESTRY

System	Branches	Nodes	Flow
Sawlog transport	Logging roads	Road intersections or log landings	Logging trucks
Hiking recreation	Trails	Campgrounds or trail intersections	Hikers
Water supply	Water pipes	Water sources or pumping stations	Water
Sawmill	Conveyor belts	Sawmill machinery (e.g., saws)	Wood

activities. Some of these activities may run in parallel; others depend on one another. Forest managers are responsible for scheduling activities in a manner that will avoid bottlenecks and meet project deadlines. Sometimes they must predict the most likely date for the completion of a project, taking into account all the things to be done and how they interact.

PERT and CPM are two techniques designed to help project managers do this. PERT (Project Evaluation and Review Technique) was developed in the late 1950s to help the U.S. Navy manage its Polaris weapons system program. PERT was designed to evaluate the probability of meeting project deadlines, given probabilistic estimates of activity durations.

CPM (Critical-Path Method) was developed by the DuPont Company and Remington Rand Univac, also in the late 1950s. CPM focused on the inverse relationship between the cost and duration of activities, and could be used to identify the least-cost allocation of resources to activities that would be capable of meeting a given project deadline.

The differences between the two techniques have become blurred over time, and neither the probabilistic elements of PERT nor the time/cost trade-offs of CPM are as important to most project managers as their developers anticipated. Accordingly, we shall emphasize the common elements of PERT and CPM that are most useful in practice, touching only briefly on the probabilistic applications of PERT.

A Slash-Disposal Project

The first step in using PERT/CPM is to identify all of the activities involved in a project, and any precedence relationships between them. A *precedence relationship* is a requirement that a particular activity be completed before work begins on some other activity. In our discussion of PERT/CPM, we shall use an example described by Davis (1968). It deals with the burning of the logging slash left by a clear-cutting operation on a tract of Douglas fir forest. Burning the slash is one way of cleaning the site to prepare it for planting or aerial seeding.

This project can be broken down into six distinct activities. These are shown in Table 11.2, along with their precedence relationships and expected durations. For example, the manager of this project expects that it will take 2 days to apply the chemical fire retardants to keep the fire from spreading to

TABLE 11.2   ACTIVITIES AND THEIR PRECEDENCE RELATIONSHIPS
                    FOR A SLASH DISPOSAL PROJECT

Task	Expected duration (days)	Activities that must be completed before work can begin on this activity
Preparation of external firebreaks	5	
Falling internal hardwoods	8	
Falling snags in vicinity	4	
Checking out pumps and equipment	2	
Application of chemical fire retardants	2	Preparation of external firebreaks
Installation of firing devices	3	Preparation of external firebreaks and falling internal hardwoods

the rest of the forest. However, that activity cannot start before the external firebreaks have been built.

Construction of a PERT / CPM Network

Once all the activities of a project, their expected duration, and their precedence relationships have been identified, they can be expressed in a PERT/CPM network model. Each *activity* is represented in the network by an arrow between two nodes. For example, in Fig. 11.1 the preparation of firebreaks is represented by the arrow from node A to node C. The nodes of a PERT/CPM network are called *events* because they refer to points in time. Each activity is named by its starting and ending event.

The network must have a single event to represent the project's start, and another to represent its end. All paths through the network must lead from the project's start to its end. PERT/CPM networks are usually drawn with the starting event at the top or left-hand side of the network, and its end on the bottom or right-hand side.

The PERT/CPM network for our slash-burning project is developed in Fig. 11.1 in four stages. In Figure 11.1(a), the beginning of the four activities that are not preceded by others are shown leading away from the project's starting event A. This is in agreement with the fact that work can start on any of these activities as soon as the project starts.

In Fig. 11.1(b), the two activities that must be preceded by others have been added to the network. Application of chemical retardants cannot begin until the external firebreaks have been prepared, so the former activity has been drawn with C as its starting event.

Similarly, installation of firing devices has been added in Fig. 11.1(b) with event D as its starting event to express the requirement that internal hardwoods be felled before installing the firing devices. There is one more precedence requirement noted in Table 11.2. Firing devices cannot be installed until the external firebreaks are prepared. This requirement has been expressed in Fig. 11.1(b) by drawing a *dummy activity*, of zero duration, as a dashed

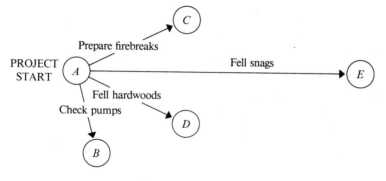

(a) Activities with no precedence requirements.

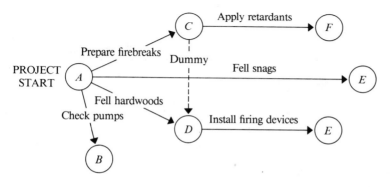

(b) Adding activities with precedence requirements and a dummy.

Figure 11.1   Construction of a PERT/CPM network. (Figure continues on p. 150.)

arrow from event C to event D. This implies that the installation of firing devices cannot start before the dummy activity is completed. But the dummy activity itself cannot start before the firebreaks have been prepared. In short, because of the dummy, firing devices cannot be installed until the external firebreaks have been prepared.

The network in Fig. 11.1(b) does not yet have a single event corresponding to the project's end. Let us call this ending event E. Work on all of the dangling activities in Fig. 11.1(b) can continue until the end of the project. Therefore, we can end all of those activities at E. This has been done in Fig. 11.1(c).

We need only one refinement to complete the network. In Fig. 11.1(c), felling the snags and checking the pumps have both the same "name": AE. To remove this ambiguity, we replace one of these two activities, say the checking of pumps, by the sum of two activities: AB, the actual checking of pumps, and a dummy, BE.

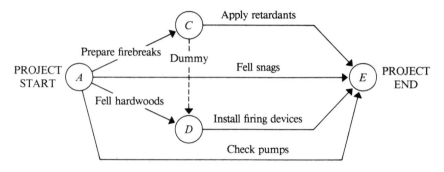

(c) Defining a finish event.

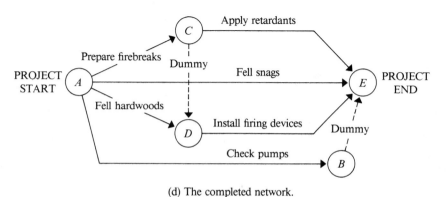

(d) The completed network.

Figure 11.1   Continued.

To summarize, the rules that must be followed in drawing a PERT/CPM network diagram are:

1. Each activity must be uniquely defined by its starting and ending event—two events may be joined by only one activity.
2. The network must have a single event corresponding to the project's start, and a single event corresponding to its end. Dangling activities are not permitted.
3. An event occurs when all activities leading to it have been accomplished.
4. An activity can begin only after its starting event has occurred.

Rules 3 and 4 together imply that activities may not form a loop.

There are actually different ways to draw PERT/CPM networks. For example, some people draw them representing activities by nodes, using branches to represent precedence relationships. There are, however, no substantive differences in the information conveyed in these alternative representations. Which system you will use will probably be determined more by the characteristics of your PERT/CPM computer software than any other factor.

PERT Computations

Constructing a PERT/CPM network is a useful exercise in and of itself for project managers. It forces them to identify what activities a project will involve, how long they should take, and what activities depend on others. However, PERT/CPM goes beyond constructing networks. It can also provide the following data:

1. The *earliest starting time* and the *earliest ending time* of each activity. That is, the earliest time at which each activity could start (end) if preceding activities were completed as quickly as possible.
2. The *earliest ending time* of the project. This is the minimum time in which a project manager can hope to complete a project if things go as planned.
3. The *latest starting time* and the *latest ending time* of each activity. That is, the latest time at which each activity could start (end) without increasing the earliest ending time of the project.
4. The *slack time* of each activity. This is the difference between the expected duration of an activity and the time available to do it without increasing the earliest ending time of the project.
5. The *critical activities* (i.e., those that do not have any slack time).

A convenient format to keep track of these times during PERT/CPM computations is shown in Fig. 11.2. The name of an activity in a general network is i, j. The earliest starting time, $ES_{i,j}$, and the latest starting time, $LS_{i,j}$ for an activity are shown in the tail of the activity's arrow. If you forget which goes where, just remember that an earliest time can't be greater than a latest time.

The earliest ending time, $EE_{i,j}$, and latest ending time, $LE_{i,j}$, for an activity are displayed in the head of the activity's arrow. The expected duration, $d_{i,j}$, and the slack time, $S_{i,j}$, for an activity are shown alongside the activity's arrow. They are separated by a comma.

All earliest times are computed by a forward pass through the network, latest times by a backward pass. Slacks and critical path are determined last.

Earliest times   The results of a *forward pass* through the network are shown in Fig. 11.3. The single number beside each activity is the activity's expected

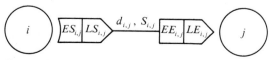

Figure 11.2   Activity earliest and latest times, duration, and slack.

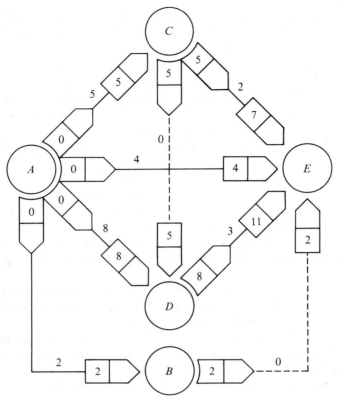

Figure 11.3   Earliest starting and ending times.

duration. The calculations begin at the project starting event and fan out through the network, first identifying each activity's earliest starting time ($ES_{i,j}$), then adding the expected duration ($d_{i,j}$) to this to determine the activity's earliest ending time ($EE_{i,j}$).

Consider Fig. 11.3. The earliest starting times for the four activities branching off from the project's start are zero, by definition. As a result, their earliest ending times are equal to their respective durations. The earliest starting time of activities CD and CE is 5 days, the earliest ending time of their preceding activity, AC. Since activity CD has no duration, its earliest ending time is also 5 days.

Now, the earliest starting time for activity DE is the latest of the earliest ending times of activities AD and CD, which is 8 days. Therefore, the earliest ending time of activity DE is $8 + 3 = 11$ days.

Proceeding in this way for all possible forward paths through the network, we find that the earliest ending times of activities AE, BE, CE, and DE are, respectively, 4, 2, 7, and 11 days. Thus, the earliest ending time of the project is 11 days.

In general, assuming that A is the starting event and N the ending event, all earliest times are found as follows:

For activities that can start immediately:

$$ES_{A,j} = 0$$

For all other activities:

$$ES_{i,j} = \max_k \left(EE_{k,i} \right)$$

The earliest starting time is the latest of the earliest ending times of all directly preceding activities.

For all activities:

$$EE_{i,j} = ES_{i,j} + d_{i,j}$$

The earliest ending time is the earliest starting time plus the activity's expected duration.

For the ending activities:

$$EET = \max_i EE_{i,N}$$

The earliest ending time of the project, EET is the latest of the earliest ending time of the activities ending at N.

Latest Times   The results of a *backward pass* through the slash-burn network are shown in Fig. 11.4. The calculations begin at the project's end event and fan out backward through the network, identifying each activity's latest ending time ($LE_{i,j}$), then subtracting the expected duration to determine the activity's latest starting time ($LS_{i,j}$).

Consider, for example, Fig. 11.4. The latest ending times for all activities ending at the project's end are by definition equal to the project's earliest ending time, 11 days. Subtracting the respective durations of the activities leads to their latest starting times. For example, the latest starting time for activity CE is $11 - 2 = 9$ days. Similarly, the latest starting time for activity DE is 8 days, and it is also 8 days for CD.

Now, the latest ending time for activity AC is the earliest of the latest starting times of activities CD and CE, which is 8 days. Note that the latest start and latest ending times for dummies are equal since they have zero duration.

In general, assuming that the event N is the project's ending event, all latest times are found as follows:

For activities that end at the project's end:

$$LE_{i,N} = EET$$

The latest ending time is equal to the earliest ending time of the project, determined in the forward pass.

For all other activities:

$$LE_{i,j} = \min_k \left(LS_{j,k} \right)$$

The latest ending time is the earliest of the latest starting times for all directly subsequent activities.

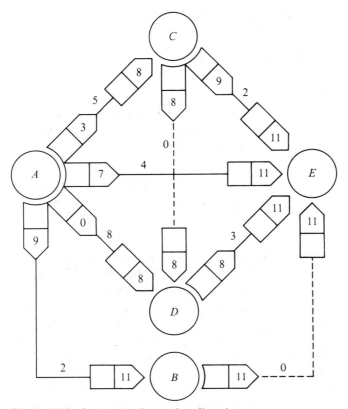

Figure 11.4 Latest starting and ending times.

For all activities:

$$LS_{i,j} = LE_{i,j} - d_{i,j}$$

The latest starting time is the latest ending time minus the activity's expected duration.

Slack Times Finally, the slack time for an activity can be calculated as either the difference between the activity's latest and earliest starting times:

$$S_{i,j} = LS_{i,j} - ES_{i,j}$$

or the difference between the latest and earliest ending times:

$$S_{i,j} = LE_{i,j} - EE_{i,j}$$

For example, the slack time for activity CE is $11 - 7 = 4$ days (using ending times) or $9 - 5 = 4$ days (using starting times). Therefore, the manager directing the slash-burn may delay the application of fire retardants for 4 days beyond its earliest start date without causing the project to take more than 11 days. Alternatively, if the preparation of firebreaks is started by its earliest start time, the project manager knows that problems lengthening this activity by as much as 4 days will not cause any increase in project duration. In fact, people could perhaps be reassigned from that task to others.

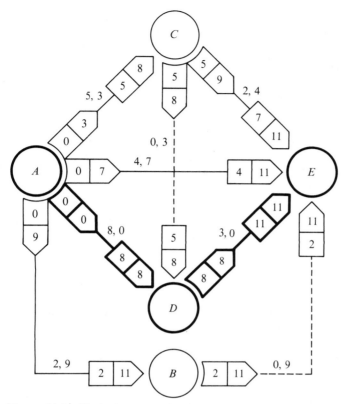

Figure 11.5 Slack times and the critical path.

Critical Path Clearly, slack times deserve careful attention. Activities with zero slack are particularly important, and are collectively referred to as a project's *critical path*. The critical path for the slash-burning project consists of activities *AD*, the felling of hardwoods, and *DE*, the installation of firing devices. It is shown in bold in Fig. 11.5, along with the earliest and latest times, duration and slack for each activity.

The activities on the critical path are critical in that if they do not start as quickly as possible (at their earliest starting times), or if their completion takes longer than expected, the project will take more than its anitcipated earliest ending time. A project manager must monitor carefully the progress of all activities on the critical path, since they have the greatest potential for becoming bottlenecks and preventing project completion on schedule.

Nearly critical activities (those with small activity slacks) must be closely watched as well, since there is always an element of error in estimating the expected duration of activities. When the completion date of critical or near-critical activities begins to slip, it is often advisable to reallocate resources away from ongoing noncritical activities to the problem areas.

The critical path for a project may change when the expected duration of any activity is revised. In the example project, if preparing external firebreaks were to require 9 rather than 5 days, the new critical path would be ACE. As estimates of activity durations are revised, a project manager must update the PERT/CPM network. In that way the network becomes a useful tool in the day-to-day administration of a project rather than a monument to the optimism of the manager.

Probabilistic PERT

The calculations done so far used the expected time of each activity. However, PERT can also give a manager the probability of finishing a project within a specified time.

    This is accomplished by using three estimates of duration for each activity: an optimistic duration O, a pessimistic duration P, and a most-likely duration L. Then, assuming a beta probability distribution for the duration, the expected duration is obtained as the following weighted average of the three:

$$d = \frac{O + 4L + P}{6}$$

and all the PERT/CPM computations proceed as above, using this estimate of the expected duration. The length of the critical path gives us an estimate of the expected earliest end time for the project, EET.

    In addition, the standard deviation of the duration of each activity is:

$$s = \frac{O - P}{6}$$

Then, as long as the activities are independent, the standard deviation of the duration of the entire project, S, is:

$$S = \sqrt{s_1^2 + s_2^2 + \cdots + s_n}$$

where $s_1, \ldots, s_n$ are the standard deviations of the duration of activities on the critical path.

    Now, let A be the time within which we would like to finish the project. Then, the probability of the project's ending time being less than A is the probability of A being $T = (A - EET)/S$ standard deviations away from EET. This probability can be read from the normal distribution in Table 11.3, as long as the number of activities on the critical path is fairly large.

    For example, assume that we have done the PERT computations of the slash-burn project using, for each activity, optimistic, pessimistic, and most-likely durations. Assume further that the expected duration of each activity remains unchanged, so that the expected end time of the project is still $EET = 11$ days. Finally, assume that the standard deviation of the project ending time is $S = 3$ days. What is the probability that the project will end in 8 days?

    To answer this we need only to observe that the target time of 8 days is $(8 - 11)/3 = -1$ standard deviations from the expected end time. Looking at

TABLE 11.3   VALUES OF THE STANDARD NORMAL
                 DISTRIBUTION FUNCTION

P	T
0.05	− 1.64
0.10	− 1.28
0.20	− 0.84
0.30	− 0.52
0.40	− 0.25
0.50	0.00
0.60	0.25
0.70	0.52
0.80	0.84
0.90	1.28
0.95	1.64

Note: P is the probability that an observation from a normal distribution be T standard deviations or less from its expected value.

Table 11.3, this means that the probability of completing the project in 8 days or less is about 15 percent. This is useful information, even though it is only a rough approximation, due to the assumptions made.

Activity Bar Charts

A PERT/CPM network is not the only way to display the important dates in the plan for a project. An activity bar chart is an alternative and somewhat less technical representation containing much of the same information. An activity bar chart for the slash-burn example project is shown in Fig. 11.6. The horizontal axis is divided into days (or some other time unit), and calendar dates may be indicated for ease of reference. Each activity in a project is represented by a bar starting at its earliest starting time and extending through its latest ending time. The activity duration is shown by the length of the white

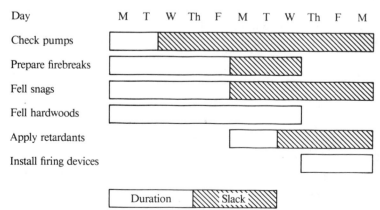

Figure 11.6   Activity bar chart for slash-burn project.

portion of this bar, and the activity slack by the length of the shaded remainder. The activities on the critical path stand out visually due to the absence of any shaded area in their bars. Activity bar charts are particularly useful for displaying the chronological development of a project.

Intangible Benefits of PERT / CPM

Pert/CPM analysis of a project requires a clear specification of project objectives and components, and it provides a realistic way to examine them in light of deadlines and resource limitations. It can help avoid major project cost overruns. It offers a clear mechanism for communicating project plans to people inside and outside the project. For people inside the project, it can let them "see" exactly where they fit into the big picture and foster a sense of teamwork. Even small projects can benefit from PERT/CPM analysis.

11.3 FINDING SHORTEST ROUTES

The Spanish Peak Trails

As a second example of a network model, one that deals with distance rather than time, consider Fig. 11.7. The branches in this network represent hiking trails of the Spanish Peak State Park. The nodes are simply intersections and are labeled with letters. The number beside each branch is the length of the trail between two nodes, in miles. Public access to the park is restricted to a single location, A. The most outstanding feature of the park is a lake at G. Figure 11.7 is not a trail map, since all of the trails are shown as straight lines, and these lines are not drawn to scale. A network diagram is an abstract representation of a system and, unlike this example, does not deal necessarily with distances.

There are several children's summer camps near Spanish Peak State Park. The counselors at these camps want to take their campers on a hike from the park entrance to the lake. However, some of these campers are quite young, so the counselors want to minimize the length of this hike. Accordingly they have asked the park ranger to show them the shortest route from the park entrance (node A) to the lake (node G).

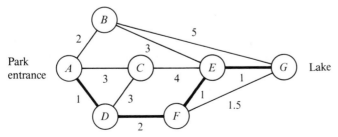

Figure 11.7 Shortest path through Spanish park trail network.

Solution Procedure

Given an origin and a destination node, a shortest route between them can be found by a simple procedure. We fan out from the origin, successively identifying the next closest node to the origin. When the destination is reached, the shortest route to it has been found. Specifically, the *shortest-route* solution algorithm works this way:

> *Step a:* Define the origin as a "solved" node, and all other nodes as "unsolved."
>
> *Step b:* Examine each solved node that is directly connected to one or more unsolved nodes. For each of these solved nodes, determine the closest unsolved nodes, including ties. These are the *candidates* for the next closest node to the origin. For each candidate node, add the shortest distance from the origin to its associated solved node to the distance between the solved node and the candidate. The next closest node to the origin is the candidate having the smallest such sum. The candidate node thus identified becomes solved. Record its shortest distance to the origin.

Repeat step (b) until the destination is selected as the closest node to the origin.

Example

The application of this procedure to the Spanish Peak State Park trail system is demonstrated in Table 11.4. The object is to find the shortest route from *A* to *G*.

> *Step a:* Node *A* is "solved"; all others remain "unsolved."
>
> *Step b1:* Node *D* is the closest node directly connected to *A*. Therefore, *D* becomes the next closest node to the origin, at a distance of 1 mile. Nodes *A* and *D* are now solved.
>
> *Step b2:* Node *A* is still directly connected to two unsolved nodes in this iteration, *B* and *C*. Since node *B* is the closer to *A*, it becomes the candidate for *A*. Similarly, *D* is directly connected to unsolved nodes *C* and *F*. Since node *F* is the closer of these to *D*, it becomes *D*'s candidate. The shortest distance of candidate *F* to the origin is 3 miles, while the shortest distance of candidate *B* is 2 miles. Thus, *B* becomes a solved node, together with *A* and *D*.
>
> *Step b3:* The candidate nodes for *A*, *B*, and *D* are *C*, *E*, and *F*, respectively. Both node *C* and node *F* are 3 miles from the origin while *E* is 5 miles off. Therefore, both *C* and *F* become solved nodes, along with *A*, *B*, and *D*.

TABLE 11.4 FINDING THE SHORTEST ROUTE THROUGH THE SPANISH PEAK STATE PARK TRAIL NETWORK

Step	Solved nodes directly connected to unsolved nodes	Candidate nodes	Distance from origin	Node closest to the origin	Shortest distance to origin	Branch to preceding node on shortest path
b_1	A	D	1	D	1	AD
b_2	A	B	2	B	2	AB
	D	F	1 + 2 = 3			
b_3	A	C	3	C	3	AC
	B	E	2 + 3 = 5			
	D	F	1 + 2 = 3	F	3	DF
b_4	B	E	2 + 3 = 5			
	C	E	3 + 4 = 7			
	F	E	3 + 1 = 4	E	4	FE
b_5	B	G	2 + 5 = 7			
	E	G	4 + 1 = 5	G	5	EG

Step b4: Node E is the closest node to the origin, at a distance of 4 miles.

Step b5: The destination (node G) is identified as the closest node to the origin. The shortest route through the network is 5 miles.

The last column of Table 11.4 shows how to recognize the branches that constitute the shortest path through the Spanish Peak trail system. Starting with the destination, we note that the branch on the shortest path leading to it is *EG*. We then find that the branch on the shortest path leading to E is *FE*, that leading to F is *DF* and to D is *AD*.

Thus the shortest path is *ADFEG*.

11.4 MAXIMIZING FLOWS

Carrying Capacity of Hiking Trails

The Spanish Peak Park has become so popular that the carrying capacity of some trails is being exceeded. The result has been overcrowding and ecological damage. The park ranger has a good idea of the carrying capacity of each trail segment, that is, of the maximum number of people that may walk it each day. Carrying capacities, in hiker trips per day (round trip), are shown along each branch in Fig. 11.8.

Given these data, the ranger would like to know the maximum number of hikers that can be admitted to the park. This is a typical *maximum-flow* problem. It can be solved by linear programming.

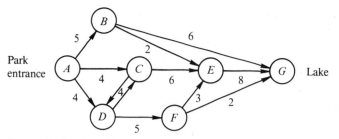

Figure 11.8   Carrying capacity of trails, in hikers per day (round trip).

Decision Variables

The variables of the linear program measure the number of hikers that walk a particular branch of the trail. All visitors to the park return before the end of the day and by the same route. Therefore, we need only consider the one-way trip. The relevant variables are:

$$X_{a,b}, X_{a,c}, X_{a,d}, X_{b,e}, X_{b,g}, X_{c,d}, X_{c,e}, X_{d,c}, X_{d,f}, X_{e,g}, X_{f,e}, X_{f,g}$$

where $X_{i,j}$ is the number of hikers that go from node i to j. Note that two variables, $X_{c,d}$ and $X_{d,c}$, apply to branch CD since hikers can take that trail in either direction on the outgoing trip, depending on whether they started along AC or along AD. For simplicity, we have ignored some other possibilities, like movements in the directions EF or EB on the outgoing trip. In fact, some of these paths may not be very realistic routes.

We shall need two additional variables: X_{in}, the number of hikers entering the park, and X_{out}, the number arriving at the lake.

Objective Function

The objective is to maximize the average daily number of hikers admitted to the park during a season. That is:

$$\max Z = X_{in} \text{ (hikers per day)}$$

Constraints

A first constraint expresses the fact that the number of hikers that enter the park is equal to the number that reach the lake, that is:

$$X_{in} - X_{out} = 0$$

Next, the number of hikers that arrive at each node along the trail is equal to the number that depart:

Node A: $X_{in} - X_{a,b} - X_{a,c} - X_{a,d} = 0$
Node B: $X_{a,b} - X_{b,e} - X_{b,g} = 0$
Node C: $X_{a,c} + X_{d,c} - X_{c,d} - X_{c,e} = 0$
Node D: $X_{a,d} + X_{c,d} - X_{d,c} - X_{d,f} = 0$
Node E: $X_{b,e} + X_{c,e} + X_{f,e} - X_{e,g} = 0$
Node F: $X_{d,f} - X_{f,e} - X_{f,g} = 0$
Node G: $X_{b,g} + X_{e,g} + X_{f,g} - X_{out} = 0$

$$(11.1)$$

TABLE 11.5   LINEAR-PROGRAMMING TABLEAU TO FIND THE MAXIMUM FLOW THROUGH THE SPANISH PEAK TRAIL NETWORK

	X_{in}	$X_{a,b}$	$X_{a,c}$	$X_{a,d}$	$X_{b,e}$	$X_{b,g}$	$X_{c,d}$	$X_{c,e}$	$X_{d,c}$	$X_{d,f}$	$X_{e,g}$	$X_{f,e}$	$X_{f,g}$	X_{out}	
Z	1													-1	$= 0$
INOU	1														$= 0$
AAAA	1	-1	-1	-1											$= 0$
BBBB		1			-1	-1									$= 0$
CCCC			1				-1	-1	1						$= 0$
DDDD				1			1		-1	-1					$= 0$
EEEE					1			1			-1	1			$= 0$
FFFF										1		-1	-1		$= 0$
GGGG						1					1		1	-1	$= 0$
CDCD							1		1						≤ 4
UPBD		5	4	4	2	6		6		5	8	3	2		

Finally, the number of hikers that use a particular trail cannot exceed the trail capacity. That is:

$$X_{a,b} \leq 5, \ X_{a,c} \leq 4, \ X_{a,d} \leq 4, \ X_{b,e} \leq 2, \ X_{b,g} \leq 6, \ X_{c,e} \leq 6,$$
$$X_{d,f} \leq 5, \ X_{f,e} \leq 3, \ X_{e,g} \leq 8, \ X_{f,g} \leq 2 \tag{11.2}$$

and

$$X_{c,d} + X_{d,c} \leq 4 \tag{11.3}$$

The last constraint means that the total number of people walking the trail branch *CD* cannot exceed 4, in either direction, during the outgoing trip.

The linear-programming tableau for this problem appears in Table 11.5. The constraints (11.2) are all shown in the same row called UPBD, for upper bounds. This reflects the fact that many computer programs have a simpler way of handling upper bounds on variables than the usual row constraints.

There are simpler methods than linear programming to model flows in networks, but they are more specialized. In particular, they cannot handle simply a constraint like (11.3).

The solution of the linear program in Table 11.5 is shown in Fig. 11.9. At most, 13 hikers a day may use the trails without exceeding the carrying

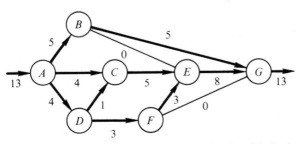

Figure 11.9   Maximum flow through the Spanish Peak trail system.

capacity of any branch. The figure shows the assignment of hikers to each trail segment. This leaves the park ranger with the problem of making sure that trails will be used in this way. It is easy to control the number of people entering the park, less to control which trail they use. The ranger could issue permits to hikers, for a specific route through the park. Or, she could close some trails temporarily when they become overused, with the aim of maintaining an average use close to that shown in Fig. 11.9.

11.5 CONCLUSIONS

Network diagrams provide a useful way of conceptualizing many forest resource management problems. Branches of networks and their corresponding nodes can have a wide variety of interpretations. In PERT/CPM, branches represent the duration of various activities in a project and nodes refer to specific points in time. The network then shows how activities depend on one another, that is, which ones must be finished before others can start. The object of PERT/CPM computations is to find the shortest time in which the project can be done and to point out the critical activities, that is, those that will lengthen the project if they are delayed. The computations are sufficiently simple that they can be done by hand, although a computer program will certainly help.

In transportation networks, branches may refer to specific roads, and nodes refer to their intersections. One then often wishes to find the shortest route from one point to another. This can also be done by manual computation, at least for reasonably small networks. Naturally, the objective function may be different; for example, if cost data are available, it would be better to seek the cheapest route rather than the shortest. This can be done with the same model and same computation procedures.

Another useful application of networks is in studying flows. Although procedures are available to maximize flows in networks, they can always be solved by linear programming with some gain in flexibility. The basic idea is to write equations expressing the conservation of flow at each node: what comes in must equal what goes out. Other constraints may be added to reflect limits on flows along specific branches. The objective is then to find the maximum flow of goods, people, information, etc., that can go through the system in a specified unit of time.

PROBLEMS

11.1. The Supervisor of a National Forest wants to decrease unexpected delays in the preparation of timber sales. Accordingly, he has directed his staff to use PERT to coordinate the next timber sale. To do this, the staff has identified the various activities involved, their precedence relationships, and the time necessary to do them:

Activity	Expected Duration (days)	Activities that must be completed before work on this activity can start
Timber inventory	4	None
Nontimber inventory	3	None
Initial sale design	2	Timber inventory
		Nontimber inventory
Transportation planning	21	Timber inventory
		Nontimber inventory
Initial environmental assessment	4	Timber inventory
		Nontimber inventory
Final environmental assessment	5	Initial sale design
		Transportation planning
		Initial environmental assessment
Final sale design	5	Final environmental assessment
Mark sale boundaries	2	Final sale design
Lay out roads	14	Final sale design
Mark timber	5	Mark sale boundaries
Cruise timber	4	Mark timber
Prepare advertisement	2	Lay out roads, Cruise timber
Advertise sale	7	Prepare advertisement
Award sale	2	Advertise sale

Draw a network diagram showing the precedence relationships between activities, using dummy activities if necessary. Remember to use dummy activities so that only one activity connects two events.

Perform the forward and backward pass calculations for this network, first by hand and then with a computer program. What are the critical activities? How much time will be needed to prepare this sale?

Summarize your results in an activity bar chart. For each activity, this chart should show the earliest start date, expected duration, latest start date, and slack time.

11.2. You have just been hired as director of the newly created Redwood National Park. The park will cover almost 80,000 acres of old-growth redwood forest. Prior to its purchase for the park, most of the land was owned by lumber companies, and was little used for recreation.

Your immediate task is to plan, schedule, and direct the numerous things that must be done before the park can be opened to the public. You plan to use PERT to manage this complex project. You have already identified the various tasks involved, their precedence relationships, and the time needed to do them.

Activity	Expected Duration (months)			Activities that must be completed before work on this activity can start
	O	L	P	
Establish ranger stations	1	1.5	2	None
Establish fire protection	0.5	1	2	Establish ranger stations
Purchase inholdings	4	6	8	Establish ranger stations
Phase out lumber operations	9	11	13	Establish ranger stations
Secure mineral rights	4	5	6	Establish ranger stations
Obtain scenic easements	8	10	12	Establish ranger stations
Construct signs	3	4	6	Establish fire protection
Construct temporary campgrounds	1	2	3	Establish fire protection
Designate temporary primitive campsites	2	4	6	Establish fire protection
Construct temporary headquarters	1	2	3	Establish fire protection
Repair existing trails	9	11	14	Establish fire protection Purchase inholdings
Repair boundary fences	10	12	16	Establish ranger stations
Post boundary	10	12	16	Establish ranger stations
Preliminary hydrological study	2	3	5	Establish ranger stations
Archaeological study	4	6	8	Phase out lumber operations
Range study	3	4	6	Phase out lumber operations
Preliminary environmental study	4	6	8	Construct signs Construct temporary campgrounds Designate temporary primitive campsites Construct temporary headquarters Repair existing trails Repair boundary fences
Preliminary master plan	3	5	7	Preliminary hydrological study Preliminary environmental study
Public hearings on master plan	1	2	3	Preliminary master plan
Final hydrological study	1	2	3	Public hearings on master plan
Final environmental study	3	4	5	Public hearings on master plan Secure mineral rights Obtain scenic easements
Final master plan	5	6	8	Archaeological study Range study Final hydrological study Final environmental study
Construct new trails	12	14	18	Public hearings on master plan
Designate permanent primitive campsites	5	6	7	Public hearings on master plan
Construct permanent campgrounds	10	12	13	Final master plan
Construct permanent headquarters	10	12	14	Final master plan
Construct vehicle access system	12	14	16	Final master plan

These data are shown above. Note that there are three time estimates for each activity: optimistic (O), most likely (L) and pessimistic (P).

Draw a network diagram showing the precedence relationships between these activities, using dummy activities where needed. Remember to use dummy activities so that only one activity connects two events.

Perform the PERT calculations for this network with a computer, using the three estimates of the duration for each activity.

What are the critical activities? How long will it take to prepare the park for the public?

Draw a bar chart showing for each activity the earliest start date, expected duration, latest start date, and slack time.

Using a table of the standard normal distribution, find the probability of getting the park ready for the public in 52 or 60 months.

11.3. A logging contractor needs to find the shortest route through a network of logging roads, shown below, from a landing at node A to a log concentration yard at node H. Nodes B through G are simply road intersections. The length of the road segments are shown in miles along the segments. Find the shortest route from A to H.

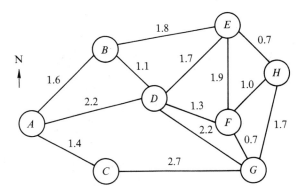

11.4. Suppose that the logging contractor alluded to in Problem 11.3 instructs his drivers to take the shortest route from the landing to the concentration yard, but then notices a definite increase in their travel times. At the contractor's request, you decide to reconsider your route recommendation.

Driving through the road network, you observe that the northern road segments are in very poor condition, making for slow travel. Realizing that you should have solved for the fastest route rather than the shortest, you take out a logging truck and time what it takes to traverse each road segment in the system. These times are given below.

From Node	To Node	Travel time (minutes)
A	B	9.6
A	C	4.2
A	D	6.6
B	E	10.8
B	D	4.4
C	G	8.1
D	E	6.8
D	F	3.9
D	G	6.6
E	F	7.6
E	H	4.2
F	G	2.1
F	H	3.0
G	H	5.1

What is the fastest route through the network? How long should it take to traverse this route? What savings in time does this represent over taking the shortest route found in Problem 11.3?

11.5. Suppose that the managers of the Spanish Peak State Park described in Sect. 11.4 of the text decide to upgrade their trail system by building new trails from nodes B to C and from C to F, each with a capacity of 4 hikers. Further suppose that the capacities of the existing trails from nodes B to G, E to G, and A to D are each increased by two hikers. How would the linear programming tableau in Table 11.5 have to be modified to reflect these changes? What would the maximum flow of hikers through the expanded trail system be?

11.6. The logging contractor of Problems 11.3 and 11.4 has become involved in a dispute with recreationists using the area in which he works. They object to the frequency with which they are disturbed by logging trucks roaring past. They ask the contractor to limit the number of trucks per hour on each road segment to the numbers shown on the network below. They especially want few trucks in the area about node F, a popular camping site. Also, because the hikers prefer the striking topography along the northern roads, their proposed limits are more generous along southern road segments.

Formulate a linear programming model to determine the largest number of logging trucks per hour that could move through the system from A to H if the desires of the recreationists were satisfied. According to that solution, how many trucks would be moving along each road segment?

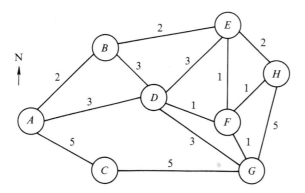

ANNOTATED REFERENCES

Carson, W. W., and D. P. Dykstra. 1978. Programs for road network planning. U.S. Forest Service General Technical Report PNW-67. Pacific Northwest Forest and Range Experiment Station, Portland. 21 pp. (Lists BASIC computer programs designed to help logging engineers to find the shortest route through a forest transportation system.)

Corcoran, T. J., and M. A. Nieuwenhuis. 1985. Modeling wood flow under salvage conditions. *In* Forest Operations in Politically and Environmentally Sensitive Areas:

A Proceedings of the Council on Forest Engineering, 18–22 August, 1985, Tahoe City, California, pp. 46–50. 162 pp. (Applies geographic information systems and shortest route methods to the harvesting of insect-damaged timber.)

Dane, C. W., C. F. Gray, and B. M. Woodworth. 1979. Factors affecting the successful application of PERT/CPM systems in a government organization. *Interfaces* 9(5):94–98. (Reasons for the success or failure of PERT/CPM methods on eighteen national forests.)

Davis, J. B. 1968. Why not PERT your next resource management problem? *Journal of Forestry* 66(5):405–408. (Basis of the PERT model presented in this chapter.)

Davis, S. S. 1967. An adaptation of the critical path method of resource allocation in timber sales planning. D.N.R. Report No. 11. Washington Department of Natural Resources. 53 pp. (Detailed example of the application of a PERT/CPM model to the administration of timber sales by a public agency.)

Dunn, R. A., and K. D. Ramsing. 1981. *Management science: A practical approach to decisionmaking.* Macmillan, New York 527 pp. (Chapter 14 introduces PERT/CPM models using an example dealing with the management of a ski resort.)

Dykstra, D. P. 1984. *Mathematical programming for natural resource management.* McGraw-Hill, New York. 318 pp. (Chapter 7 discusses resource-related applications of minimum-spanning trees, shortest route, maximum flow, and PERT/CPM models.)

Hillier, F. S., and G. J. Lieberman. 1986. *Introduction to operations research.* Holden-Day, Oakland. 888 pp. (Chapter 10 is a good general introduction to minimum spanning trees, shortest route, maximum flow, and PERT/CPM models.)

Husch, B. 1970. Network analysis in FAO international assistance forestry projects. *Unasylva* 24(4) No. 99:18–28. (Use of PERT/CPM at the Food and Agriculture Organization of the United Nations to plan and monitor forestry development projects. Several examples.)

Mandt, C. I. 1973. Network analysis in transportation planning. *In* Planning and decisionmaking as applied to forest harvesting. (J. E. O'Leary, ed.) pp. 95–101. Oregon State University, School of Forestry, Corvallis. 158 pp. (Describes a shortest-route application to the allocation of harvests between several sawmills in the harvest area.)

Mater, M. H. 1967. PERT: A new technique for reducing sawmill modernization costs. *Forest Industries* 94(7):36–39. (Application of PERT to control construction costs.)

Martin, A. J. 1977. A computer program for analyzing PERT networks. U.S. Forest Service General Technical Report NE-32. Northeastern Forest Experiment Station, Upper Darby. 10 pp. (FORTRAN program for PERT computations, applies the program to award U.S. Forest Service timber sale contracts.)

Ramsing, K. D. 1966. How the critical path method can assist road construction: *Forest Industries* 93(13):66–69. (Application of PERT/CPM models to the construction of logging roads.)

____1967. How the critical path method can assist road construction: Part II. *Forest Industries* 94(1):180–183. (Continuation of previous citation.)

Taha, H. A. 1982. *Operations research: An introduction.* Macmillan, New York. 848 pp. (Chapter 6 is a good general introduction to minimum-spanning trees, shortest route, maximum flow, and network models, including the linear programming representation of network models. Chapter 12 is a good general introduction to PERT/CPM models, especially with respect to the time-cost tradeoff analysis associated with CPM models.)

Multistage Decision Making with Dynamic Programming

12.1 INTRODUCTION

In the preceding chapters we solved many forest management problems using linear programming. Linear programming is a very powerful method because standard computer programs are available to get solutions. However, linear programming has some limitations. First, it applies only to variables that are continuous. In Chap. 10 we saw how integer programming could be used to bypass this limitation, but integer programs are not easy to solve. Second, linear programming applies only to problems that can be expressed with linear equations.

Dynamic programming is an approach to optimization that can readily handle nonlinear relationships and discrete variables. Despite the name, many dynamic-programming applications have nothing to do with time. For example, the problem of how to allocate funds to competing projects can be solved by dynamic programming. This approach consists in decomposing the problem into a sequence of subproblems, or stages, one for each project. The solutions of each subproblem are found first, and then these solutions are put together to get the solution of the overall problem.

The disadvantage of dynamic programming is that, in contrast to linear and integer programming, it does not have a standard form. Although the general approach is always the same, the actual details of the solution depend on the specific case. The best way to learn how forestry problems can be solved by dynamic programming is to study many examples.

We shall start with one of the earliest applications of dynamic programming in forestry: the determination of thinnings and final harvest in even-aged stands. From this simple example we shall be able to infer the common characteristics of problems solvable by dynamic programming, as well as the method of solution.

We shall then proceed with two more examples. First, trimming rolls of paper in a paper mill to maximize value, and then the allocation of funds to projects to minimize the probability of extinction of an endangered species.

12.2 BEST THINNING OF AN EVEN-AGED FOREST STAND

A forester in northern California plans to cut a mixed conifer stand to maximize the total yield from thinning and final harvest. He has decided already to do the harvest in three stages: an immediate thinning, a second thinning 20 years later, and a clear-cut 20 years after that.

However, he is undecided as to how much to thin and will consider three possibilities: no thinning, a light thinning that removes approximately 50 ft^2 of basal area per acre, or a heavy thinning that removes approximately 100 ft^2 of basal area per acre.

Stages, States, and Decisions

The different ways of treating the stand in the next 40 years can be depicted as a network, as in Fig. 12.1. Following the dynamic-programming terminology, we refer to the time when a decision is made as a *stage*.

The condition of the stand at a particular stage, just before the decision, is called a *state*. In Fig. 12.1 a state is represented by a lettered node of the network.

A decision is represented in the network by a branch between nodes. The consequence of a decision is to move the stand from a particular stage and state to a different state at the subsequent stage. The change is due in part to the thinning and in part to the growth of the timber that remains after thinning.

The numbers along the branches in Fig. 12.1 refer to the immediate yield resulting from a decision. For example, at stage 1, a heavy thinning yields 15 thousand board feet per acre (Mbft/a) and a light thinning 5 Mbft/a.

Management Alternatives

A path through the network represents one possible way to manage the stand. Thus, starting from state A at stage 1, not thinning leads to state D at stage 2. At stage 2, state D, a heavy thinning yields 20 Mbft/a and leads to state G at stage 3. At that stage and state the final harvest yields 110 Mbft/a. The total yield of this management regime would then be 130 Mbft/a.

Clearly, the best management could be found by following all possible paths through the network and finding the one with the largest total yield. This indeed would be the best procedure for this small problem. However, the number of paths would become extremely large were one to consider the possibility of thinning in any one of the 40 years of management. In that case, the dynamic programming approach would be very advantageous.

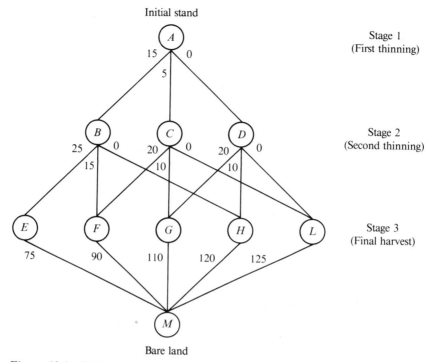

Figure 12.1 Different ways of harvesting a forest stand.

A Myopic Solution

One intuitive way of solving the thinning problem would be to choose at each stage, starting with stage 1, the decision that gives the largest immediate yield. This would lead to thin the stand heavily at stages 1 and 2. The total yield from this sequence would then be 15 + 25 + 75 = 115 Mbft/a.

However, this solution cannot be optimal, since at least one path, from state A to B to F to M, has a higher yield (15 + 15 + 90 = 120 Mbft/a). Thinning at an early stage can accelerate growth and reduce mortality in later stages, but it can also leave too little growing material. The decision of how much to thin at each stage can't be made independently of what has been done earlier, or of what will be done later. A correct solution must take into account this dependence between decisions at various stages.

Dynamic Programming Solution

Consider the possible decisions at stage i and state s.

Let x_i be the decision variable. The value of x_i is the destination state selected at stage i. For example, $x_2 = E$ means that at stage 2 the stand is thinned to reach state E at stage 3.

Let $y_i(s, x_i)$ be the immediate yield of decision x_i at stage i and state s. For example, $y_2(B, E) = 25$ Mbft/a.

Let $Y_i(s, x_i)$ be the highest yield that can be obtained from stage i and all subsequent stages, given state s and decision x_i at stage i.

Furthermore, let x_i^* be the decision that maximizes $Y_i(s, x_i)$, and let $Y_i^*(s)$ be the corresponding maximum value of $Y_i(s, x_i)$.

Thus, $Y_i^*(s)$ is the highest yield from stage i and beyond, given state s at stage i. The object is to find $Y_1^*(A)$, the highest yield from stages 1, 2, and 3, given the initial stand state.

The dynamic-programming approach works *backward*. Thus, we first determine the highest yield at stage 3, for every possible state, and the corresponding best decision:

$$Y_3^*(s) \quad \text{and} \quad x_3^* \tag{12.1}$$

This is a trivial problem because there is only one possible decision for each state at stage 3. From this we then determine the highest yield from stage 2 and stage 3, for each possible state at stage 2. That is, we find the decisions x_2^* such that:

$$Y_2^*(s) = \max_{x_2} \left[y_2(s, x_2) + Y_3^*(x_2) \right] \tag{12.2}$$

From this we finally determine the highest yield from stages 1, 2, and 3 given the initial state at stage 1, that is, we find the decision x_1^* such that:

$$Y_1^*(A) = \max_{x_1} \left[y_1(A, x_1) + Y_2^*(x_1) \right]$$

$Y_1^*(A)$ is the highest total yield that can be obtained from the stand, and x_1^* is the best decision at stage 1. The decision x_1^* determines the best state at stage 2. For that state, we know the best decision x_2^* from the solution of (12.2). The decision x_2^* determines in turn the best state at stage 3. For that state we find, from (12.1), the best decision x_3^*.

The specific computations proceed as follows, stage by stage:

Stage 3: As shown in Fig. 12.1, five states are possible: E, F, G, H, and L. Regardless of the state, the best (in fact, the only possible) decision is $x_3^* = M$. The corresponding maximum yields for each state are shown in Table 12.1.

Stage 2: The computations for this stage appear in Table 12.2.

The highest yield obtainable from stages 2 and 3, for a particular state s and

TABLE 12.1   YIELDS OF THE FINAL HARVEST (STAGE 3)

s	$Y_3^*(s)$	x_3^*
E	75	M
F	90	M
G	110	M
H	120	M
L	125	M

TABLE 12.2 BEST SECOND THINNING AS A FUNCTION OF STATE (STAGE 2)

	$Y_2(s, x_2) = y_2(s, x_2) + Y_3^*(x_2)$						
s	$x_2 = E$	$x_2 = F$	$x_2 = G$	$x_2 = H$	$x_2 = L$	$Y_2^*(s)$	x_2^*
B	100 = 25 + 75	105 = 15 + 90	—	120 = 0 + 120	—	120	H
C	—	110 = 20 + 90	120 = 10 + 110	—	125 = 0 + 125	125	L
D	—	—	130 = 20 + 110	130 = 10 + 120	125 = 0 + 125	130	G or H

decision x_2, is:

$$Y_2(s, x_2) = y_2(s, x_2) + Y_3^*(x_2)$$

For example, assume that the stand is in state B at stage 2 and that $x_2 = E$. Then, the highest yield obtainable from stages 2 and 3 is:

$$Y_2(B, E) = y_2(B, E) + Y_3^*(E)$$
$$= 25 \qquad + 75 = 100 \text{ Mbft/a}$$

The complete row of Table 12.2 corresponding to state B is obtained by repeating these calculations for the two other possible decisions at stage 2, $x_2 = F$ and $x_2 = H$. This leads to:

$$Y_2(B, F) = 105 \text{ Mbft/a} \quad \text{and} \quad Y_2(B, H) = 120 \text{ Mbft/a}$$

Therefore, the highest yield from stages 2 and 3, given state B at stage 2 is $Y_2^*(B) = 120$ Mbft/a, and the best decision is $x_2^* = H$.

Repeating these computations for the other possible states at stage 2 leads to, for state C:

$$Y_2^*(C) = 125 \text{ Mbft/a} \qquad x_2^* = L$$

and for state D:

$$Y_2^*(D) = 130 \text{ Mbft/a} \qquad x_2^* = G \text{ or } H$$

Stage 1: The calculation for stage 1 appear in Table 12.3. The highest yield obtainable from stages 1, 2, and 3, for a particular state s and decision x_1, is:

$$Y_1(s, x_1) = y_1(s, x_1) + Y_2^*(x_1)$$

There is only one possible state at stage 1, $s = A$. If the decision is $x_1 = B$, the highest yield obtainable from the three stages is:

$$Y_1(A, B) = y_1(A, B) + Y_2^*(B)$$
$$= 15 \qquad + 120 = 135 \text{ Mbft/a}$$

TABLE 12.3 BEST FIRST THINNING AS A FUNCTION OF STATE (STAGE 1)

	$Y_1(s, x_1) = y_1(s, x_1) + Y_2^*(x_1)$				
s	$x_1 = B$	$x_1 = C$	$x_1 = D$	$Y_1^*(s)$	x_1^*
A	135 = 15 + 120	130 = 5 + 125	130 = 0 + 130	135	B

Repeating these calculations for $x_1 = C$ and $x_1 = D$ leads to:

$$Y_1(A, C) = 130 \text{ Mbft/a} \quad \text{and} \quad Y_1(A, D) = 130 \text{ Mbft/a}$$

Therefore, the highest yield from the three stages is $Y_1^*(A) = 135$ Mbft/a, and the best first decision is $x_1^* = B$.

The subsequent best decisions are obtained as follows: since the best first decision is $x_1^* = B$, the best state at stage 2 is B. At stage 2 and state B the best decision is $x_2^* = H$ (see Table 12.2). This decision in turn leads to state H at stage 3. At stage 3 and state H there is but one possible decision, $x_3^* = M$ (see Table 12.1).

In summary, given a stand of initial state A and a final harvest in 40 years, the best management regime requires only an immediate heavy thinning.

Tables 12.1 to 12.3 can also be used to determine the optimal sequence of harvests starting from any stage and state. For example, assume the crew doing the first thinning did not cut enough. The stand might then be in state C at stage 2. Table 12.2 shows that $x_2^* = L$ for $s = C$ at stage 2, so the optimal decision would still be to skip the second thinning.

Naturally, the practical value of this particular dynamic solution is limited, due to the few alternatives considered. Nevertheless, the same method could be used to investigate more thinning alternatives, at more frequent intervals. Besides thinning, clear-cutting could be an option at every stage, thus making the rotation a decision variable. The best rotation could then be found simultaneously with the best thinning regime.

12.3 GENERAL FORMULATION OF DYNAMIC PROGRAMMING

Despite its simplicity, the thinning problem of the previous section has all the features of more complex dynamic-programming problems. Problems of this kind are defined in terms of stages, states, and decisions, and they are solved recursively.

Stages, States, and Decisions

Problems that can be solved by dynamic programming can be divided in stages, where some decision must be made at each stage. In the thinning example, stages were points in time, but this is not always the case, as we shall see in subsequent examples.

Each stage has one or more states associated with it. In defining the state variables it is helpful to think of what changes from stage to stage and what is affected by decisions. In the thinning problem, the state was the structure of the stand. Stand structure could be defined by a number of variables, such as number of trees, basal area, or volume.

The effect of a decision is to move from a stage and state to another state at the next stage. There is an immediate *return* associated with a decision. For any given stage and state, the optimal sequence of decisions for the remaining stages must be independent of the decisions made in previous stages. That is to say, "no matter where we are, how we got here doesn't have any bearing on where we need to go." In the thinning problem, the stand structure at any stage is sufficient to predict the growth of the stand, regardless of how that structure was reached.

Recursive Solution

The objective of a dynamic-programming problem is to maximize (or minimize) the returns from all decisions. The solution starts by finding the optimum solution for each possible state at the last stage. This is usually a trivial problem. The solution proceeds backward, one stage at a time, using a recursive equation. For the thinning problem, the recursive equation was:

$$Y_i^*(s) = \max_{x_i} \left[y_i(s, x_i) + Y_{i+1}^*(x_i) \right]$$

In general, the function within brackets reflects the immediate returns at stage i and the maximum returns from stage $i + 1$ onward that result from the decision x_i.

The recursive equation is used to find $Y_i^*(s)$ and x_i^* for all possible states, from the last to the first. The maximum return over all stages, $Y_1^*(s)$ and the best decision at stage 1, x_1^*, are obtained when the first stage is reached. From there, it is a simple matter to determine the best decisions at all stages, by using the relationship between states and decision variables.

12.4 TRIMMING PAPER ROLLS TO MAXIMIZE VALUE

This second example of dynamic programming differs from the thinning problem in that the stages are not points in time. The relationship between states and decisions is also different.

Problem Definition

The Maine pulp-mill cooperative considered in Chaps. 2, 3, and 9 has been so successful that it has added a paper machine to its mill. The machine produces a continuous sheet of high-quality coated book paper. The sheet is 15 ft wide and must be trimmed to narrower dimensions before it is shipped to customers. All paper is sold in large rolls of same diameter, but of different widths.

Currently, the selling price of paper of this quality is $40, $70, $130, and $150 for rolls 3, 5, 7, and 9 ft wide, respectively. Note that price is not directly proportional to width. The premium per additional foot is highest between 5 and 7 ft, less between 3 and 5 ft, and still less between 7 and 9 (Fig. 12.2).

There are many ways of trimming the sheet coming out of the paper machine to produce rolls with a total width of 15 ft or less. The problem is to

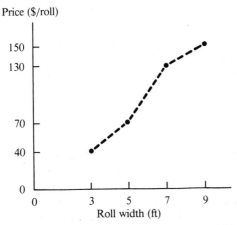

Price ($/roll)

Roll width (ft)

Figure 12.2 Relationship between the width of a roll of paper and its price.

find the combination that yields the highest value. We shall do this by dynamic programming.

Stages, States, and Decision Variables

The trimmers located at the end of a paper-making machine cut the outcoming sheet simultaneously to specified widths. However, for our purpose it will be helpful to think of the process as a sequence of stages. Each stage corresponds to choosing the width of one roll of paper. Only five stages are needed since, at most five rolls can be cut, each one 3 ft wide. We shall denote a stage by i, where i varies from 1 to 5. A natural choice of a decision variable, then, is the width of the roll cut at each stage, x_i. The only possibilities are:

$$x_i = 3, 5, 7, \text{ or } 9 \text{ ft} \qquad \text{for any } i$$

The state variable must describe the change that takes place from stage to stage, in response to a decision. A possible state variable, then, is the width of the sheet of paper that remains to be cut at stage i; call it s. Consequently: if s is the state at stage i, then $s - x_i$ is the state at stage $i + 1$.

Description of Alternatives

The different ways of cutting the sheet of paper can be represented by a network, as in Fig. 12.3. Each node corresponds to a particular state. A row of nodes is a stage. The branches between nodes correspond to possible decisions.

At stage 1, 15 ft of paper remain to be cut; therefore, the initial state is $s = 15$. The first roll may be cut at any of the possible widths. Let $x_1 = 3$ ft, then $s = 15 - 3 = 12$ ft at stage 2. Now, given $s = 12$ ft at stage 2, let the width of the second roll be $x_2 = 5$ ft. Then, $s = 12 - 5 = 7$ ft at stage 3.

The complete network in Fig. 12.3 is obtained in this way, by trying each possible value of x_i at each stage while keeping into account the fact that s cannot decrease further if it is less than 3 ft.

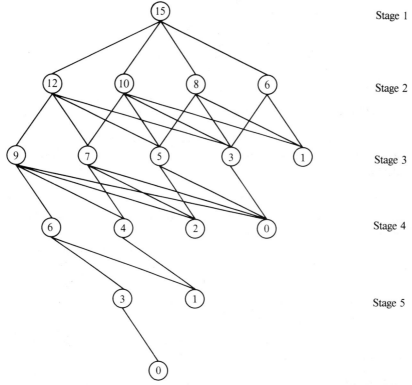

Figure 12.3   Different ways of trimming a 15-ft wide roll of paper into 3-, 5-, 7-, or 9-ft widths.

Dynamic-Programming Solution

Consider the possible decisions at stage i and state s. Let $v(x_i)$ be the immediate return from decision x_i. This is just the price of a roll of paper x_i ft wide. Let $V_i(s, x_i)$ be the highest value of the rolls of paper cut at stage i and beyond, given the state s at stage i and the decision x_i. Furthermore, let x_i^* be the decision that maximizes $V_i(s, x_i)$ and let $V_i^*(s)$ be the corresponding maximum of $V_i(s, x_i)$. Thus:

$$V_i^*(s) = \max_{x_i} \left[v(x_i) + V_{i+1}^*(s - x_i) \right] \tag{12.3}$$

The object is to determine $V_1^*(15)$, the highest value that can be gotten from trimming a 15-ft wide sheet of paper. We do this by applying the recursive relation (12.3) stage by stage, from stage 5 to stage 1.

Stage 5: Figure 12.3 shows two possible states at stage 5, $s = 3$ and $s = 1$ ft. It is possible to obtain a fifth roll of paper only if $s = 3$ ft. In that state, the best decision is to cut a 3 ft roll and get a return of $40, that is:

$$V_5^*(3) = \$40 \quad \text{and} \quad x_5^* = 3 \text{ ft}$$

TABLE 12.4 BEST WIDTH OF THE FOURTH ROLL OF PAPER AS A FUNCTION OF REMAINING SHEET WIDTH (STAGE 4)

	$V_4(s, x_4) = v(x_4) + V_5^*(s - x_4)$			
s (ft)	$x_4 = 3$ ft	$x_4 = 5$ ft	$V_4^*(s)$ ($)	x_4^* (ft)
6	80 = 40 + 40	70	80	3
4	40	—	40	3

Stage 4: The computations for this stage appear in Table 12.4. The highest value obtainable from stages 4 and 5, for a particular state and decision at stage 4 is:

$$V_4(s, x_4) = v(x_4) + V_5^*(s - x_4) \qquad (12.4)$$

Figure 12.3 shows that the possible states are $s = 6, 4, 2,$ or 0 ft. More rolls can be cut only if $s = 6$ or 4 ft.

For example, assume $s = 6$ ft, then cutting a 3-ft roll would give an immediate return of $40 and lead to $s = 3$ ft at stage 5, which in turn would give a maximum return of $40 at stage 5. In terms of equation (12.4) we have:

$$V_4(6, 3) = v(3) + V_5^*(6 - 3)$$
$$= \$40 + \$40 = \$80$$

still assuming $s = 6$ ft, but cutting a 5-ft roll would give an immediate return of $70 and lead to $s = 1$ ft at stage 5, with no further return. Thus:

$$V_4(6, 5) = v(5) + V_5^*(6 - 5)$$
$$= \$70 + 0 = \$70.$$

Therefore, the highest value obtainable from stages 4 and 5, given $s = 6$ ft at stage 4, is $V_4^*(6) = \$80$, and the best decision is $x_4^* = 3$ ft.

Repeating these calculations for $s = 4$ ft leads to:

$$V_4^*(4) = \$40 \qquad \text{and} \qquad x_4^* = 3 \text{ ft}$$

Stages 3, 2, and 1: The calculations for stages 3, 2, and 1 are similar to those for stage 4. The results for each stage appear in Tables 12.5 through 12.7.

Consider Table 12.7, which refers to stage 1. It shows that $V_1^*(15) = \$260$ and $x_1^* = 7$ ft. Thus, the maximum value that can be obtained by trimming the sheet of paper is $260. The best solution includes cutting the first roll 7 ft wide.

TABLE 12.5 BEST WIDTH OF THE THIRD ROLL OF PAPER (STAGE 3)

	$V_3(s, x_3) = v(x_3) + V_4^*(s - x_3)$					
s (ft)	$x_3 = 3$ ft	$x_3 = 5$ ft	$x_3 = 7$ ft	$x_3 = 9$ ft	$V_3^*(s)$ ($)	x_3^* (ft)
9	120 = 40 + 80	110 = 70 + 40	130	150	150	9
7	80 = 40 + 40	70	130	—	130	7
5	40	70	—	—	70	5
3	40	—	—	—	40	3

TABLE 12.6   BEST WIDTH OF THE SECOND ROLL OF PAPER (STAGE 2)

	$V_2(s, x_2) = v(x_2) + V_3^*(s - x_2)$					
s (ft)	$x_2 = 3$ ft	$x_2 = 5$ ft	$x_2 = 7$ ft	$x_2 = 9$ ft	$V_2^*(s)$ ($)	x_2^* (ft)
12	190 = 40 + 150	200 = 70 + 130	200 = 130 + 70	190 = 150 + 40	200	5 or 7
10	170 = 40 + 130	140 = 70 + 70	170 = 130 + 40	150	170	3 or 7
8	110 = 40 + 70	110 = 70 + 40	130	—	130	7
6	80 = 40 + 40	70	—	—	80	3

TABLE 12.7   BEST WIDTH OF THE FIRST ROLL OF PAPER (STAGE 1)

	$V_1(s, x_1) = v(x_1) + V_1^*(s - x_1)$					
s (ft)	$x_1 = 3$ ft	$x_1 = 5$ ft	$x_1 = 7$ ft	$x_1 = 9$ ft	$V_1^*(s)$ ($)	x_1^* (ft)
15	240 = 40 + 200	240 = 70 + 170	260 = 130 + 130	230 = 150 + 80	260	7

The length of the other rolls are obtained as follows: since the state at stage 1 is $s = 15$ and the best decision is $x_1^* = 7$ ft, the best state at stage 2 is:

$$s = 15 - 7 = 8 \text{ ft}$$

Now, at stage 2 and state 8 ft, the best decision is $x_2^* = 7$ (see Table 12.6). The resulting state at stage 3 is:

$$s = 8 - 1 = 1 \text{ ft}$$

and no other roll can be cut. Therefore, the best solution is to cut two rolls of 7 ft each, for a total value of $260. The remaining foot of paper can be sent back to the pulpmill for recycling.

12.5 MINIMIZING THE RISK OF LOSING AN ENDANGERED SPECIES

The two previous examples of dynamic programming involved additive returns. The highest returns at stage i were in both cases the highest of the immediate returns at stage i plus the highest of the returns at stage $i + 1$ and beyond. However, dynamic programming can also be applied to problems with nonlinear objective functions. The following example uses a multiplicative objective function.

Problem Definition

Consider a nonprofit organization whose main objective is the protection of wildlife. This organization is particularly concerned by the status of a species that is close to extinction. Three projects have been set up to try to save this species. Each project is in a different area and uses a somewhat different approach. The species is doomed if all the projects fail.

TABLE 12.8 RISK OF PROJECT FAILURE AS A FUNCTION OF FUNDING

Project	Probability of failure as a function of funding		
	$0	10^6	2×10^6
1	0.50	0.30	0.20
2	0.70	0.50	0.30
3	0.80	0.50	0.40

The organization has $2 million to assist the three projects. This money should be used to minimize the probability that all three projects will fail. Note that the probability of total failure is the product of the probabilities of failure for each individual project.

The organization's managers believe strongly in the effectiveness of large grants. Therefore, they will consider only three funding levels for each project: $0, $1, or $2 million.

The organization has hired a consultant to determine the probability that each project will fail, conditional on the amount of money granted. The result of the consultant's work is summarized in Table 12.8. The table shows, for example, that if project 1 is granted nothing, there is a 50 percent chance that it will fail. A $1-million grant will decrease that probability to 30 percent, and $2 million to 20 percent. There are many possible combinations of projects and funding levels. We shall use dynamic programming to find the best combination.

Stages, States, and Decision Variables

Again, as in the paper-trimming example, it is useful to think of the allocation of money to each project as a sequence of decisions or stages. Consequently, stages 1, 2, and 3 refer to the allocation of money to project 1, 2, and 3, respectively.

The decision variable x_i is the amount of money allocated at stage i. The decision variable can take only three values, regardless of the stage: $x_i = 0, 1,$ or 2 million dollars.

A decision at a particular stage changes the amount of money left at the next stage. A natural state variable, s, is then the amount of money remaining for allocation at stage i and beyond. If s is the state at stage i, then $s - x_i$ is the state at stage $i + 1$.

Dynamic Programming Solution

Consider the possible decisions at stage i and state s. Let $p_i(x_i)$ be the immediate return of decision x_i (probability of failure of project i if it is granted x_i million dollars). Let $P_i(s, x_i)$ be the smallest probability of failure at stage i and beyond, given the state s at stage i and the decision x_i. Furthermore, let x_i^* be the decision that minimizes $P_i(s, x_i)$, and let $P_i^*(s)$ be the corresponding smallest value of $P_i(s, x_i)$. Thus:

$$P_i^*(s) = \min_{x_i} p_i(x_i) P_{i+1}^*(s - x_i) \tag{12.5}$$

The object is to determine $P_1^*(2)$, the smallest probability of failure that can be gotten from \$2 million. We do this by applying the recursive relation (12.5) stage by stage, from stage 3 to stage 1.

Stage 3: Three states are possible at stage 3, $s = 0$, 1, or 2. If $s = 0$, no money is left for the third project and the only possible decision is $x_3^* = 0$, the probability that the third project will fail is then (from Table 12.8) $P_3^*(0) = 0.80$. If $s = 1$, the best decision is $x_3^* = 1$ and the probability of failure is $P_3^*(1) = 0.50$. If $s = 2$, the best decision is $x_3^* = 2$ and the probability of failure is $P_3^*(2) = 0.40$. These results for stage 3 are summarized in Table 12.9.

Stage 2: The computations for this stage appear in Table 12.10. The three possible states are $s = 0$, 1, or \$2 million. Assume for example that $s = 1$, the two possible decisions are $x_2 = 0$ or 1. If $x_2 = 0$, then, the probability of failure of project 2 is 0.70 and the state at stage 3 is $s = 1$, which in turn leads to a probability of failure of project 3 of 0.5 (see Table 12.9).

In terms of equation (12.5) we have:

$$P_2(1, 0) = p_2(0) P_3^*(1)$$
$$= 0.7 \times 0.5 = 0.35$$

If $s = 1$, but $x_2 = 1$, then the probability of success of project 2 is 0.50. No money is left for the third project, so that its probability of failure is 0.80. Thus:

$$P_2(1, 1) = p_2(1) P_3^*(0)$$
$$= 0.50 \times 0.80 = 0.40$$

Therefore, the smallest probability of failure for stages 2 and 3, given $s = 1$ at stage 2 is $P_2^*(1) = 0.35$, and the best decision is $x_2^* = 0$.

TABLE 12.9 BEST FUNDING OF THIRD PROJECT (STAGE 3)

s (10^6 \$)	$P_3^*(s)$	x_3^* (10^6 \$)
0	0.8	0
1	0.5	1
2	0.4	2

TABLE 12.10 BEST FUNDING OF SECOND PROJECT (STAGE 2)

	$P_2(s, x_2) = p_2(x_2) P_3^*(s - x_2)$				
s (10^6 \$)	$x_2 = 0$ (10^6 \$)	$x_2 = 1$ (10^6 \$)	$x_2 = 2$ (10^6 \$)	$P_2^*(s)$	x_2^* (10^6 \$)
0	$0.56 = 0.7 \times 0.8$			0.56	0
1	$0.35 = 0.7 \times 0.5$	$0.40 = 0.5 \times 0.8$		0.35	0
2	$0.28 = 0.7 \times 0.4$	$0.25 = 0.5 \times 0.5$	$0.24 = 0.3 \times 0.8$	0.24	2

TABLE 12.11 BEST FUNDING OF FIRST PROJECT (STAGE 1)

	$P_1(s, x_1) = p_1(x_1)P_2^*(s - x_1)$				
s (10^6 \$)	$x_1 = 0$ (10^6 \$)	$x_1 = 1$ (10^6 \$)	$x_1 = 2$ (10^6 \$)	$P_1^*(s)$	x_1^* (10^6 \$)
2	$0.120 = 0.50 \times 0.24$	$0.105 = 0.30 \times 0.35$	$0.112 = 0.20 \times 0.56$	0.105	1

Repeating these calculations for $s = 0$ leads to:

$$P_2^*(0) = 0.56 \quad \text{and} \quad x_2^* = 0$$

and for $s = 2$:

$$P_2^*(2) = 0.24 \quad \text{and} \quad x_2^* = \$2 \text{ million}$$

Stage 1: The calculations for stage 1 follow the same procedure as those for stage 2. However, there is only one state at stage 1, $s = \$2$ million, meaning that no money has been allocated yet. The results of the computations appear in Table 12.11. They show that:

$$P_1^*(2) = 0.105 \quad \text{and} \quad x_1^* = \$1 \text{ million}$$

Thus, the lowest probability of failure that the organization can achieve is 0.105. This can be done by granting \$1 million to the first project. The grants to the other projects are obtained as follows:

Since the state at stage 1 is $s = \$2$ million and the best decision is $x_1^* = 1$ million, the best state at stage 2 is $s = 2 - 1 = 1$ million dollars. Now, at stage 2 and state 1, the best decision is $x_2^* = 0$ (see Table 12.10). The resulting state at stage 3 is $s = 1 - 0 = \$1$ million. For that stage and state, the best decision is $x_3^* = 1$ (Table 12.9). Therefore, the best solution is to grant \$1 million each to projects 1 and 3, and nothing to project 2.

12.6 CONCLUSIONS

The examples used in this chapter illustrate the fact that many forest-management problems can be solved by dynamic programming. The method is attractive because it is very general. Although we have dealt with discrete state variables in our example, dynamic programming has been used to solve forest-management problems with continuous state variables as well. The method can also handle stochastic return functions. For example, the growth of the stand in the thinning example could be a function of the state of the stand and of a random variable.

However, it should be kept in mind that dynamic-programming solutions become difficult as the number of state variables increases. In addition, many problems that can be solved by dynamic programming can also be solved by other methods. For example, as suggested in this chapter, comparing all alternatives (the so-called exhaustive-search approach) may be a good way to solve even fairly large problems, regardless of how much computer time it takes.

Ultimately, an efficient method is one that gives the correct solution at minimum cost. In this cost, computer time is negligible compared to the time spent in formulating a problem, developing a model, and writing the computer code to solve it.

PROBLEMS

12.1. Consider the problem of optimizing the management of an even-aged stand discussed in Section 12.2 of the text. Assume that the forester managing this stand wants to maximize the present value of harvests rather than their volume. Assume further that the forester expects the real price of mixed conifer stumpage to remain at $100 per thousand board feet over the next 40 years, and that the guiding rate of interest used by his firm is 3 percent per year.

Use dynamic programming to determine the sequence of harvests that would maximize their present value. Assume that the management alternatives remain the same as in Figure 12.1.

12.2. Redo Problem 12.1 using a real discount rate of 6 percent per year. How does the optimal sequence of management activities change? What is the reason for this change?

12.3. The following table describes different ways of managing a red pine plantation, from bare land to final harvest:

Age (Years)	Starting state	Action	Harvest (100 ft^3 / acre)	Ending state
0	Bare land	Plant 200 trees/acre	0	B
		Plant 400 trees/acre	0	C
		Plant 800 trees/acre	0	D
10	B	Thin	0	E
		None	0	F
	C	Thin	0	F
		None	0	G
	D	Thin	0	G
		None	0	H
30	E	Thin	5	I
		None	0	K
	F	Thin	7	J
		None	0	L
	G	Thin	8	K
		None	0	M
	H	Thin	9	L
		None	0	N
60	I	Clearcut	40	O (Bare land)
	J	Clearcut	45	O
	K	Clearcut	47	O
	L	Clearcut	55	O
	M	Clearcut	49	O
	N	Clearcut	48	O

When the plantation is started, the initial density may be of 200, 400, or 800 trees per acre. After 10 years, the plantation may be precommercially thinned, or left as is. At age 30, a commercial thinning may be done as shown in the table, the yield of the thinning depends on the state of the stand, and thus on earlier decisions. Finally, when the trees are 60 years old, the entire stand is cut.

Reorganize the data in the table into a network diagram, with nodes corresponding to states and arcs to decisions. Show the stages and the returns from each decision. Use dynamic programming to determine the sequence of decisions that would maximize the volume produced by this plantation.

12.4. Modify the analysis done in Problem 12.3 to determine the sequence of decisions that would maximize the present value of harvests rather than the volume. Assume a constant real price for red pine stumpage of $15 per hundred cubic feet and a real guiding rate of interest of 3 percent per year. Also assume costs of site preparation and planting of $100, $150, and $200 for densities of 200, 400, and 800 trees per acre, respectively. Finally, assume a cost of $40 per acre for precommercial thinning.

12.5. Consider the paper trimming discussed in Section 12.4 of the text. Assume that a new market has developed for 6-foot-long rolls of paper selling for $110 per roll.

Redraw Figure 12.3 to reflect this additional opportunity. Use dynamic programming to determine the best way of trimming a 15-foot roll of paper in this new situation.

12.6. A logging contractor sells oak logs in the local log market. To maximize the profits from this business, he must pay careful attention to how his crews do the bucking, i.e., how they cut the trees they fell into logs. In the local market, logs are divided into three grades on the basis of length and small end diameter. Grade 1 logs must be 12-feet long and at least 10 inches in diameter at the small end, grade 2 logs must be 10- or 12-feet long and at least 8 inches in diameter, and grade 3 logs must be 8-, 10-, or 12-feet long and at least 6 inches in diameter. The value of logs, by grade and length, is:

Log grade	Length (ft) 8	10	12
1	—	—	$75
2	—	$55	$60
3	$25	$30	$40

Consider a fallen tree that is 24-feet long with a 30-inch large end diameter. Moving from the large to the small end of the tree, the diameter decreases by one inch every foot.

Use dynamic programming to determine the best way to buck this tree. (The formulation of this problem is similar to that of the paper trimming problem. Be sure to consider small end diameter in determining what kinds of bucking patterns are possible at each stage.)

12.7. The logging foreman for a hardwood veneer mill has been authorized to spend up to two extra hours of work every time he fells a particularly valuable tree in order to reduce losses due to breakage. The foreman is trying to decide how to allocate this time between three modifications of the usual felling procedure: (1) felling or limbing trees over which the tree being cut may break, (2) preparing a "bed" for trees to fall in, and (3) using greater care in skidding fallen trees. The foreman estimates that extra time spent on each modification would lead to the following probabilities of avoiding breakage:

Modification	Time spent (hours)		
	0	1	2
Fell or limb trees	0.80	0.95	0.96
Prepare bed	0.90	0.92	0.93
More careful skidding	0.91	0.96	0.96

For example, if no extra time is used to fell or limb surrounding trees, the probability of not breaking the tree when it falls is 0.80, but this probability increases to 0.95 if one extra hour is spent on this modification.

To obtain a sound tree, the foreman must avoid breakage while the tree falls, when it hits the ground, and while it is being skidded. Thus, the probability of avoiding breakage altogether is the product of the probabilities of avoiding breakage due to each modification contemplated by the foreman.

Use dynamic programming to find how the two hours of extra time should be allocated to each modification to get the highest probability of not breaking a tree.

ANNOTATED REFERENCES

Amidon, E. L., and G. S. Akin. 1968. Dynamic programming to determine optimum levels of growing stock. *Forest Science* 14(3):287–291. (One of the earliest and simplest applications of dynamic programming in forest management.)

Brodie, J. D., D. M. Adams, and C. Kao. 1978. Analysis of economic impacts on thinning and rotation of Douglas-fir, using dynamic programming. *Forest Science* 24(4):513–522. (Determines optimal thinning schedules and rotations as a function of regeneration costs, initial stocking levels, site, quality premiums, and variable logging costs.)

Cawrse, D. C. 1979. Dynamic system modeling in timber management: A selected annotated bibliography. Department of Forestry and Wood Sciences, Colorado State University. 20 pp. (Bibliography and comparison of the use of differential equations, linear and nonlinear programming, dynamic programming, and optimal control theory in timber management models.)

Chen, C. M., D. W. Rose, and R. A. Leary. 1980. How to formulate and solve optimal stand density over time problems for even-aged stands using dynamic programming. U.S. Forest Service General Technical Report NC-56. North Central Forest and Range Experiment Station, St. Paul. 17 pp. (Tutorial, less difficult to understand than many papers on the subject.)

Dykstra, D. P. 1984. *Mathematical programming for natural resource management*. McGraw-Hill, New York. 318 pp. (Chapter 10 introduces the basics of dynamic programming using optimal thinning and log bucking examples.)

Hillier, F. S., and G. J. Lieberman. 1986. *Introduction to operations research*. Holden-Day, Oakland. 888 pp. (Chapter 11 covers deterministic and probabilistic dynamic programming models.)

Hool, J. N. 1968. An univariate allocation algorithm for use in forestry problems. *Journal of Forestry* 66(6):492–493. (A simple application of dynamic programming to optimize the allocation of effort between several different markets by a Christmas tree distributor.)

Kennedy, J. O. S. 1981. Applications of dynamic programming to agriculture, forestry, and fisheries: Review and prognosis. *Review of Marketing and Agricultural Economics* 49(3):141–173. (Potential and limitations of dynamic programming in resource-related applications.)

Lembersky, M. R., and U. H. Chi. 1986. Weyerhaeuser decision simulator improves timber profits. *Interfaces* 16(1):6–15. (A graphics-oriented computer program simulates the bucking and sawing decisions made by a user and compares these to optimal decisions generated by a dynamic programming model.)

Martin, G. L., and A. R. Ek. 1981. A dynamic programming analysis of silvicultural alternatives for red pine plantations in Wisconsin. *Canadian Journal of Forest Research* 11(2):370–379. (Determines optimum thinning schedules for red pine. Results compared to previously reported red pine growth rates.)

O'Regan, W. G., P. H. Kourtz, and S. Nozaki. 1975. Patrol route planning for an airborne infrared forest fire detection system. *Forest Science* 21(4):382–389. (Application of dynamic programming to selecting the flight patterns that will maximize the number of forest fires detected.)

Pnevmaticos, S. M., and S. H. Mann. 1972. Dynamic programming in tree bucking. *Forest Products Journal* 22(2):26–30. (Similar to Problem 12.6, but much more detailed.)

Riitters, K., J. D. Brodie, and D. W. Hann. 1982. Dynamic programming for optimization of timber production and grazing in ponderosa pine. *Forest Science* 28(3):517–526. (Optimizes the joint production of timber and forage in ponderosa pine.)

Taha, H. A. 1982. *Operations research: An introduction*. Macmillan, New York. 848 pp. (Chapter 9 covers dynamic programming, including the solution of linear-programming models by dynamic programming.)

Chapter 13

Simulation of Uneven-Aged Stand Management

13.1 INTRODUCTION

Past chapters have dealt mostly with optimization models. The common theme throughout these chapters was to find management strategies that were best for specific criteria. The criteria were represented either by an objective function, by constraints, or by both. Optimization is indeed a fundamental goal in analyzing forestry operations. Ideally, one wishes always to find a decision that is not only good, but better than any other decision.

Unfortunately, optimization methods such as linear, goal, and dynamic programming force us to design models of very specific forms. For example, linear programming requires that the constraints and the objective function be linear in the variables. Sometimes, heroic assumptions must be made to cast a forest-management problem into such a linear form.

Simulation allows much more flexibility in modeling. Any phenomenon that can be represented by mathematical relationships of any form is tractable by simulation. Simulation can be described as the process of developing a model of a real system and conducting experiments with the model. In a sense, optimality is still the goal, since by experimenting we hope to discover the best way of managing a system. But, in contrast with programming models, there are no built-in algorithms, like the simplex, that lead to an optimal solution. In a simulation experiment, all we do is observe the consequences of a specific set of actions corresponding to a management strategy. In essence, simulation allows us to bring the real world to the laboratory for intensive study. For that reason, simulation has become one of the most powerful and versatile tools for problem solving in forest management.

13.2 TYPES OF SIMULATION

In simulation, time can be handled in two ways: fixed-time incrementing and next-event incrementing. *Fixed-time incrementing* is most suitable for systems that change continuously over time, say the growth of a tree, a stand, or an entire forest. The smaller the time increment, the smoother the evolution of the system, since changes from one instant to the next are small. For this reason fixed-time incrementing simulations are sometimes called continuous simulations.

In *next-event incrementing* only the time when an interesting event occurs is recorded, then the time of the next event is computed and the simulation clock is advanced by that time interval. This kind of simulation is well suited to discrete events. The occurrence of fire in a forest is a good example of a discrete event. Next-event incrementing avoids doing a lot of calculations during time intervals when nothing happens.

Most next-event simulations are also stochastic, that is, they involve random events. For example, fires occur at random. Stochastic processes are ideally suited to simulation. In fact, for complex stochastic problems, simulation is often the only possible approach.

Continuous simulation systems may also have stochastic elements. For example, the laws that govern the growth of a forest stand are not exact, and for some purposes it may be desirable to represent this uncertainty explicitly with random variables.

The distinction between continuous and discrete, deterministic and stochastic models is not absolute. Continuous models may have discrete elements, and vice versa. Some of the variables in a stochastic model may be treated as if they were known exactly. This will often lead to a model simpler to build and use. The art of the model builder is to recognize the key features of a system, avoiding detail that would just complicate the model without making it necessarily more useful. "Small is beautiful" is a good precept to guide model building and model selection.

To understand simulation, more perhaps than for any other technique, one must do it. With this in mind we will study in detail three short examples of simulation. The first one, treated in this chapter, is a continuous deterministic simulation of uneven-aged forest stand management. It uses essentially the same growth equations as the model that was solved by linear programming in Chap. 8. This will help clarify the differences between simulation and optimization models. The second example, in Chap. 14, deals with even-aged management. Even-aged forests were among the first to be studied with simulation models.

The third example, given in Chap. 15, is a next-event-incrementing stochastic model of a plantation subject to random fires. It will illustrate the principle of next-event-incrementing simulation and it will also show how to handle probability distributions to model stochastic systems.

13.3 THE SIMULATION PROGRAM UNEVEN

As in Chap. 8, the condition of an uneven-aged stand at a particular instant in time is described by the number of trees per acre in each diameter class. The purpose of the simulation model that we shall study is to predict the condition of the stand at any point in time in the future, given (1) its initial condition, (2) the laws that predict how the stand grows over short time intervals, and (3) the harvests that the forester applies to the stand.

The simulator will also compute the net present value of the returns and costs obtained from the stand. In that manner, we shall be able to compare different management regimes in economic terms.

The model used for our purpose is a computer program named Uneven. Its structure appears in Fig. 13.1, in the form of a flow chart that describes how the major subroutines of the program are related.

The program starts by reading the data defining the initial condition of the stand and the management strategy. After this, the current condition of the

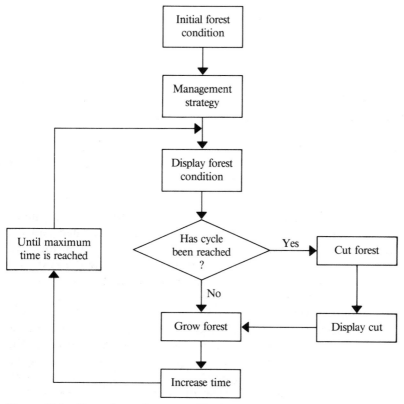

Figure 13.1   Flow chart of program Uneven.

```
'-------------------------------
'          Uneven
'-------------------------------
'   Program to simulate the management
'   of an uneven-aged forest
'-------------------------------
main:
   GOSUB initia            'initiate forest
   GOSUB manage            'define management
   WHILE year<=xyear       'until maximum time is reached
      GOSUB showstock             'display current forest condition
      IF tlast=cycle THEN GOSUB cut    'if cycle reached, cut forest
      year=year+ 5                'current time
      tlast=tlast+5               'time since last cut
      GOSUB growth                'predict forest growth
   WEND
END


'-------------------------------
'   Read initial forest condition
'-------------------------------
initia:
   year=0                  'initial time
   pval=0                  'initial present value
   FOR iclass=1 TO 7
      READ trb(iclass)           'initial trees/acre
   NEXT iclass
   DATA 278, 141,73,32,12,4,3
   FOR iclass=1 TO 7
      READ trv(iclass)           'value of a tree
   NEXT iclass
   DATA 0.04,0.10,0.18,0.26,0.97,2.8,5.04
RETURN
```

Figure 13.2   Computer code of program Uneven.

stand is displayed on the computer screen. Then, if the time since the last cut is equal to the cutting cycle, the effect of the harvest is simulated and the results are displayed; otherwise this procedure is skipped. After this, the simulated time is increased and the growth of the stand during the next time unit is calculated. Then, the new condition of the stand is displayed. This cycle continues until the maximum simulated time is reached.

The program that describes this process in a way that is comprehensible to the computer is listed in Fig. 13.2. The particular computer language used is a dialect of BASIC, a language available on most microcomputers. The program consists of a main program and seven subroutines. It is good programming technique to decompose a program in several subroutines. Each subroutine should correspond to a specific function of the program. In that way, the structure of the program is well defined and the program is easier to

```
'---------------------------------
'   Define management regime
'---------------------------------
manage:
    READ xyear,tlast,cycle          'max years, years since last cut, cycle
    DATA 200,0,10
    READ rate, fcost                'interest rate, harvest cost/acre
    DATA 0.05,10
    FOR iclass=1 TO 7
        READ trd(iclass)            'desired number of trees/acre
    NEXT iclass
    DATA 250,100,40,20,5,0,0
RETURN


'---------------------------------
'   Print current forest condition
'---------------------------------
showstock:
    PRINT "year";year
    PRINT " stock";
    FOR iclass=1 TO 7
        PRINT USING "####."; trb(iclass),
    NEXT iclass
    PRINT
RETURN


'---------------------------------------
'   Cut all trees in excess of desired number
'---------------------------------------
cut:
    FOR iclass=1 TO 7
        trc(iclass)=trb(iclass)-trd(iclass)     'trees cut
        IF trc(iclass)<0 THEN trc(iclass)=0
        trb(iclass)=trb(iclass)-trc(iclass)     'trees left
    NEXT iclass
    tlast=0                                      'years since last cut
    GOSUB pvalue                                 'compute present value
    GOSUB showcut                                'display data for current cut
RETURN
```

Figure 13.2   Continued.

write, understand, and maintain. All the variables used in the program are
defined in Table 13.1.

Main Program

Named Main, it corresponds closely to the flowchart in Fig. 13.1. It keeps
track of the number of years that have been simulated and stops when the
maximum simulation time has been reached. At the same time it keeps track

```
'-------------------------------------
'   Present value of cumulated harvests
'-------------------------------------
pvalue:
    disc=(1+rate)^year
    FOR iclass=1 TO 7
        pval=pval+trv(iclass)*trc(iclass)/disc
    NEXT iclass
    pval=pval-fcost/disc
RETURN
'-------------------------------------
'   Display data for current cut
'-------------------------------------
showcut:
    PRINT " cut   ";
    FOR iclass=1 TO 7
        PRINT USING"####.";trc(iclass),
    NEXT iclass
    PRINT
    PRINT USING" present value####.";pval
RETURN


'-------------------------------
'   Predict growth of forest
'-------------------------------
growth:
    tre(1)=.81*trb(1)-.043*trb(2)-.22*trb(3)-.43*trb(4)-.69*trb(5)
        -.98*trb(6)-1.3*trb(7)+109
    IF tre(1)<0 THEN tre(1)=0
    tre(2)=.23*trb(1)+.7*trb(2)
    tre(3)=.26*trb(2)+.67*trb(3)
    tre(4)=.3*trb(3)+.65*trb(4)
    tre(5)=.3*trb(4)+.66*trb(5)
    tre(6)=.3*trb(5)+.81*trb(6)
    tre(7)=.19*trb(6)+.86*trb(7)
'-------------------------------
'   Set number of trees at the beginning
'   of the next period equal to number
'   at the end of this period.
'-------------------------------
    FOR iclass=1 TO 7
        trb(iclass)=tre(iclass)
    NEXT iclass
RETURN
```

Figure 13.2   Continued.

TABLE 13.1 DEFINITION OF VARIABLES IN PROGRAM UNEVEN

Variable	Definition
year	Current time, increased by 5-year intervals
xyear	Maximum simulated time
tlast	Time since the stand was last cut
cycle	Cutting cycle
rate	Discount rate, per year
fcost	Fixed cost of harvesting ($/acre)
pval	Cumulated net present value of harvests ($/acre)
trb (*iclass*)	Number of trees per acre at the beginning of a time interval
tre (*iclass*)	Number of trees per acre at the end of a time interval
trc (*iclass*)	Number of trees cut per acre
trd (*iclass*)	Desired number of trees per acre
trv (*iclass*)	Value of a tree ($)
iclass	Index of diameter class (varies from 1 to 7)

of the time interval elapsed between harvests. Main also directs the action of the subroutines. Each subroutine performs the following functions.

Subroutine Initia

This subroutine sets the initial condition of the stand. First, the year and the present value of the harvests are set to zero. Then, the subroutine Initia reads the number of trees in each of seven diameter classes. In Fig. 13.2, there are 278 trees per acre in the smallest-diameter class and 3 in the largest. Next, the program reads the value of an average tree in a diameter class (stumpage value). In Fig. 13.2, each tree in the smallest-diameter class is worth $0.04, each one in the largest is worth $5.04. At the end of the subroutine, control is returned to the main program.

Subroutine Manage

This subroutine begins by reading the maximum simulation time, the time since the last harvest and the length of the cutting cycle. Next the subroutine reads the interest rate (a fraction per year) and the fixed harvest cost. The latter is the cost to the owner of preparing a timber sale, in dollars per acre, independent of the stumpage value. Finally, subroutine Manage reads the number of trees that the owner wants to leave in each diameter class, after the cut.

Subroutine Showstock

This subroutine displays the current year and, under it, the current growing stock, defined by the number of trees in each diameter class at that point in time (see Fig. 13.3).

```
year  0
  stock   278.  141.   73.   32.   12.    4.    3.
year  5
  stock   282.  163.   86.   43.   18.    7.    3.
year  10
  stock   270.  179.  100.   53.   24.   11.    4.
  cut      20.   79.   60.   33.   19.   11.    4.
  present value  54.
year  15
  stock   286.  128.   53.   25.    9.    2.    0.
year  20
  stock   305.  155.   69.   32.   14.    4.    0.
  cut      55.   55.   29.   12.    9.    4.    0.
  present value  64.
year  25
  stock   286.  128.   53.   25.    9.    2.    0.
year  30
  stock   305.  155.   69.   32.   14.    4.    0.
  cut      55.   55.   29.   12.    9.    4.    0.
  present value  71.
```

Figure 13.3 Output of program Uneven.

Subroutine Cut

Subroutine Cut is called by the main program only if the number of years since the last cut is equal to the cutting cycle. This subroutine simulates the removal of the trees that exceed the desired number of trees in each class. The trees that have been cut are displayed on the screen in the same manner as the growing stock (see Fig. 13.3). Subroutine Cut itself calls subroutines Pvalue and Showcut.

Subroutine Pvalue and Showcut

Subroutine Pvalue computes the cumulative present value of revenues generated by harvests up to the current year, net of fixed harvesting costs. In calculating present value, the harvest is assumed to occur at the beginning of the current year. Subroutine Showcut displays the number of trees cut and the present value of the cut.

Subroutine Growth

This subroutine computes the number of trees that will be in each diameter class at the end of the next 5-year interval, given the current condition of the stand. Subroutine Growth uses stand growth equations that are similar to Eqs. (8.3), except that seven diameter classes are used to describe the stand instead of three.

The growth equations state that, except for the smallest diameter class, the number of trees in a diameter class 5 years hence is directly proportional to the number of trees in that diameter class and to the number of trees in the next smaller diameter class.

The number of trees in the smallest diameter class at the end of the current 5-year interval is also related directly to the number of trees in that class, but is related inversely to the number of trees in all other classes, reflecting the process of ingrowth (see Chap. 8). An IF statement is used to make sure that the number of trees in the smallest diameter class, and thus also in the larger diameter classes, never becomes negative. This is a very simple requirement, but one that is not represented as easily in nonsimulation models.

Note that we are not restricted to this specific way of calculating the growth of the stand. Any mathematical expression that gives the number of trees in each diameter class at the end of a 5-year interval as a function of the current number of trees is acceptable. Parts of the growth equations may even be random variables. This flexibility is one advantage of simulation with respect to mathematical programming. Slightly different forms of the growth model would have led to serious difficulties in solving the optimization problems that were solved by linear programming in Chap. 8.

13.4 OUTPUT AND APPLICATIONS OF PROGRAM UNEVEN

Part of the output of the program Uneven is shown in Fig. 13.3. It consists of two lines for each simulated year when no cut occurs and of four lines when the stand is cut.

The first line shows the current year; it progresses from year 0 to 30 at 5-year intervals. The second line shows growing stock of the stand at the beginning of the current year, measured by the number of trees in each of the seven diameter classes, from the smallest to the largest. For example, when the simulation starts, there are 278 trees per acre in the smallest diameter class and 3 in the largest.

In the years when a cut occurs, the number of trees that have been cut in each diameter class is shown under the growing stock. In Fig. 13.3 this happens in years 10, 20, and 30. The net present value of the returns from harvesting up to that year is also shown.

Stand Dynamics

Many different questions can be explored using the program Uneven. The simple output in Fig. 13.3, which corresponds to a portion of a short simulation, is itself informative. It shows how a stand managed under the specific strategy, defined in Fig. 13.2 (see data in subroutine Manage) is expected to evolve during the first 30 years.

Present value ($/acre)

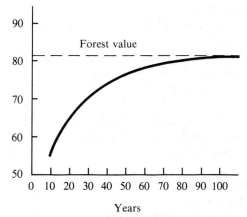

Figure 13.4   Years

Figure 13.4   Present value approaches forest value as the simulated time increases.

The data show, for example, that the stand, cut systematically in that way, would quickly reach a steady state. The growing stock and the harvests in years 20 and 30 are equal. This means that the growth of the stand in a decade just replaces what was removed by the harvest at the beginning of the decade. Barring disturbances, this level of production could be maintained indefinitely.

Forest Value

Figure 13.3 shows a present value that rises from $4 per acre for a management plan of 10 years to $71 per acre for a plan of 30 years. However, the rate of growth of the present value tends to decline over time. In fact, lengthening the simulation shows that present value reaches a maximum of $80 per acre for plans of 70 to 80 years (see Fig. 13.4). This $80 is the per-acre value of the forest, including land and initial trees, given the simulated management regime and an infinite time horizon.

This observation implies that we can compare different management regimes by comparing the different forest values that they lead to. To do this, the time horizon need not be very long. As shown by Fig. 13.4, a maximum simulated time of 100 years is usually enough.

We shall now explore how forest value changes with the management strategy. Specifically, we shall study the effect of changing the length of the cutting cycle, the intensity of the cut, or both.

Best Cutting Cycle

For simplicity, let us consider only one type of harvest, defined by the minimum diameter of the trees that are cut. For example, one could prescribe that every time the stand is cut, every tree in diameter class 7 and above would be cut. This would be achieved by setting the desired number of trees to zero

TABLE 13.2   FOREST VALUES PREDICTED BY THE SIMULATION
PROGRAM UNEVEN FOR DIFFERENT CUTTING
CYCLES AND DIAMETER CLASS LIMITS

	Cutting cycle (years)			
Diameter class limit	5	10	15	20
7 (17″ +)	59	61*	55	48
6 (15″ to 17″)	92†	101‡	96†	87
5 (13″ to 15″)	67	88	92*	89†
4 (11″ to 13″)	42	66	75	78*

Note: Every tree in the diameter class limit or above is cut.
* The best cutting cycle, given a diameter limit.
† The best diameter limit, given a cutting cycle.
‡ The best combination.

for diameter class 7, and to an arbitrarily large number for smaller diameter classes, in the last DATA statement of subroutine Manage. The lower diameter-class limit, the more intense the cut.

Different cutting intensities can in turn be combined with different cutting cycles. One may then wonder whether it is better to cut the stand lightly and often, or heavily and at long intervals. The program Uneven can be used to answer this question. The results of simulations for cutting cycles of 5 to 10 years and for diameter limits corresponding to diameter classes 4 to 7 are shown in Table 13.2.

A row of the table shows the effect on forest value of changing the cutting cycle, other things remaining equal. For example, if only trees in diameter class 7 are cut, and the cutting cycle is progressively increased, present value increases, reaches a maximum for a cutting cycle of 10 years, and then declines. There is an optimum cutting cycle for each cutting intensity, but the optimum varies with the cutting intensity. For example, the best cutting cycle changes to 20 years if all trees in diameter class 4 and above are cut.

Best Cutting Intensity

Similarly, for any given cutting cycle, the forest value rises with the intensity of the cut, reaches a maximum, and then declines. For example, given a cutting cycle of 20 years, the best strategy is to cut all trees in diameter class 5 and above. The best cutting intensity changes with the cutting cycle. For a cutting cycle of 5 years, the optimum would consist in removing the two largest diameter classes only.

Optimum Combination

The simulation results in Table 13.2 show clearly that there is one overall best management strategy, given the assumptions made. It consists of removing all trees in the two largest diameter classes every 10 years. This yields a forest value of $101 per acre.

Sensitivity Analysis

Note that choosing the correct diameter limit seems more critical than the cutting cycle. Increasing or decreasing the cutting cycle by 5 years would change the forest value by less than 10 percent, relative to the optimum. On the other hand, removing the largest-diameter class only would reduce forest value by close to 40 percent. Removing the three largest diameter classes instead of two would reduce present value by 13 percent.

13.5 CONCLUSIONS

A forest simulator like Uneven can be developed quickly, with less knowledge than that needed for the optimization model of Chap. 8. And yet, despite its simplicity, it is a powerful tool. Numerous other management experiments can be done with the Uneven program. The general principle remains the same as for the analysis of the cutting cycle and cutting intensity. To study the effect of one parameter, do a series of simulations in which all parameters, except the one being studied, remain the same. Then, observe how selected management criteria, such as forest value, respond to changes in the parameter.

One difficulty is that many parameters can be changed. To keep the number of experiments reasonably small, the analyst must use considerable judgment and intuition in guessing which parameters are important and in defining management strategies that are likely to yield good results.

PROBLEMS

13.1. Which of the following systems do you think might be better simulated using fixed-time or next-event incrementing? Using deterministic or stochastic simulation? Why?

forest fires	timber harvesting
sawmill operations	big game hunting
whaling	logging machinery
insect populations	tree growth

13.2. The data in Figure 13.2 result in a stand that moves quickly to a stable steady state, given the particular harvesting rule used. Apply the program Uneven to predict the growth of a stand that starts in the same initial condition but is never cut. There are two ways of doing this: making the cutting cycle very long, or the desired number of trees in each age class very high.

After changing the data of program Uneven in this way, run the program and study the results. Graph the number of trees in each diameter class over time. What do you observe?

13.3. Repeat the simulation done in Problem 13.2, for a stand that starts in the following initial condition:

Diameter class	1	2	3	4	5	6	7
Trees per acre	0	0	0	0	0	0	100

What kind of stand does this diameter distribution describe? Observe the results of the simulation and compare them to those of Problem 13.2.
Repeat this simulation for the following initial condition:

Diameter class	1	2	3	4	5	6	7
Trees per acre	300	0	0	0	0	0	0

What kind of stand does this diameter distribution describe? Compare the results of this simulation with those obtained with the other two initial conditions.

Based on these simulations, how does the initial condition of a stand influence its subsequent growth and steady state?

13.4. Consider the stand described by the data in Fig. 13.2. Suppose that the owner of this stand wants to try the following management regime. He will cut the stand every 10 years, and take trees only from the three largest diameter classes, leaving at most five trees per acre in diameter class 5 and none in diameter classes 6 and 7.

Use the program Uneven to predict the per acre present value of the returns that the owner should get. Keep prices and interest rates as in Fig. 13.2 and assume a planning horizon of 100 years. Compare this present value with that obtained from the management regime described by the data in Fig. 13.2. What is the best regime?

13.5. The manager of the stand described by the data in Fig. 13.2 has been offered $1.00 per acre per year to allow several dozen cattle to graze on his land. Unfortunately, the cattle would cause many young trees to die, thus reducing ingrowth. Suppose that this damage reduces the number of trees in diameter class 1 by about 100 trees per acre, every five years. Change one parameter of the equations in subroutine Growth of program Uneven to reflect this damage. Leave all other data as in Fig. 13.2.

Run this modified version of program Uneven to determine the per acre net present value of the returns from the stand if cattle grazing is allowed. Use a planning horizon of 100 years. Use the fact that the present value of x received for every year for that long is approximately x/r, where r is the interest rate expressed as a fraction per year.

Compare the result with the present value obtained from an ungrazed stand. Should the owner allow cattle grazing at this price? If not, what minimum price should he charge to recover his losses?

13.6. A veneer mill has just opened in the vicinity of the stand described by the data in Fig. 13.2. As a result, the values of trees in ages classes 6 and 7 have increased to $5.80 and $9.04, respectively.

Modify the data in Fig. 13.2 to reflect this change. Run this new version of program Uneven for each cutting cycle and diameter class limit combination in Table 13.2 in the text.

What combination of cutting cycle and diameter class limit maximizes the present value of returns from the stand? Assume a planning horizon of 100 years.

What has been the effect of the opening of the mill on the value of the stand, including bare land?

13.7. A chronic pathogen is causing heavy mortality in the stand described by the data in Fig. 13.2, especially in the largest trees. A biometrician has found that the effect of the disease can be simulated by changing the growth equations for diameter classes 5, 6, and 7 in subroutine Growth of program Uneven to:

$$tre(5) = 0.2 * trb(4) + 0.49 * trb(5)$$
$$tre(6) = 0.1 * trb(5) + 0.41 * trb(6)$$
$$tre(7) = 0.05 * trb(6) + 0.3 * trb(7)$$

According to the first equation, what fraction of the trees that are alive and in diameter class 4 in year t are still alive and in the same diameter class in year $t + 5$? What fraction of the trees that are alive and in diameter class 4 in year t are still alive and in diameter class 5 in year $t + 5$? You may want to refer to Chapter 8 to answer these questions.

Use this modified version of program Uneven to compute the present value of the returns from the stand. Leave all data but the growth equations as in Fig. 13.2.

How much will the disease damage cost the stand's owner over the next 30 years?

Would complete sanitation harvesting (taking all trees in the four largest diameter classes each time the stand is cut) reduce these losses?

By how much did the disease decrease the value of this forest stand, including land?

ANNOTATED REFERENCES

Baker, F. A., D. W. French, and D. W. Rose. 1982. DMLOSS: A simulator of losses in dwarf mistletoe infested black spruce stands. *Forest Science* 28(3):590–598. (Deterministic model of a pathogen's spread and the resulting mortality.)

Belcher, D. W., M. R. Holdaway, and G. J. Brand. 1982. A description of STEMS: The stand and tree evaluation and modeling system. U.S. Forest Service General Technical Report NC-79. North Central Forest Experiment Station, St. Paul. 18 pp. (Deterministic model for Lake States forests based on simulation of individual tree growth.)

Boothby, R. D., and J. Buongiorno. 1985. UNEVEN: A computer model of uneven-aged forest management. CALS Research Report R3285. University of Wisconsin, Madison. 62 pp. (A refined version of the Uneven program used in this chapter, includes optimization procedures.)

Boyce, S. G. 1985. Forestry decisions. U.S. Forest Service General Technical Report SE-35. Southeastern Forest Experiment Station, Asheville. 318 pp. (Discusses the merits of using simulation rather than optimization models to manage forests, emphasizes fixed-time incrementing models and graphical output.)

Christy, D. P., and H. J. Watson. 1983. The application of simulation: A survey of industry practice. *Interfaces* 13(5):47–52. (A survey of industrial users of simulation models, level of use, areas of application, verification methods, and programming languages used.)

Crandall, D. A., and R. J. Luxmoore. 1982. Simulated water budgets for an irrigated sycamore phytomass farm. *Forest Science* 28(1):17–30. (Deterministic simulation model to assess irrigation needs of a biomass plantation.)

Goulet, D. V., R. H. Iff, and D. L. Sirois. 1979. Tree-to-mill forest harvesting simulation models: Where are we? *Forest Products Journal* 29(10):50–55. (State-of-the-art review of the simulation of harvesting and transportation systems.)

Grant, W. E. 1986. *Systems analysis and simulation in wildlife and fisheries sciences.* Wiley, New York. 338 pp. (Contains many examples of deterministic models of wildlife populations.)

Hansen, G. D. 1984. A computer simulation model of uneven-aged northern hardwood stands maintained under the selection system. School of Forestry Miscellaneous Publication No. 3 (ESF 84-017). SUNY College of Environmental Science and Forestry, Syracuse. 21 pp. (A more complex, multispecies simulation model than the one considered in this chapter.)

Starfield, A. M., and A. L. Bleloch. 1986. *Building models for conservation and wildlife management.* Macmillan, New York. 253 pp. (Chapter 2 contains an example of a deterministic model of a wildlife population.)

Chapter 14

Simulation of Even-Aged Forest Management

14.1 INTRODUCTION

This chapter presents a second example of simulation which deals with the scheduling of harvests in an even-aged forest. The purposes of the simulation model that we shall develop are to:

1. Describe the evolution of the forest over time when it is managed according to a variant of area control
2. Predict the effects of changing the allowable cut on the value of the forest

As in Chaps. 6 and 7, the state of the forest at a specific point in time is described by the area in each age class. The silviculture consists of clear-cutting followed by immediate artificial regeneration. The volume of timber in a particular age class is strictly a function of the age of the stand.

In the first simulation we shall assume that the price of timber is fixed, independent of the volume cut. Later we shall modify the model for the case where an increase in volume cut lowers the price of timber.

We shall also assume throughout that the management policy is a variant of area control. Specifically, the manager fixes the area to be cut during each time interval. In addition, oldest stands are always cut first. This implies a rotation that is equal to the total area of the forest divided by the average area cut every year. One of the applications of the program will be to investigate the effect of the choice of the allowable cut, and thus of the rotation, on the value of the forest.

14.2 THE MODEL EVEN

The simulation program used to investigate even-aged forest management is named Even. The code, written in BASIC, is listed in Fig. 14.1. It consists of one main program and seven subroutines. The variables used in the program are defined in Table 14.1.

Main Program

The role of the program called Main is to direct the flow of information between subroutines and to update the simulation clock. The main program first reads the initial condition of the forest and the management data. Then, for each decade it displays successively the current status of the forest, calculates the harvest and its present value, displays the results of these calculations, and predicts the growth of the remaining forest during the next decade. The program then increases the time by 10 years. This cycle is repeated until the desired maximum simulation time is reached.

Subroutine Initia

This subroutine sets the initial time and the initial present value of the harvests to zero. It then reads the initial area in each one of the 10 age classes. The ages of trees within an age class span a decade. In the example of Fig. 14.1, there are 250 acres in age class 1,150 acres in age class 2, and so on, up to 120 acres in age class 10. The total area of the forest is 2280 acres. Any stand older than 100 years is included in the oldest age class. In contrast with the model that we used in Chap. 6, the number of age classes remains the same throughout the projection period, although the area in each age class varies.

Subroutine Initia then reads the volume of timber as a function of age, in thousand cubic feet per acre. For example, stands of timber 50 years old carry some 9300 ft³/a. The data are for Douglas fir in the Pacific Northwest on site 180. We shall assume that this relationship between volume per acre and age remains constant over time.

Subroutine Manage

This subroutine reads the management data, beginning with the desired length of the simulation. It is set at 200 years in Fig. 14.1. The subroutine then reads the price of timber, which in Fig. 14.1 is $250 per thousand cubic feet. The interest rate is set at 5 percent per year and the reforestation cost is $150 per acre. The last information read by subroutine Manage is the maximum allowable cut. In Fig. 14.1 this is 380 acres. This is the area that would be cut every decade if the forest were regulated and the rotation age set at 60 years, since $(2280/60) \times 10 = 380$ acres per decade.

```
'------------------------------------------
'                    Even
'------------------------------------------
'   Simulation of even-aged forest management
'   under area control
'------------------------------------------
main:
    GOSUB initia              'initiate forest
    GOSUB manage              'define management
    WHILE year<=xyear         'until max time is reached
        GOSUB showstock              'display current growing stock
        GOSUB cut                    'cut forest
        GOSUB pvalue                 'determine present value
        GOSUB showcut                'display cut data
        GOSUB growth                 'predict growth
        year=year+10                 'increase time
    WEND
END


'------------------------------------------
'   Read initial forest condition
'------------------------------------------
initia:
    year=0                  'initial time
    pval=0                  'initial present value
    FOR iclass=1 TO 10
        READ areab(iclass)      'initial area (acres)
    NEXT iclass
    DATA 250, 150, 320, 400, 0, 100, 300, 110, 530,120
    FOR iclass=1 TO 10
        READ vpa(iclass)           'volume per acre (1000cft)
    NEXT iclass
    DATA 0.5,1.1,3.6,6.8,9.3,11.6,13.5,15.2,16.7,17.9
RETURN
'------------------------------------------
'   Define management regime
'------------------------------------------
manage:
    READ xyear               'max simulated time (years)
    DATA 200
    READ price,rate, rcost
    DATA 250, 0.05, 150
    READ xarea               'allowable cut area (acres)
    DATA 380
RETURN
```

Figure 14.1 Computer code of program Even.

```
'-------------------------------------------
'  Display current growing stock
'-------------------------------------------
showstock:
    PRINT "year";year
    PRINT" stock";
    FOR iclass=1 TO 10
      PRINT USING"####.";areab(iclass),
    NEXT iclass
    PRINT
RETURN
'-------------------------------------------
'  Cut forest
'-------------------------------------------
cut:
    tareac=0              'total area cut during decade
    tvolc=0              'total volume cut during decade
    FOR iclass=1 TO 10
      areac(iclass)=0       'area cut in age class during decade
    NEXT iclass
    iclass=10
    WHILE tareac<xarea      'total area cut less than allowable cut
      areac(iclass)=xarea-tareac
      IF areac(iclass)>areab(iclass) THEN areac(iclass)=areab(iclass)
      areab(iclass)=areab(iclass)-areac(iclass)    'area left after cut
      tareac=tareac+areac(iclass)
      tvolc=tvolc+areac(iclass)*vpa(iclass)
      iclass=iclass-1
    WEND
RETURN
```

Figure 14.1 Continued.

Subroutine Showstock

This subroutine displays on the computer screen the current year and, under it, the area in each age class at the beginning of that year (see Fig. 14.2).

Subroutine Cut

This subroutine first initializes the total area and the total volume cut in the next 10 years to zero. Then it cuts the allowed area in the following steps, starting with the oldest age-class:

1. The area to be cut in the current age class is set equal to the allowable cut minus the total area already cut in the current decade.

```
'-------------------------------------------
'   Compute cumulative net present value
'-------------------------------------------
pvalue:
    disc=(1+rate)^(year+5)                  'discount factor
    pval=pval+(tvolc*price-tareac*rcost)/disc  'present value
RETURN
'-------------------------------------------
'   Display area, volume of cut and net present value
'-------------------------------------------
showcut:
    PRINT" cut    ";
    FOR iclass=1 TO 10
        PRINT USING"####.";areac(iclass),
    NEXT iclass
    PRINT
    PRINT USING" volume cut#####. present value#######.";tvolc,pval
RETURN


'-------------------------------------------
'   Predict growth of forest during next decade
'-------------------------------------------
growth:
    areae(1)=tareac                         'area reforested
    FOR iclass=2 TO 9
        areae(iclass)=areab(iclass-1)  'area moves up one age class
    NEXT iclass
    areae(10)=areab(10)+areab(9)       'area in oldest age class
'-------------------------------------------
'   Area at beginning of next decade is equal to
'   area at end of current decade
'-------------------------------------------
    FOR iclass=1 TO 10
        areab(iclass)=areae(iclass)
    NEXT iclass
RETURN
```

Figure 14.1 Continued.

2. If the area to be cut is greater than the area that is available in the current age class, then the cut can only be equal to the area available.

3. Next, the area left in the current age class after the cut is determined.

4. Finally, the total area and the total volume that have been cut in the current decade are computed.

These steps are repeated for younger and younger age classes, until the total area cut in the decade equals the allowable cut.

TABLE 14.1 DEFINITION OF VARIABLES IN
PROGRAM EVEN

Variable	Definition
year	Current time, increased by 10-year intervals
xyear	Maximum simulated time (years)
rate	Discount rate, per year
rcost	Regeneration cost ($/acre)
pval	Cumulated net present value ($)
iclass	Age-class index, varies from 1 to 10
areab (*iclass*)	Area at the beginning of a decade (acres)
areae (*iclass*)	Area at the end of a decade (acres)
areac (*iclass*)	Area cut in a decade (acres)
tareac	Total area cut in a decade
vpa	Volume per acre (1000 ft^3)
tvolc	Total volume cut in a decade
iclass	Age class, varies from 1 to 10, by decades.

year 0

stock 250. 150. 320. 400.   0. 100. 300. 110. 530. 120.

cut   0.   0.   0.   0.   0.   0.   0.   0. 260. 120.

volume cut 6490. present value 1226610.

year 10

stock 380. 250. 150. 320. 400.   0. 100. 300. 110. 270.

cut   0.   0.   0.   0.   0.   0.   0.   0. 110. 270.

volume cut 6670. present value 2001289.

year 20

stock 380. 380. 250. 150. 320. 400.   0. 100. 300.   0.

cut   0.   0.   0.   0.   0.   0.   0. 80. 300.   0.

volume cut 6226. present value 2444096.

....

year 60

stock 380. 380. 380. 380. 380. 380.   0.   0.   0.   0.

cut   0.   0.   0.   0.   0. 380.   0.   0.   0.   0.

volume cut 4408. present value 2925852.

year 70

stock 380. 380. 380. 380. 380. 380.   0.   0.   0.   0.

cut   0.   0.   0.   0.   0. 380.   0.   0.   0.   0.

volume cut 4408. present value 2952762.

Figure 14.2 Output of program Even. (Volumes are in 1000 ft^3.)

Subroutine Pvalue

This subroutine computes the cumulative net present value of all harvests up to the last one. The net returns in the current decade are the stumpage value of the volume cut, minus the reforestation cost. These net returns are discounted to the present and added to the cumulative present value up to that year. Note that harvest is assumed to proceed continuously throughout the current decade. For simplicity, however, all revenues and costs during a decade are accounted for in the middle of the decade. Therefore, the time used in the discount formula is the current year plus 5.

Subroutine Showcut

This subroutine displays the area cut in each age class during the coming decade, as well as the volume cut and the cumulative net present value of the returns up to and including those generated during the coming decade (see Fig. 14.2).

Subroutine Growth

This subroutine simulates the growth of the part of the forest that will not be cut during the coming decade. The area cut during the coming decade will constitute age class 1 at the end of the decade. Simultaneously, the areas in age class 1 to 8 grow into age classes 2 to 9. The new age class 10 at the end of the decade consists of what is left of the old age class 10 after the cut, plus what was in age class 9 at the beginning of the decade.

14.3 OUTPUT AND APPLICATIONS OF PROGRAM EVEN

Forest Dynamics

Part of the results of a simulation run with the program Even appear in Fig. 14.2. The input data are those shown within subroutines Initia and Manage in Fig. 14.1. Every decade, 380 acres are cut from the forest, as required by the area-control strategy. This corresponds to a rotation of 60 years. The oldest age classes are always cut first, so that the number of age classes decreases over time. Due to the presence of old timber on the initial forest, more volume is cut during the first decades than later on. Sixty years after the beginning of the simulation, the forest is regulated. Thereafter, it remains in a steady state, producing always the same amount and retaining the same growing stock, although the location of each age class changes.

Forest Value

The data in Fig. 14.2 show that a large part of the net present value of the returns from this forest is generated during the first decades. By the time the forest has been regulated, 60 years after the beginning of management, the net present value of the forest increases very slowly. In fact, continuing the simulation shows that the net present value approaches gradually a maximum of approximately $3 million. This is the value of the forest, inclusive of land and growing stock, given the specified management regime and all other assumptions. Given these assumptions, a buyer could pay $3 million for the forest and be ensured a real rate of return on the investment of 5 percent per year.

Best Rotation

An interesting problem concerns the rotation that is optimum given the management strategy that we are simulating. Specifically, what is the rotation that maximizes the forest value? A potential buyer of the forest would want to know this to determine the most he could pay for the forest. Someone who owns the forest already could use this information to choose the management regime that maximizes the present value of his future income.

This question can be answered readily with the simulator Even. This is done by changing the values of the allowable cut variable, *xarea*, in subroutine Manage in Fig. 14.1.

For example, *xarea* = 2280 acres implies a rotation age of 10 years, and that all the forest is cut and regenerated during one decade. Similarly, *xarea* = 1140 acres implies a rotation of 20 years, half of the forest being cut every decade. Finally, *xarea* = 22.8 implies a rotation of 100 years, which leads to one-tenth of the forest being cut and replanted every decade.

The results of different simulations, leaving everything but the allowable cut area constant, are shown in Table 14.2. It is clear from this table that the best rotation is 20 years. This rotation leads to a forest value of about $4.2 million. Note that this is not the rotation that results from the soil expectation formula. To check this, redo the computations of Table 7.1, with the data used in this simulation. You should find that the rotation that maximizes soil expectation value is 40 years.

The shorter rotation found with the simulations is due to the fact that the area-control formula limits the area that can be cut every year to a constant. A rotation of 20 years allows a cut of 1140 acres, against 570 acres for a rotation of 40 years. The larger area allows more timber to be cut quickly from the valuable old growth, which leads to the higher present value. The

TABLE 14.2 FOREST VALUE FOR DIFFERENT ROTATION AGES

Rotation (years)	Allowable cut (acres)	Forest value (10^6 $)
10	2280	3.98
20 (best rotation)	1140	4.19
30	760	4.08
40	570	3.77
50	456	3.35
60	380	3.00

rotation of 20 years turns out to be superior because of the way the allowable cut is set.

This result illustrates a general principle. In defining an optimum, whether for rotation or any other management parameter, one must define precisely the *context* within which the optimization is to be done. The context includes the status of the forest, the management regime that is applied, and the economic and social environment within which the management takes place. The latter point is worth stressing, since a rotation of 20 years implies, under area control, liquidation of the entire old-growth timber in 20 years. For many reasons, this may not be acceptable. In making the allowable-cut decision, a manager would want to weigh carefully the economic gain resulting from shorter rotations against the loss of other values that, although they are more difficult to quantify, are not less real.

14.4 DOWNWARD-SLOPING DEMAND FUNCTIONS

To illustrate the importance of context in choosing a management strategy let us consider how variations in price may influence the choice of a rotation, still within the area-control framework that we have assumed up to now. Specifically, we will assume that the amount of timber sold from the forest influences price. This is often referred to as the case of the "downward-sloping demand curve," since it implies that as the volume offered increases, the price received declines.

In the next simulations we will assume that the demand equation has the following form:

$$P = aQ^{-0.5} \tag{14.1}$$

where P is the price of the timber, in dollars per thousand cubic feet, and Q is the volume of timber cut per year, in thousand cubic feet. Equation (14.1) implies:

$$\frac{dP}{P} = -0.5\frac{dQ}{Q} \quad \text{or} \quad \frac{dQ}{Q} = -2.0\frac{dP}{P} \tag{14.2}$$

That is to say, an increase of the volume sold of 10 percent leads to a decline in price of 5 percent. Symmetrically, a rise in price of 10 percent causes a decline in demand of 20 percent. Since the relative change in quantity is greater than the relative change in price, in absolute value, the demand for timber is said to be elastic with respect to price. Precisely, the elasticity of demand with respect to price is -2.0. To define the demand equation completely, we need to estimate the coefficient a. This can be done if we know one point of the demand curve. Assume that when the volume sold from the forest is 450,000 ft^3/y the price received is \$250 per thousand cubic feet. Then:

$$250 = a450^{-0.5}$$

that is:

$$a = 250 \times 450^{0.5} = 5303$$

Price ($/1000 ft³)

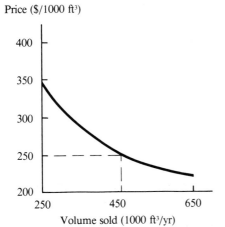

Figure 14.3 Demand curve for timber
with a price elasticity of −2.0.

Volume sold (1000 ft³/yr)

so that the demand equation is:

$$P = 5303Q^{-0.5} \tag{14.3}$$

The geometric representation of Eq. (14.3) appears in Figure 14.3. Equation (14.3) can now be added to program Even, within subroutine Pvalue, as shown in Fig. 14.4. Note that the volume cut, *tvolc*, must be divided by 10 because *tvolc* refers to the volume cut during a decade, while the quantity in the demand equation (14.3) refers to the volume cut per year. For simplicity we assume that the volume cut every year within a decade is constant.

The new version of the program Even, with the subroutine Pvalue in Fig. 14.4 was used to simulate the effect of different rotations on the value of the forest given a downward-sloping demand curve. The results are shown in Fig. 14.5. Two things can be observed from this figure. First, given the assumed demand equation, forest value is lower, regardless of rotation age. Second, the optimum rotation is 30 years, when a price-elastic demand is assumed, instead of 20, when the prices was assumed to be independent of the volume cut.

The reason for the difference in forest value is that volumes sold are the same, regardless of the assumption on demand, but unit prices are lower when a price-elastic demand equation is assumed. This is so because the volume sold in the first decades exceeds 450,000 ft³/y (Fig. 14.2) and therefore the price is less than the $250 per thousand cubic feet assumed previously (Fig. 14.3).

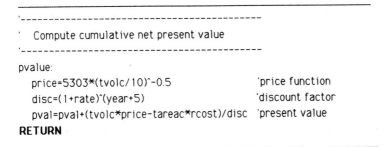

```
'----------------------------------------------
'  Compute cumulative net present value
'----------------------------------------------
pvalue:
    price=5303*(tvolc/10)^-0.5                    'price function
    disc=(1+rate)^(year+5)                        'discount factor
    pval=pval+(tvolc*price-tareac*rcost)/disc     'present value
RETURN
```

Figure 14.4 Subroutine Pvalue modified to reflect a downward-sloping demand curve.

Forest value ($ millions)

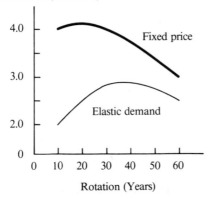

Figure 14.5 Forest value and optimum rotation vary with the elasticity of the demand for the timber.

This explains also why it is better to have a rotation of 30 years when the demand is price-responsive, for although a longer rotation leads to lower volume cut in the early years, it leads to higher prices. The net result is, for the price elasticity used here, an increase in total revenues and, thus, in forest value.

14.5 CONCLUSIONS

The simulation model of this chapter offers a straightforward approach to evaluating some management strategies for even-aged forest management. It has illustrated the importance of context in choosing management parameters like rotation age. For example, under area-control management, the economic rotation tends to increase when the demand for timber is elastic with respect to its price.

Although the model dealt only with area-control management, it is not hard to see how it could be adapted to volume control by simply changing the allowable cut from a specified area to a volume (see Problem 14.5). Other features could be added to the model in the same way that we added a downward-sloping demand curve. There is a natural desire to add such refinements to simulation models to make them as realistic as possible, but this must be resisted. Added features make a model more difficult to understand and more prone to errors. Paradoxically, perhaps, realism is not a characteristic of good models. Abstraction is best—a level of abstraction that concentrates on the key characteristics of the problem being investigated.

PROBLEMS

14.1. The object of this problem is to determine the effect of the interest rate on the best economic rotation for a forest that is managed and grows according to the simulation program Even shown in Fig. 14.1.

Change the data in that program to reflect a guiding rate of interest of 2 percent per year, leaving all other data unchanged.

Run this modified version of Even to determine the value of this forest when managed under area control, with rotations of 10, 20, 30, 40, 50, or 60 years. Recall that the forest is managed under area control and that the rotation length is set by changing the value of the area cut every decade.

Compare your results with those in Table 14.2. What is the best economic rotation? How has the value of the forest changed?

14.2. The program Even examined in this chapter simulated the growth of a forest that had many acres of old timber. Consider instead a forest of the same size and productivity that has been recently cut-over. It has 1900 acres in age class 1, 300 acres in age class 2, 80 acres in age class 3, and nothing in older age classes.

Change the data of the program Even to reflect this new initial condition, leave all other data as in Fig. 14.1.

Run this modified version of Even to determine the value of the forest managed on rotations of 10, 20, 30, 40, 50, and 60 years.

Compare these results to those in Table 14.2. Is the best rotation still 20 years? Why? How important is initial stocking in determining the value of the forest?

14.3. Consider a forest of same characteristics as the one described in Fig. 14.1, but growing on a better site. On this site, the yield of each age class is:

Age class	1	2	3	4	5	6	7	8	9	10
1000 ft^3 / acre	0.55	1.3	4.3	8.5	12.1	15.7	19	22	25	27.7

Modify the data of the program Even to reflect this higher yield. Keep all other data as in Table 14.1.

Run this modified version of Even to determine the value of this new forest when managed on rotations of 10, 20, 30, 40, 50, and 60 years.

Compare your results to those in Table 14.4 in the text. What is the new best economic rotation?

14.4. Consider the forest examined in section 14.4. It faced a downward-sloping demand curve for its timber. Assume that population and income changes in the region where the forest is located have led to an increase in the demand for houses. This in turn has caused a permanent shift in the demand for timber. Viewed another way, the forest can now sell a specific amount of timber at a higher price. For example, the forest could sell 450,000 cubic feet of wood a year for $300 per thousand cubic feet, rather than for $250.

Assuming that the elasticity of the demand for timber with respect to price has remained at -2.0, what is the new value of a in the price equation $P = aQ^{-0.5}$?

Modify the subroutine Pvalue shown in Fig. 14.4 to reflect this shift in demand. Run the program Even thus changed to determine the value of the forest when managed on 10, 20, 30, 40, 50, and 60 year rotations. Find the best rotation and compare your results to those in Table 14.2.

14.5. The version of program Even shown in Fig. 14.1 can easily be modified to allow for volume control rather than area control. First, change the second **READ**

statement in subroutine Manage to:

> **READ** xvol

Then change the **WHILE** statement in subroutine Cut to:

> **WHILE** tvolc < xvol

Finally, change the next statement in subroutine Cut to:

> areac(iclass) = (xvol − tvolc)/vpa(iclass)

Even, thus modified, recognizes the value in the second **DATA** statement in subroutine Manage as the allowable cut, in thousand cubic feet per decade. To determine the allowable cut under volume control, divide the total initial volume of the forest (22,043 thousand cubic feet for the data in Fig. 14.1) by the rotation length, in decades. For example, with a rotation length of 60 years the allowable cut would be:

> $22043/6 = 3647(1000 \text{ ft}^3/\text{decade})$

Change the version of program Even in Fig. 14.1 to simulate volume control management.

Run this modified version of Even to determine the present value of the forest with rotations of 50 and 60 years.

Compare your results to those in Table 14.2 in the text. What happens for a rotation of 40 years? Why?

ANNOTATED REFERENCES

Betters, D. R. 1975. A timber-water simulation model for lodgepole pine watersheds in the Colorado Rockies. *Water Resources Research* 11(6):903–908. (Deterministic model for evaluating the impacts of alternative management activities on the output of water and timber from a forested watershed.)

Buongiono, J., and D. E. Teeguarden. 1973. An economic model for selecting Douglas-fir reforestation projects. *Hilgardia* 42(3):35–120. (Includes a deterministic simulation program, FOREST, to determine economic initial density, thinning and rotation in even-aged stands.)

Gould, E. M., and W. G. O'Regan. 1965. Simulation, a step toward better forest management. Harvard Forest Paper 13. Harvard Forest, Petersham. 86 pp. (One of the first applications of simulation in forest management, uses the same principles of the program Even described in this chapter, but has also stochastic elements.)

Gould, E. M., Jr. 1977. Harvard Forest management game. *Journal of Forestry* 75(9):587–589. (A noncomputerized version of the simulation described in Gould and O'Reagan.)

Olson, D., C. Schallau, and W. Maki. 1984. IPASS: An interactive policy analysis simulation system. U.S. Forest Service, General Technical Report PNW-170. Pacific Northwest Forest and Range Experiment Station, Portland. 70 pp. (Deterministic model of the interactions between regional industries, labor force, population, and forest production.)

Schmidt, J. S., and P. L. Tedder. 1981. A comprehensive examination of economic harvest optimization simulation methods. *Forest Science* 27(3):523–536. (Comparison of harvest scheduling models that incorporate some form of downward-sloping demand function.)

Chapter 15

Forest Simulation with Random Events

15.1 INTRODUCTION

According to the general classification of simulation models given in Sec. 13.2, the models we dealt with in Chaps. 13 and 14 were deterministic and continuous. They were deterministic in that all the underlying functions assumed that the future values of variables, or at least their expectations, were known exactly. They were continous because the simulations consisted of forecasting how a forest system changed at regular time intervals. The length of the time interval could vary, depending on the application, but it never changed within a simulation.

The purpose of this chapter is to give an example of a simulation model that is stochastic and event oriented. That is, the future is now represented as it really is, very vague and best described by probabilistic statements and relationships. In addition, the simulation clock is not advanced by constant amounts, say 5 or 10 years as in Chaps. 13 and 14. Instead, only the dates when an interesting event occurs are recorded. The main advantage of doing this is that it reduces the number of calculations considerably. This is especially important in stochastic models because they involve many more computations than deterministic models, given the same problem.

15.2 PLANTATIONS THAT BURN

To illustrate the method of stochastic next-event simulation we will use a simple model of the growth of a forest plantation in a region that is ravaged by frequent fires. We shall assume that little can be done to suppress these fires. The fires occur randomly.

The model has two purposes: first, to determine how the presence of fires influences the value of plantations in this area; second, to find out how the plantation should be managed in order to maximize the returns to the owner.

In this model, only two kinds of events occur: a fire or a harvest. When a fire occurs, the entire crop of trees is lost and the plantation must be started again. When the crop is harvested, the forest is replanted immediately. The amount harvested is a deterministic function of the age of plantation. The only stochastic element in this model is the occurrence of fires. Since this is a rather different type of model from those we have studied so far, let us examine it in detail.

15.3 MODELING RANDOM FIRES

Although the times at which fires occur are random, the random process itself follows specific probabilistic laws. The laws that are assumed in simulation models are necessarily simple. This is consistent with the kind of information generally available.

In the case of forest fires, recorded or unrecorded memory may lead to statements of the following sort: "In this area, disastrous fires occur approximately once every 25 years." This of course does not mean that a fire will occur regularly every 25 years, but that over a very long time-span, the average interval between fires is 25 years. Some fires may actually occur at 5-year intervals, others every 50 years only.

In this specific example, the mean rate of fire occurrence is one-twenty-fifth per year. It is reasonable to assume that every time period of fixed length has the same chance of having a fire, regardless of when the previous fire happened. The exponential distribution is a probability distribution that has this property. In general, let m be the mean rate of fire occurrence, per year. Then, according to the exponential law, the probability p of having a fire during a period of time t is:

$$P(T \leq t) = 1 - \exp(-mt) \tag{15.1}$$

where T is the time interval between two fires. The graph of this function appears in Fig. 15.1. The figure shows that the probability that a fire occurs in a time span of 10 years is about 33 percent. The probability of having a fire within 25 years is about 63 percent, while it is nearly certain that a fire will occur during a time span of 100 years.

Equation (15.1) can be used to generate a random observation for t, the time between two fires. This is done by setting the right-hand side of Eq. (15.1) equal to a random number between 0 and 1, denoted by R. This leads to:

$$1 - \exp(-mt) = R \quad \text{or} \quad \exp(-mt) = 1 - R$$

and, taking the natural logarithm of both sides:

$$\ln[\exp(-mt)] = \ln(1 - R)$$

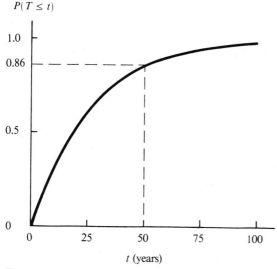

$P(T \le t)$

Figure 15.1 Probability of having a fire within t years, given an average fire incidence of once every 25 years.

so that $-mt = \ln(1 - R)$, which yields:

$$t = -\ln\frac{(1 - R)}{m} \qquad (15.2)$$

This relationship is illustrated in Fig. 15.1. For example, to a random number of 0.86 corresponds a time interval between fires of 50 years.

15.4 THE SIMULATION PROGRAM FIRE

The computer program used to implement the principles outlined above is named Fire. The BASIC code of the program appears in Fig. 15.2. It consists of a main program and five subroutines. The names and definitions of the variables used in the program are given in Table 15.1.

Main Program

The main program first calls the subroutine Dat to read the basic data. It then calls the function RANDOMIZE to set the seed of the random number generator at 3333. Changing the seed changes the series of random numbers produced by the program. The main program then calls subroutine Initia to initiate the actual simulation. Then, as long as the simulated time is less than or equal to the time horizon the following steps are taken:

First, the program displays on the computer screen the current time, the time when the next fire will occur, the time of the next

```
'--------------------------------------------------------------------
'                          Fire
'--------------------------------------------------------------------
'  Simulates a plantation that may be destroyed by fire.
'--------------------------------------------------------------------
main:
   GOSUB dat
   RANDOMIZE 3333                    'random number seed
   GOSUB initia
   WHILE year<=yearMax               'until time horizon is reached
     PRINT USING"#####.";year;tnFire;tnHarvest;pval
     IF tnFire<=tnHarvest THEN GOSUB burn ELSE GOSUB harvest
   WEND
END
'--------------------------------------------------------------------
'   Read data
'--------------------------------------------------------------------
dat:
   yearMax=200         'time horizon (years)
   afireInter=25       'average time interval between fires (years)
   rate=.03            'interest rate per year (fraction)
   reforCost=50        'cost of reforestation ($/acre)
   price=250           'price of timber ($/1000cft)
   rotation=30         'rotation, in years (must be a multiple of ten)
   GOSUB yield
RETURN


'--------------------------------------------------------------------
'   Read expected volume per acre of plantation in function of age
'--------------------------------------------------------------------
yield:
   FOR iage=1 TO 10        'at 10 year intervals, up to 100 years
     READ vpa(iage)        'volume (1000cft/acre)
   NEXT iage
   DATA 0.5,1.1,3.6,6.8,9.3,11.6,15.5,15.2,16.7,17.9
RETURN
'--------------------------------------------------------------------
'   Initiate simulation
'--------------------------------------------------------------------
initia:
   year=0                             'initial time
   tnFire=-LOG(1-RND)*afireInter      'time to first fire (years)
   tnHarvest=rotation                 'time to first harvest (years)
   pval=-reforCost                    'initial present value
RETURN
```

Figure 15.2 Computer code of program Fire.

```
'-------------------------------------------------------------------
'   Next event is a fire
'-------------------------------------------------------------------
burn:
   year=tnFire                              'current time
   pval=pval-reforCost/(1+rate)^year        'discounted reforestation cost
   ttnFire=-LOG(1-RND)*afireInter           'time to next fire
   tnFire=year+ttnFire                      'year of next fire
   tnHarvest=year+rotation                  'year of next harvest
RETURN
'-------------------------------------------------------------------
'   Next event is a harvest
'-------------------------------------------------------------------
harvest:
   year=tnHarvest                                          'current time
   indexRot=rotation/10                                    'age-class
   pval=pval+(vpa(indexRot)*price-reforCost)/(1+rate)^year 'present value
   tnHarvest=year+rotation                                 'next harvest
RETURN
```

Figure 15.2   Continued.

TABLE 15.1   VARIABLE NAMES AND DEFINITIONS FOR PROGRAM FIRE

Variable name	Definition
year	Current time (years)
yearMax	Maximum simulated time (years)
tnFire	Time of occurrence of the next fire (years)
tnHarvest	Time of occurrence of the next scheduled harvest (years)
afireInter	Average time interval between fires (years)
rate	Interest rate per year
reforCost	Reforestation cost ($/a)
price	Price of timber ($/1000 ft^3)
rotation	Rotation age (years)
vpa	Volume per acre (1000 ft^3)
pval	Discounted value of future costs and revenues ($/a)
ttnFire	Time to next fire (years)

harvest, and the net present value of returns from the plantation, so far.

Then, if the next event that will occur is a fire, the subroutine Burn is caled into action, otherwise control is passed to the subroutine Harvest. The functions of these two subroutines are described below.

Subroutines Dat and Yield

In the specific example shown in Fig. 15.2, subroutine Dat sets the time horizon at 200 years, the average time interval between fires at 25 years, the interest rate at 3 percent per year, the reforestation cost at $50 per acre, the price of timber at $250 per thousand cubic feet, and the rotation at 30 years.

Then, subroutine Dat calls subroutine Yield that reads the volume of timber at different ages from a DATA statement. The volume per acre is defined in thousand cubic feet and is read at 10-year intervals, starting with the volume at age 10.

Subroutine Initia

As shown in Fig. 15.2, this subroutine initiates the current time, *year*, at 0. For simplicity, the time origin is set just after a fire has occurred. The subroutine Initia then computes the time when the first fire will occur, *tnFire*. This is done by applying Eq. (15.2). The standard function RND returns a random number between 0 and 1. Note that instead of dividing by the fire frequency as in Eq. (15.2), the formula in subroutine Initia multiplies by the mean time interval between fires, which achieves the same purpose.

Subroutine Initia then determines the time of the first harvest, *tnHarvest*, assuming no fire occurs before it. This is equal to the rotation, given that the simulation starts just after a fire has occurred.

The final calculation of subroutine Initia is the initial present value of the plantation. This is negative and just equal to cost of reforestation, which is assumed to be done immediately after a fire.

Subroutine Burn

This subroutine is activated if the result of the IF test in the main program indicates that a fire will occur before the next scheduled harvest. The first statement of subroutine Burn sets the value of the current year to the time of the fire.

The next statement calculates the present value of the plantation, which is the present value so far minus the discounted value of the cost of reforesting immediately after the fire.

The third and fourth statements in subroutine Burn calculate the time of the next fire, *tnFire*. This is done by first generating a random value of the time interval between fires, using formula (15.2) (Note that every time the function RND is called by the computer program it generates a new random number.) Then, this random time interval is added to the current time.

The last statement of subroutine Burn calculates the time of the next harvest, assuming no fire occurs earlier.

Subroutine Harvest

This subroutine is activated when the IF test in the main program shows that the next event is a regularly scheduled harvest. The first statement sets the current time, *year*, to the time of the next harvest.

The next two statements calculate the present value of the plantation, after the harvest, assuming that the land is replanted immediately. Given the assumptions made, the forest generates an income only when a harvest occurs.

The last statement of subroutine Harvest determines the time of the next scheduled harvest, assuming no fire occurs before.

15.5 OUTPUT OF PROGRAM FIRE

The results obtained by running the program Fire with the data in Fig. 15.2 appear in Table 15.2. It is easy to see how the program works by reading this table line by line.

In year 0, the present value of the forest is $-$50$ per acre, which is the cost of the initial plantation. The next fire will occur in 34 years. This is the first random event. The next harvest is in year 30; this is simply equal to the rotation, assuming no fire happens before then.

Since the next harvest happens before the next fire, the next event is a harvest. It occurs on the thirtieth year. At that time, the forest is cut and replanted immediately. This leads to a present value of $300 per acre. The next scheduled harvest is at year 60. However, a fire occurs in the thirty-fourth year. This destroys the forest totally and requires replanting. As a result, the present value of the forest declines to $282 per acre.

Forest Value

The simulation continues in this way until the time horizon is reached. Table 15.2 shows that the present value of the returns from the forest fluctuates greatly at the beginning of the simulation. However, after a long period of

TABLE 15.2 OUTPUT OF PROGRAM FIRE WHEN THE SEED IS EQUAL TO 3333

Year	tnFire (year)	tnHarvest (year)	pval ($/a)
0	34	30	$-$50
30	34	60	300
34	38	64	282
38	74	68	265
68	74	98	380
74	96	104	375
96	115	126	372
115	121	145	370
121	136	151	369
136	137	166	368
137	206	167	367
167	206	197	373
197	206	227	376

time, the present value stabilizes at approximately $375 per acre. This is due to the exponential growth of the discounting factor as time increases. Returns and costs that occur a long time in the future have little effect on present value. Therefore, when the simulation is sufficiently long, say 200 years, the last present value that is obtained is, for all practical purposes, the present value of the returns over an infinite horizon. Since the simulation starts from bare land, this forest value is also the soil-expectation value, the value of land used for this kind of forestry.

Forest Value as a Stochastic Variable

It must be stressed that the forest value calculated in this way is a random variable. It depends on the series of random numbers that occurs in a particular simulation of forest fires. To see how much the forest value may change, let us do another simulation with the Fire model. The data remain the same as in Fig. 15.2, but the seed in the RANDOMIZE function is set to 1111 instead of 3333. The results of this simulation appear in Table 15.3. They are very different from those in Table 15.2. Now, the value of the forest is about − $130 per acre. The reason for this can be seen readily from the data in Table 15.3. A series of fires occurs during the first century of the plantation so that the first harvest happens in year 114. The net result is an economic loss.

It must be noted that the sequences of events in both simulations are consistent with the assumed probability distribution of fires. Both sequences may happen, leading either to a handsome return or a considerable loss. Clearly, a forester should not make a decision based on any single simulation. In a risky environment, forest value is a random variable. Therefore, enough information must be obtained to describe that random variable as well as possible. In general, one would like to have at least some measure of central

TABLE 15.3 OUTPUT OF PROGRAM FIRE WHEN THE SEED IS EQUAL TO 1111

Year	tnFire (year)	tnHarvest (year)	pval ($/a)
0	13	30	− 50
13	23	43	− 84
23	33	53	− 110
33	53	63	− 128
53	60	83	− 139
60	74	90	− 148
74	84	104	− 153
84	138	114	− 157
114	138	144	− 128
138	155	168	− 129
155	157	185	− 130
157	176	187	− 130
176	185	206	− 130
185	208	215	− 131

tendency and of spread. That is, what should we expect the forest value to be, on average, and how far may individual observations be from that average? This information can be obtained from simulation experiments.

15.6 STATISTICAL ANALYSIS OF SIMULATED FOREST VALUE

A simulation run is no different from a classical physical experiment. For example, when we run the program Fire, we set the constants at some values, in the same manner as we control the ingredients of a chemical reaction, and observe the result. Because the experiment has errors, the measures of the results are random variables. Therefore, the statistical principles and formulas used in designing and analyzing physical experiments apply directly to simulation.

Again, using the Fire model as an example, each result of a run gives a random observation of forest value, call it $fval_i$, where the subscript i refers to a particular run. A set of runs with different series of random numbers gives us a sample of random observations on forest value. Let the number of runs, that is the sample size, be n. Then, an unbiased estimate of the expected value of forest value is the sample mean:

$$aFval = \frac{\sum\limits_{i=1}^{n} fval_i}{n} \tag{15.3}$$

while an unbiased estimate of the variance of present value is:

$$varFval = \left(\frac{1}{n-1}\right) \sum\limits_{i=1}^{n} (fval_i - aFval)^2$$

or:

$$varFval = \left(\frac{1}{n-1}\right) \sum\limits_{i=1}^{n} fval_i^2 - \frac{\sum\limits_{i=1}^{n} fval_i^2}{n(n-1)} \tag{15.4}$$

which leads to the following estimate of the standard error of the mean of forest value:

$$seaFval = \sqrt{\frac{varFval}{n}} \tag{15.5}$$

This standard error will be smaller with larger numbers of observations, n. However, note that for the standard error to decrease by half, the number of observations must quadruple.

Finally, one may compute an alpha-confidence interval for the mean forest value, as follows:

$$[aFval - Z(\alpha)seaFval, aFval + Z(\alpha)seaFval] \tag{15.6}$$

where α is the probability that a standard normal deviate be between $-Z(\alpha)$ and $Z(\alpha)$. Therefore, the probability that the true mean forest value be in the interval defined by (15.6) is α.

For example, for $\alpha = 0.95$, $Z(0.95) = 1.96$ and, therefore, the 95 percent confidence interval for the mean is:

$$[aFval - 1.96seaFval, \ aFval + 1.96seaFval] \tag{15.7}$$

Given such confidence intervals, one may then determine whether changes in mean forest value that result from changes in management variables are statistically significant, at the specified confidence level, or whether they just stem from pure chance.

15.7 THE SIMULATION PROGRAM FIRESTAT

The objective of this computer program is to compute the statistics defined by Eqs. (15.3) to (15.5) for a forest plantation that burns at random intervals. Program Firestat is an extension of program Fire. Instead of simulating the growth of a plantation for a certain number of years, it repeats several such simulations a large number of times. Each simulation gives a different observation on forest value. The program Firestat shows each observation and calculates summary statistics for all of them.

```
'------------------------------------------------------------
'                         Firestat
'------------------------------------------------------------
'   Computes mean and variance of soil expectation value of a plantation
'   that may be destroyed by fire.
'------------------------------------------------------------
main:
   nobs=100
   sFval=0
   ssqFval=0
   RANDOMIZE 3333                 'random number seed
   GOSUB dat
   FOR iobs=1 TO nobs             'for each observation
      GOSUB initia
      WHILE year<=yearMax         'until time horizon is reached
         IF tnFire<=tnHarvest THEN GOSUB burn ELSE GOSUB harvest
      WEND
      GOSUB currentStat
   NEXT iobs
      GOSUB summaryStat
END
```

Figure 15.3 Computer code of program Firestat. (Subroutines not listed are the same as in Fig. 15.2.)

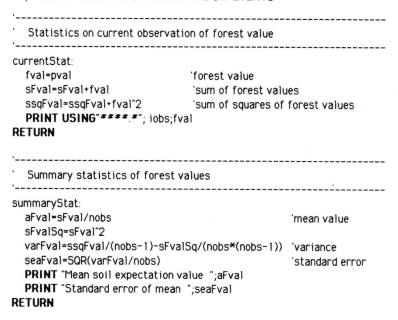

```
'-------------------------------------------------------------------
'  Statistics on current observation of forest value
'-------------------------------------------------------------------
currentStat:
    fval=pval                        'forest value
    sFval=sFval+fval                 'sum of forest values
    ssqFval=ssqFval+fval^2           'sum of squares of forest values
    PRINT USING"####.#"; iobs;fval
RETURN


'-------------------------------------------------------------------
'  Summary statistics of forest values
'-------------------------------------------------------------------
summaryStat:
    aFval=sFval/nobs                             'mean value
    sFvalSq=sFval^2
    varFval=ssqFval/(nobs-1)-sFvalSq/(nobs*(nobs-1))  'variance
    seaFval=SQR(varFval/nobs)                    'standard error
    PRINT "Mean soil expectation value ";aFval
    PRINT "Standard error of mean ";seaFval
RETURN
```

Figure 15.3 Continued.

The computer code of program Firestat appears in Fig. 15.3, except for the subroutines that are the same as in program Fire. The definitions of the variables are given in Table 15.4.

As in program Fire, the core of the main program of Firestat is a WHILE loop that controls the succession of fires and harvests in a plantation. In addition, however, program Firestat has a FOR loop that causes the simulation to be repeated a specified number of times, designated as *nobs*. Each pass through this loop generates one observation on forest value, *fval*. This observation is displayed by subroutine CurrentStat together with the

TABLE 15.4 NAMES AND DEFINITIONS OF VARIABLES IN PROGRAM FIRESTAT

Variable	Definition
nobs	Number of observations on forest value, each observation corresponds to a different series of random numbers
iobs	Index of observation, varies from 1 to *nobs*
fval	Forest value ($/acre)
sFval	Sum of forest values over *nobs* observations
ssqFval	Sum of squares of forest value
aFval	Mean of forest value
varFval	Variance of forest value
seaFval	Standard error of the mean of forest value

observation number, *iobs*. Subroutine CurrentStat then calculates the sum of forest values and the sum of squared forest values, up to the last observation.

When the FOR loop is completed, *nobs* random observations on forest value have been generated. The program Firestat then calls subroutine SummaryStat to calculate the summary statistics for the sample of observations. This subroutine calculates the mean of forest value over all observations, *aFval*; the variance of forest value, *varFval*; and the standard error of the mean of forest value, *seaFval*. The formulas used by subroutine SummaryStat are those in Eqs. (15.3) to (15.5). Finally, the subroutine SummaryStat displays these summary statistics on the screen.

15.8 BEST ROTATION UNDER RISK

To illustrate one application of the program Firestat, we have used it to calculate forest value under different rotations. If there were no fire, the economic rotation for a plantation, using the data in Fig. 15.2 (subroutine Dat) would be 40 years. Verify that this is the rotation that maximizes the soil expectation value by doing the computations in Table 7.1.

Assuming that fires may occur with a frequency of 1 : 25 per year, should the rotation be shortened, and by how much?

Figure 15.4 shows the means and standard errors of means of forest value for rotations of 20, 30, 40, and 50 years. These data were obtained by running Firestat with the data in Figs. 15.2 and 15.3. In particular, the number

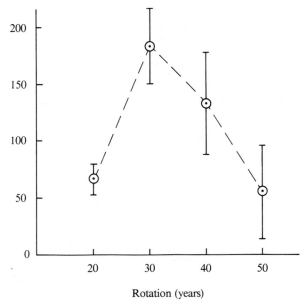

Figure 15.4 Mean and 95 percent confidence interval of mean of forest value for different rotations.

of observations was set at 100 and the time horizon at 200 years. Therefore, each mean in Fig. 15.4 is computed from 100 independent simulations of plantations, harvests, and fire sequences extending over a period of 200 years. Also shown in Fig. 15.4 are the 95 percent confidence intervals of the means. For example, there is a 95 percent probability that the true mean forest value for a rotation of 30 years lies between $170 and $205 per acre.

The largest mean forest value occurs for a rotation of 30 years, but because the 95 percent confidence intervals for the mean forest value at 30 and 40 years overlap, one cannot in principle reject the hypothesis that the two means are equal, at the 95 percent confidence level. Note however that a decision maker may not want to use such a high confidence level. He might well decide on the evidence of Fig. 15.4 that in the presence of fires, shortening the rotation by 10 years is indeed a good strategy. On the other hand, there is little doubt that a rotation of 30 years will on average bring higher forest values than rotations of 20 or 50 years.

In judging Fig. 15.4, one must keep in mind that the confidence intervals refer to the mean of forest value. The spread of individual observations of forest value is much larger. On average, a forester is unlikely to lose money on this kind of plantation, regardless of the rotation, since no confidence interval in Fig. 15.4 includes 0. Nevertheless, there will be individual plantations that will indeed lead to a loss. One such possibility was described in Table 15.3.

15.9 CONCLUSIONS

Stochastic-event simulation is an attractive way of analyzing forest-management problems that involve risk. The inclusion of random elements reflects the uncertain environment that surrounds decision makers. Recognizing risk explicitly leads to a picture of the world that is much different from the one conveyed by deterministic models. Standard errors of measures of efficiency, like present value, convey information that is undoubtedly useful to decision makers.

Stochastic models, however, can quickly become extremely complex. Focusing the simulation on important events does decrease considerably the number of calculations, especially the number of times random distributions must be sampled. In addition, risk should be recognized explicitly where it matters. For example, in our simple model, we chose deliberately to recognize the randomness of fires, and to treat forest growth as deterministic. How the forest will grow is also uncertain, but much less than the time when a fire shall occur. This principle should be followed in larger models, risk should be introduced reluctantly and only when it is the only reasonable way to formulate a problem.

PROBLEMS

15.1. The data of the program Fire shown in Fig. 15.2 assume an average interval between fires of 25 years. Set the average fire interval at 10, 20, ..., 90, and 100 years, leaving all other data as in Fig 15.2, and run the program Fire for each interval.

What is the relationship between the per acre value of the forest and the average interval between fires? What important parameters or assumptions are your conclusions contingent upon?

15.2. Program Firestat can be used to better define the relationship between the per acre value of the forest and the average interval between fires. Run the version of Firestat shown in Fig. 15.3 with the average interval between fires set at 10, 20, ... , 90, and 100 years, leaving all other data as in Fig 15.3. Do the results obtained confirm or disprove the conclusions you reached in Problem 15.1?

15.3. Careful examination of cost records has shown that reforestation costs per acre are 25 percent lower on burned areas than on harvested areas of the forest. The reason is that it is easier for planting crews to move about in burned areas—in fact, areas that are harvested must often be burned before they are planted to eliminated residues and brush (see also Chap. 12).

Modify the subroutine Burn of program Fire to reflect this difference in costs, assuming that the reforestation costs in Fig. 15.2 refer to reforestation on cut-over land. Run the version of Fire shown in Fig. 15.2 with and without this modification. What effect does the refinement of reforestation cost data have on the value of the forest? (Note: On a given computer the same seed will always result in the same sequence of random numbers, and, therefore, the same pattern of harvests and fires. The same seed on different computers, however, may generate a different sequence of random numbers.)

15.4. The simulations discussed in this chapter assumed an interest rate of 3 percent and a timber price of $250 per thousand cubic feet. Suppose instead that real interest rates are expected to increase to 6 percent and stay there for a long time, and that housing construction will drop as a result. Forest economists anticipate that the new price of timber will be only $175 per 1000 ft^3.

Run the program Firestat with and without changing the interest rate and timber price to these new values. Leave all other data as in Fig. 15.3. How seriously will this weakening of timber markets affect the value of the forest?

Calculate a 95 percent confidence interval for the forest value under the weak market assumptions. In these conditions, would you invest in this forest? Why?

15.5. The forest value calculated in Problem 15.4 under weak market conditions assumed a 30 year rotation. Run the program Firestat again assuming weak market conditions (6 percent interest and $175 per thousand cubic feet), but with rotations of 20, 40, and 50 years.

Calculate a 95 percent confidence interval for the forest value for each rotation. Does any one rotation have a 95 percent chance of yielding a profit? Which rotation seems to be best?

15.6. To better understand the difference between programs Firestat and Fire, run Firestat with several different random number seeds. On most computers, seeds can be any integer between −30,000 and 30,000. Comparing Tables 15.2 and 15.3, it is clear that the output of Fire is quite dependent upon the value of the seed.

Consider instead the outputs of Firestat with different seeds. How much do the estimates of the average forest value and their standard errors change with the seed? Why?

ANNOTATED REFERENCES

Dunn, R. A. and K. D. Ramsing. 1981. *Management science: A practical approach to decision making.* Macmillan, New York. 527 pp. (Chapter 13 describes a stochastic model of the log handling equipment for a multiproduct mill producing paper, plywood, and lumber.)

Grant, W. E. 1986. *Systems analysis and simulation in wildlife and fisheries sciences.* Wiley, New York. 338 pp. (Contains many examples of stochastic models of wildlife populations.)

Hillier, F. S., and G. J. Lieberman. 1986. *Introduction to operations research.* Holden-Day, Oakland. 888 pp. (Chapter 23 covers the basics of stochastic simulation modeling.)

Osawa, A., C. A. Shoemaker, and J. R. Stedinger. 1983. A stochastic model of balsam fir bud phenology utilizing maximum likelihood parameter estimation. *Forest Science* 29(3):478–490. (Stochastic model of bud development.)

Reynolds, M. R., Jr., H. E. Burkhart, and R. F. Daniels. 1981. Procedures for statistical validation of stochastic simulation models. *Forest Science* 27(2):349–364. (Develops a framework for testing the validity of models of natural resource systems, and applies this framework to a stochastic model of forest growth.)

Smith, V. K., and J. V. Krutilla. 1974. A simulation model for management of low density recreational areas. *Journal of Environmental Economics and Management* 1:178–201. (Describes a stochastic model of dispersed recreation use patterns, and the model's application to evaluating congestion problems.)

Starfield, A. M., and A. L. Bleloch. 1986. *Building models for conservation and wildlife management.* Macmillan, New York. 253 pp. (Chapters 3 and 4 describe stochastic models of wildlife populations.)

Stedinger, J. R. 1984. A spruce budworm-forest model and its implications for suppression programs. *Forest Science* 30(3):597–615. (Stochastic model of the population dynamics of a forest pest under different management programs.)

Winsaur, S. A. 1982. Simulation of grapple skidders and a whole-tree chipper. U.S. Forest Service Research Paper NC-221. North Central Forest Experiment Station, St. Paul. 42 pp. (Stochastic model of a logging system. Includes computer code.)

Chapter 16

Analysis of Forestry Investments

16.1 INTRODUCTION

Many of the things a forester does are investments, that is, projects that may produce results only far into the future. In fact, it is the very long time required to grow trees to commercial value that distinguishes forestry from other economic endeavors.

This chapter studies methods of judging the economic value of forestry investments. We shall start with a brief review of the concepts of investment and interest rate. These concepts will then be used to justify the objective of present value maximization. This will be followed by the study of practical criteria to evaluate and compare investments. We shall then examine how inflation should be handled in investment analysis. Finally we shall make some suggestions regarding the choice of appropriate interest rates for forestry investments.

16.2 INVESTMENT AND INTEREST RATE

In past chapters we have often suggested, without justifying it, that to judge the economic value of different courses of action, a forest manager should compare their net present value, that is, the discounted value of future benefits minus future costs. To understand why this is appropriate we need a broader view of the concepts of investment and interest rate.

To this end we shall use a model of a very simple economy, that of Robinson Crusoe. Wheat is his essential crop and we shall ignore the rest. Every year, Robinson must decide how much wheat to consume and how

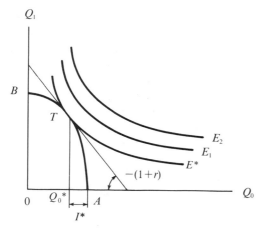

Figure 16.1 Optimum investment and interest rate.

much to set aside as seed. The amount of wheat he saves for planting is his investment. How much should he invest?

The factors that influence the decision of Robinson Crusoe are summarized in Fig. 16.1. The amount of wheat he consumes this year is denoted by Q_0, and Q_1 is the amount he will have next year.

Productivity of Investments

The amount of wheat that Robinson Crusoe invests depends in part on how much will grow from what he plants. In Fig. 16.1, this is represented by the curve AB, the *production possibility frontier* of Robinson Crusoe. Point A refers to zero investment: he consumes everything this year and has nothing the next. Point B is the case where he does not eat any bread this year and invests all his wheat in the future crop.

The curve AB is very steep close to A. This shows that the first pounds of seed saved and planted yield much future wheat per pound. However, the yield of each additional pound of seed decreases gradually as the quantity planted increases. Returns diminish because the resources of Robinson are limited. He can take great care of the first square feet he plants, but the more he plants, the more he loses to birds, drought, etc. Ultimately he reaches a point where he can barely recover the seed he plants. Of course, there is no reason for Robinson to invest that much. It is the high productivity of the first pounds planted, the fact that Robinson gets much more next year than what he sacrifices now, that incites him to set at least some of his wheat aside for planting.

Time Preference

Robinson Crusoe does not have all the wheat he wants. It is a great sacrifice for him to put aside some of his crop. Many a day he is tempted to give up part of the potential future harvest to make a good loaf of bread. A pound of wheat next year is worth less to him than a pound now. This time preference for wheat is represented in Fig. 16.1 by *indifference curves*. The indifference curve E_1, for example, represents a set of combinations of current and future wheat among which Robinson is indifferent. The curve is steeper as Q_0 decreases. This means that the less wheat Robinson has now, the more valuable it is to him, so that any more sacrifice in current consumption must be compensated by considerable increase in future consumption for Robinson to accept the trade. Note also that the farther up the indifference curve is from the origin, the higher the level of well-being along that curve. For example, along E_2 the amount of future consumption available is greater than along E_1, for any level of current consumption. Therefore, any point along E_2 is better than any one along E_1.

Optimum Investment

The best level of investment for Robinson Crusoe should allow him to reach the highest indifference curve, given his technique of production. Thus, the optimum investment is defined by the point where the production possibility frontier AB is just tangent to an indifference curve, E^*. This is the point T in Fig. 16.1. The optimum investment is I^*, to which the optimum current consumption Q_0^* corresponds.

Interest Rate

The slope of the tangent to AB and E^* at T defines the interest rate. Precisely, let r be the rate of interest expressed as a fraction per year, then:

$$\frac{dQ_1}{dQ_0} = -(1 + r) \tag{16.1}$$

where the derivative of Q_1 with respect to Q_0 is taken at T either along AB or along E^*. The equation simply means that at the optimum investment level, a one-unit decrease in current consumption for purpose of investment must be compensated by a $1 + r$ increase in future consumption. That is to say, the interest rate is the *trade-off rate* at which Robinson Crusoe is willing to exchange this year's consumption for next year's.

The simple economy we have used so far can be generalized to many time periods and many goods. The principles remain the same. At least part of what every economic system produces can be either consumed or saved. What is saved can in turn be invested in a process that will produce something in the future. Investment is thus a sacrifice in current consumption. The sacrifice is induced by the net productivity of investments: they promise to return more than what they cost. On the other hand, the amount invested is limited by the time preference of people, the fact that one unit of anything tomorrow is worth less than the same today. The rate at which current consumption is traded for future consumption at the optimum is the interest rate.

Present-Value Maximization

We are now ready to answer the question we posed at the beginning of this section. In making investment decisions, why should one maximize present value?

Let us again consider the economy symbolized by Fig. 16.1. Assume that we know the interest rate r. Then, the present value of consumption over the two time periods is, by definition:

$$PV(Q_0) = Q_0 + \frac{Q_1(Q_0)}{1 + r} \qquad (16.2)$$

The notations $PV(Q_0)$ and $Q_1(Q_0)$ mean that PV and Q_1 are functions of Q_0. Different Q_0's define different levels of investment. These in turn lead to different values of Q_1. In Fig. 16.1 the relationship between future and current consumption is represented by the production possibility frontier AB.

In order to maximize PV, Q_0 must be such that the first derivative of PV with respect to Q_0 is zero:

$$\frac{dPV(Q_0)}{dQ_0} = 0$$

that is, by differentiating the right-hand side of Eq. (16.2):

$$1 + \frac{dQ_1(Q_0)/dQ_0}{1 + r} = 0$$

or

$$\frac{dQ_1(Q_0)}{dQ_0} = -(1 + r) \qquad (16.3)$$

But, this is Eq. (16.1), which holds true at the level of consumption Q_0^*, to which corresponds the optimum investment I^*. Therefore, maximization of present value does lead to the best level of investment, within the assumptions of the model. Note, however, that the reasoning we have followed assumes that the "correct" interest rate r is known. It is difficult to choose an interest rate, but no more than any other price. We shall return to this problem shortly. Meanwhile, let us assume that we have proper *guiding rate of interest* to evaluate forestry investments.

We now turn to the study of practical criteria for investment analysis. In doing this we shall apply the principle we have just established: a good criterion should be consistent with present-value maximization.

16.3 INVESTMENT CRITERIA

Net Present Value

The net present value criterion simply applies Eq. (16.2) to a project that generates costs and benefits over many years. Let B_t be the economic benefits in year t and let C_t be the corresponding costs, both measured in dollars. In addition, let r be the guiding rate of interest (per year) and n be the duration of the project (in years). Then the present value of all costs is:

$$PV(\text{costs}) = \sum_{t=0}^{n} \frac{C_t}{(1 + r)^t}$$

while that of all benefits is:

$$PV(\text{benefits}) = \sum_{t=0}^{n} \frac{B_t}{(1 + r)^t}$$

The net present value of the project is then:

$$NPV = PV(\text{benefits}) - PV(\text{costs}) = \sum_{t=0}^{n} \frac{B_t}{(1 + r)^t} - \sum_{t=0}^{n} \frac{C_t}{(1 + r)^t} \tag{16.4}$$

or:

$$NPV = \sum_{t=0}^{n} \frac{B_t - C_t}{(1 + r)^t} \tag{16.5}$$

The criterion is extremely simple to apply. Any project with a positive net present value is worth doing.

An example of calculation is given in Table 16.1. The example deals with a reforestation project for a tract of land of 100 acres planted to ponderosa pine. Costs are incurred to plant the land and subsequently for precommercial thinning, commercial thinning, and final harvest. Benefits due to thinnings occur at age 30, 50, and 65 years. The main benefit comes from a final harvest expected at age 65. The total discounted value of costs at 3 percent is $2101, while that of benefits is $3724. Therefore, the net present value of this project is $3724 − $2101 = $1623.

TABLE 16.1 BENEFITS AND COSTS FOR A PONDEROSA-PINE REFORESTATION PROJECT

Operation	Year	$(1.03)^{year}$	Cost ($) Current	Cost ($) Discounted	Benefit ($) Current	Benefit ($) Discounted
Planting	0	1	1,460	1,460		
Precommercial thinning	10	1.344	610	454		
Thinning	30	2.427	200	82	2,270	935
Thinning	50	4.384	200	46	2,280	520
Final harvest	65	6.830	400	59	15,500	2,269
Total				2,101		3,724

Benefit-Cost Ratio

The benefit-cost ratio of a project is the present value of the benefits expected throughout the life of the project, divided by the present value of the costs. With the definitions used above this is:

$$BC = \frac{\sum\limits_{t=0}^{n} B_t/(1+r)^t}{\sum\limits_{t=0}^{n} C_t/(1+r)^t}$$

For example, the benefit-cost ratio of the ponderosa pine reforestation project described in Table 16.1 is $3724/2101 = 1.77$.

A project that has a benefit-cost ratio of unity has a net present value equal to 0. To see this, set $BC = 1$ in Eq. (16.6). This leads to:

$$\sum_{t=0}^{n} \frac{B_t}{(1+r)^t} = \sum_{t=0}^{n} \frac{C_t}{(1+r)^t}$$

and, from Eq. (16.4), $NPV = 0$.

Similarly, a project that has a benefit-cost ratio greater than unity has a positive net present value. One with a benefit-cost ratio less than unity has a negative net present value.

We know already that only projects of positive NPV are worth doing, thus a project evaluated with the benefit-cost ratio criterion should be accepted only if its benefit-cost ratio is greater than one.

Internal Rate of Return

The internal rate of return of a project is the interest rate such that the net present value of the project is equal to zero.

Given the definition of net present value (16.5), the internal rate of return is the interest rate that solves the equation:

$$\sum_{t=0}^{n} \frac{B_t - C_t}{(1+r)^t} = 0 \tag{16.6}$$

This equation shows that the internal rate of return is the interest rate for which the present value of returns just balances the present value of costs.

Let $r*$ be the internal rate of return, that is, the particular value of r that solves Eq. (16.6). Unfortunately, Eq. (16.6) is a polynomial equation of degree n in r, thus it may have up to n roots. Therefore, the definition of the internal rate of return is ambiguous. But this is not crucial in most practical applications because the root we are seeking is an interest rate, that is, a number usually between 0 and 1. In that interval, the net present value of most projects decreases regularly as the interest rate increases.

An example of this is shown in Fig. 16.2. The figure was drawn using Eq. (16.5) with the cost and benefit data in Table 16.1. Therefore, the equation

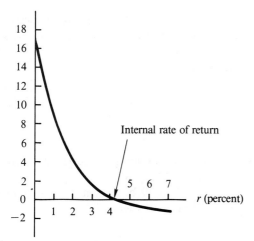

Figure 16.2   Graphic determination of internal rate of return.

was:

$$NPV(r) = -1460 - \frac{610}{(1+r)^{10}} + \frac{2070}{(1+r)^{30}} + \frac{2080}{(1+r)^{50}} + \frac{15,100}{(1+r)^{65}}$$

Figure 16.2 shows that the net present value declines regularly as the interest rate increases. The internal rate of return is about 4 percent per year, since at that rate the net present value is zero. Figure 16.2 suggests a simple graphic method of determining the internal rate: Draw the graph of the function $NPV(r)$ for a few values of r. The point where the graph intersects the horizontal axis is the internal rate of return. We will show in Sec. 16.7 how this idea can be applied simply in a computer program.

Another use of Fig. 16.2 is to derive the investment decision rule for the internal rate of return. The figure shows that the net present value of a project at a rate of interest smaller than the internal rate of return is positive. Conversely, the net present value at a rate of interest greater than the internal rate of return is negative.

Consequently, the rule is: accept a project if its internal rate of return is greater than the guiding rate of interest. In that case, the net present value of the project is positive.

Shortcomings of Benefit-Cost Ratio and Internal Rate of Return

The conclusion of the previous section is that net present value, benefit-cost ratio, and internal rate of return all discriminate correctly projects that contribute to present value from those that do not. For that purpose, it does not matter which criterion we choose.

However, projects that have a positive net present value cannot always be done. Limited resources usually force a choice among projects that could, if implemented, increase present value. In that case, ranking projects according to their benefit-cost ratio or internal rate of return may lead to the wrong decision.

Benefit-Cost Ratio   To illustrate how the largest benefit-cost ratio may fail to maximize present value, let us consider two projects, a and b. Only one of the two projects can be done. Let BC_i be the benefit-cost ratio, PVB_i the present value of benefits, PVC_i the present value of costs, and let NPV_i be the net present value of project i $(i = a, b)$. Assume the following data for the two projects:

Benefits: $PVB_a = \$150,000$ $PVB_b = \$250,000$
Costs: $PVC_a = \$50,000$ $PVC_b = \$100,000$

Thus, the benefit-cost ratios are:

$$BC_a = \frac{PVB_a}{PVC_a} = 3 \quad \text{and} \quad BC_b = \frac{PVB_b}{PVC_b} = 2.5$$

while the net present values are:

$$NPV_a = PVB_a - PVC_a = \$100,000$$

and

$$NPV_b = PVB_b - PVC_b = \$150,000$$

Choosing the project with the largest benefit-cost ratio criterion would lead to choosing project a. But this would be wrong because project b has in fact a higher net present value.

Internal Rate of Return   The largest internal rate of return may also select a project that does not maximize present value. Figure 16.3 illustrates how this may happen. The figure shows the graphs of the net present value of two projects, $NPV_a(r)$ and $NPV_b(r)$, as a function of the interest rate, r. The

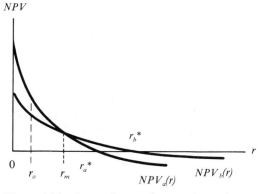

NPV

Figure 16.3   Internal rate of return inconsistent with net present value.

graphs cross at the interest rate r_m. By definition, the internal rate of return of project a is r_a^*, that of project b is r_b^*. Since r_b^* is greater than r_a^*, selecting the project with the largest internal rate of return leads to reject project a.

Assume, however, that the proper guiding rate of interest is r_0. Then, at that rate, the net present value of project a is greater than that of b, and project a should be selected.

Figure 16.3 shows that the internal rate of return criterion leads to the wrong decision when the guiding rate of interest is less than r_m, the rate at which the graphs of net present value cross. If the guiding rate is greater than r_m or if the graphs never cross, then the internal rate of return leads to a choice that is consistent with net present value.

In summary, projects with the highest benefit cost ratio or internal rate of return do not necessarily have the highest present value. But this does not mean that benefit-cost ratios and internal rates of return are useless. First, as seen earlier, they correctly separate projects that are economical from those that are not. Second, they provide information that complements net present value. In particular, people are familiar with the concept of rates of return. For example, the statement that a eucalyptus plantation has a rate of return of 5 percent per year has more meaning to most people than the fact that its net present value is $350 per acre.

16.4 CHOICE OF PROJECTS UNDER CONSTRAINTS

The previous section showed a sure way of choosing between two projects: select the one with highest net present value. The problem is more difficult if there are many projects to choose from and many that can be done. Still, this is a situation that foresters face regularly. For example, in any given year, several tracts of land may be suitable for reforestation but, due to a limited stock of seedlings or to a limited budget, or both, only a few of the tracts can be planted.

Projects Limited by One Resource

If a single resource limits the number of projects, then a simple method can be used to select those that maximize total net present value. Let R_m be the amount of the constraining resource, say the number of seedlings in stock. Let R_i be the amount of that resource needed for project i ($i = 1, \ldots, n$ where n is the number of projects). In our example R_i would be the number of seedlings necessary to plant the ith tract. Finally, let NPV_i be the net present value of project i if it is all done. In our example, this would be the present value of the expected returns from the ith tract of land, minus all the costs that will be incurred up to the final harvest. Then, define the *net present value-resource ratio* for project i, NPR_i, as:

$$NPR_i = \frac{NPV_i}{R_i}$$

In our example, NPR_i would be the net present value per seedling. There is a simple way to determine the subset of projects that maximizes total net present value, given the resource limit R_m. It consists in ranking all projects in decreasing order of their net present value-resource ratio and going down the list until the resource is exhausted. This procedure is a steepest-ascent algorithm (like the one used in the simplex method in Chap. 3). Each additional unit of resource is used in the project where it increases net present value the most.

This method works regardless of the resource involved, whether it is money, land, hours of labor, seedlings, etc. Suppose, to pursue the previous example, that the limiting resource is not the stock of seedlings but the budget for reforestation in the current year. Then, NPR_i would be the ratio of net present value to the money needed this year to reforest tract i. Note, however, that NPR_i is not the benefit-cost ratio since the denominator is this year's cost only, not the present value of the costs over the life of the project.

One limitation of this simple method is that it works perfectly only if projects are divisible, that is, if it is possible to do only part of a project. We shall examine below the case of indivisible projects.

Projects Limited by Many Resources

If the number of projects that can be done is limited by more than one resource, then a more general linear-programming model must be used. The purpose of the model is to find the set of projects that maximizes total net present value without exceeding the resources available.

Let X_i be a decision variable that indicates to what extent project i should be done. There are n projects in total; thus, $i = 1, \ldots, n$. Assume again that projects are divisible; thus, X_i is a continuous variable of value between zero and 1. Project i is all done if X_i is equal to 1, not done at all if $X_i = 0$, and partly done otherwise.

Let R_k be the amount of resource k available to do the projects. There are m such resources; thus $k = 1, \ldots, m$. Furthermore, let $R_{i,k}$ be the amount of resource k needed to complete project i.

Finally, let NPV_i be the net present value of project i if it is completed. We shall assume that the net present value of a project is directly proportional to its level of completion. Thus, the net present value of project i is: $X_i NPV_i$. Consequently, the expression of the objective function, the total net present value of all projects is:

$$\max_{X_i} Z = \sum_{i=1}^{n} X_i NPV_i \tag{16.7}$$

while the constraints are:

$$\sum_{i=1}^{n} X_i R_{i,k} \le R_k \qquad k = 1, \ldots, m \tag{16.8}$$

where the left-hand side of each constraint expresses the use of resource k by all projects. Thus, each constraint states that the total amount of resource used cannot exceed what is available.

The optimum solution $X_1^*, X_2^*, \ldots, X_n^*$ shows how much of each project should be done to maximize total net present value.

Indivisible Projects

The methods discussed so far should suffice for most cases of project selection in forestry. However, there may be a few situations where projects are not divisible. That is, projects must be done completely or not at all. In that case, the linear program of Eqs. (16.7) and (16.8) may have to be changed into an integer-programming program. This can be done by changing the variables X_i to integer variables that take the value 1 if project i is selected, 0 otherwise.

Forcing a variable to take only integer values is an option on some computer programs. Otherwise, rounding the solution of an ordinary linear program should give results that are close to the optimum if a large number of projects is being considered. The same is true of the ranking method that uses the net present value-resource ratio.

16.5 INFLATION AND INVESTMENT ANALYSIS

Up to now, we have assumed that the net present value of a forestry investment could be computed without ambiguity once appropriate prices and interest rates were known. However, the fact that prices change over time causes some difficulties. This is especially troublesome for forestry investments that take many years to mature.

Nominal and Real Price Changes

In calculating price changes over a specific time interval $[0, t]$ one must distinguish nominal from real changes. *Nominal price* changes are just changes of observed market prices. *Real price* changes refer instead to the change in the price of a commodity relative to the price of other goods and services.

To define real prices, we need an indicator of the general price level. In the United States, the producer price index can be used to that effect for an intermediate good, such as timber. The consumer price index would be preferred to calculate the real price of a consumer good, such as forest recreation.

Let I_0 and I_t be the level of the producer price index in years 0 and t, respectively. Let P_0 and P_t be the nominal prices of the good of interest, say softwood lumber. Finally, let P_t' be the real price of softwood lumber at time t. Then:

$$\frac{P_t'}{P_0} = \frac{P_t/P_0}{I_t/I_0} \tag{16.9}$$

That is, the real price change is equal to the nominal price change divided by the change in the general price level. Consequently, if there is no inflation or deflation, so that $I_t = I_0$, the real and the nominal price change are equal.

If there is inflation, $I_t > I_0$, and the real price change is less than the nominal change. If there is deflation, the reverse is true. In the remainder of this section we will talk about inflation only, but it should be clear that deflation has just the opposite effect of inflation.

EXAMPLE ■

Let us determine the real change of the price of softwood lumber between 1947 and 1979. Statistics of the U.S. Department of Labor show that the nominal producer price index for softwood lumber was 72.5 in 1947 and 380 in 1979. The producer price index for all commodities was 76.5 in 1947 and 235.6 in 1979.

$$\text{Nominal price change of softwood lumber:} \quad \frac{P_{79}}{P_{47}} = \frac{380}{72.5} = 5.24$$

$$\text{Change in general price level:} \quad \frac{I_{79}}{I_{47}} = \frac{235.6}{76.5} = 3.08$$

Thus, over those years, softwood lumber has become more costly relative to all goods represented by the producer price index. Precisely, the real price of softwood lumber has increased by:

$$\frac{P'_{79}}{P_{47}} = \frac{5.24}{3.08} = 1.70$$

that is, 170 percent.   ■ ■

Rates of Price Change

Price changes are often expressed in rates per unit of time, say in percent per year, like interest rates. Let f be the rate of inflation, expressed as a fraction per year. Then, using the index I_t as the measure of inflation, the average value of f over the interval $[0, t]$ follows the well-known interest formula:

$$I_t = I_0(1 + f)^t$$

Similarly, let G be the yearly rate of change of the nominal price of lumber. G is defined by the relationship:

$$P_t = P_0(1 + G)^t$$

Finally, let g be the real rate of price change for lumber. Then, g is defined by:

$$P'_t = P_0(1 + g)^t$$

Replacing I_t, P_t, and P_t' by their new expressions in Eq. (16.9) leads to the following relationship between rates of change:

$$(1 + g)^t = \frac{(1 + G)^t}{(1 + f)^t}$$

or

$$g = \frac{1 + G}{1 + f} - 1 \tag{16.10}$$

Equation (16.10) may be simplified if the rates of real price change and the rate of inflation, g and f, are "small," say under 10 percent. This can be seen by multiplying both sides of equation (16.10) by $1 + f$, leading to:

$$g + gf = G - f$$

If g and f are small, the product gf can be neglected, giving the approximate formula:

$$g \simeq G - f$$

EXAMPLE ■

Using the data of the previous example, the annual rate of change of the nominal price of softwood lumber between 1947 and 1979, G, was:

$$\frac{P_{79}}{P_{47}} = 5.24 = (1 + G)^{32}$$

that is, by taking the logarithms:

$$\ln(1 + G) = \frac{\ln 5.24}{32}$$

and since, when G is small, $\ln(1 + G) \simeq G$ we get:

$G \simeq 0.052$ per year

Similar calculations using the fact that $I_{79}/I_{47} = 3.08$ show that the rate of inflation f was:

$f \simeq 0.035$ per year

so that the real rate of price increases of lumber was:

$g \simeq G - f = 0.017$ per year

Equation 16.10 gives the real rate of change of any price in terms of the nominal rate and of the rate of inflation. The same formula can also be used to obtain the real rate of interest, namely:

$$r = \frac{1 + R}{1 + f} - 1 \tag{16.11}$$

where r and R are, respectively, the real and nominal rate of interest during a period with an average rate of inflation of f. If r and f are "small," the relationship is, approximately:

$r \simeq R - f$ ■■

Investment Criteria in Nominal and Real Terms

We are now ready to show that forestry investments may be evaluated indifferently at nominal or real prices and interest rate. The results will be the same using either system, as long as we are consistent. That is, if nominal prices are used, then a nominal interest rate must also be used, while a real interest rate is necessary if project evaluation is done with real prices.

To illustrate why this is so, let's consider a precommercial thinning that is expected to increase the volume of timber produced by a stand by the amount Q_t in t years. The cost of the operation is C. Let the expected nominal price of timber in year t be P_t. The nominal net present value of this project, given a nominal rate of interest R, is:

$$NPV = \frac{Q_t P_t}{(1 + R)^t} - C$$

Note that the nominal rate of interest R is used in discounting. This is consistent with the nominal price P_t. Let G be the expected rate of change of the nominal price of timber during the period of the project, and let f be the expected rate of inflation. Then:

$$NPV = \frac{Q_t P_0 (1 + G)^t}{(1 + R)^t} - C$$

or, by applying Eqs. (16.10) and (16.11):

$$NPV = \frac{Q_t P_0 (1 + g)^t (1 + f)^t}{(1 + r)^t (1 + f)^t} - C$$

$$= \frac{Q_t P_0 (1 + g)^t}{(1 + r)^t} - C$$

but, because $P_0 (1 + g)^t$ is the real timber price in year t and r is the real rate of interest, NPV is also the real net present value of the project.

This result is general, net present value calculated in real or nominal terms are the same, as long as consistent prices and interest rates are used. Similarly, benefit-cost ratios are the same in real or nominal terms. Finally, the internal rate of return applied correctly will give the same decision whether real or nominal prices are used. But again, the guiding rate of interest must be consistent with the price system used.

Thus, if the internal rate of return of a project is computed at nominal prices, then the project should be accepted if the nominal guiding rate is greater than the internal rate of return. On the other hand, if the internal rate of return is computed from real prices, then the guiding rate of interest must also be expressed in real terms, using Eq. (16.11), before comparing it to the internal rate of return.

16.6 CHOICE OF THE INTEREST RATE

Should the Interest Rate be Zero?

Choosing an appropriate interest rate to evaluate forestry investments is difficult, but probably no more than choosing any other price. The market can serve as a guide, especially for private firms, but still considerable judgment and guesswork is needed. Before suggesting practical ways of choosing interest rates, it is worth noting that—whether projects are public or private, and the forester's love of big trees notwithstanding—it is difficult to argue for a zero interest rate. To see this, let us return to Fig. 16.1 and to Eq. (16.1) which defines the interest rate:

$$\frac{dQ_1}{dQ_0} = -(1 + r) \tag{16.1}$$

A zero interest rate would imply $dQ_1/dQ_0 = -1$. Since dQ_1/dQ_0 is the first derivative along the production possibility frontier AB, this implies that the productivity of investments is zero. Every opportunity to invest and thereby reap more in the future than what is sacrificed now has been exhausted. Furthermore, since dQ_1/dQ_0 is also the first derivative along the indifference curve E^*, the time preference is zero; people are totally indifferent between current and future consumption. A situation where both a zero productivity of investment and a zero time preference occur simultaneously is difficult to imagine.

Private Investments

For a private firm, the interest rate is to a large extent determined by the market for capital. If the money needed for a project is borrowed, the guiding rate of interest should be at least equal to the rate charged by the lender. But it may be higher, depending on the other investment opportunities of the firm.

If, instead, all the money needed comes from profits, then the guiding rate of interest is defined by the best investment opportunity open to the firm. A great deal of judgment must be used, however, since investments may differ widely in terms of timing and risk. For long-term forestry investments, like buying forest land or starting new plantations, it is the rate of return of alternative investments over long time periods that matter. For a few investments it is possible to calculate such rates from published statistics.

For example, Table 16.2 shows the rates of return on Aaa corporate bonds over the period 1958 to 1984. The second column shows nominal rates, R, while the third shows the yearly rates of change of the consumer price index, f. The real rate of return for every year was computed by applying Eq. (16.11). The results show that the average real rate of return over that period was 2.5 percent per year. This is probably less than most people would expect, which shows the importance of adjusting for inflation. Many forestry projects are capable of yielding higher real rates of return than 2.5 percent per year.

TABLE 16.2 NOMINAL AND REAL RATES OF RETURN ON Aaa CORPORATE BONDS

Year	Nominal Aaa returns	Changes in CPI	Real Aaa returns
1958	3.8	1.8	2.0
1959	4.4	1.5	2.9
1960	4.4	1.5	2.9
1961	4.4	1.0	3.4
1962	4.3	1.1	3.2
1963	4.3	1.2	3.1
1964	4.4	1.3	3.1
1965	4.5	1.7	2.8
1966	5.1	2.9	2.1
1967	5.5	2.9	2.5
1968	6.2	4.2	1.9
1969	7.0	5.4	1.5
1970	8.0	5.9	2.0
1971	7.4	4.3	3.0
1972	7.2	3.3	3.8
1973	7.4	6.2	1.1
1974	8.6	11.0	−2.6
1975	8.8	9.1	−0.3
1976	8.4	5.8	2.5
1977	8.0	6.5	1.4
1978	8.7	7.7	0.9
1979	9.6	11.3	−1.5
1980	11.9	13.5	−1.4
1981	16.2	10.4	3.4
1982	13.8	6.1	7.3
1983	12.0	3.2	8.5
1984	12.7	4.3	8.0
Average			2.5

Source: Economic Report of the President, 1985, U.S. Government Printing Office, Washington D.C. 356 pp.

Often, investments are financed with funds from a variety of sources. The interest rates used in evaluating investments should reflect this. For example, if a corporation plans to buy forest land by borrowing part of the money and financing the rest from profits, then the rate of interest should be a weighted average of the rates appropriate for the two sources of funds, that is,

$$r = r_b B + (1 - B)r_p$$

where:
r is the proper guiding rate of interest
r_b is the interest rate on borrowed funds
r_p is the rate of return on the best possible use of profits
B is the fraction of funds that are borrowed

Public Projects

In the public sector, such as on lands administered by the U.S. Forest Service and the Bureau of Land Management, one possibility is to use the rate of return on government bonds, r_g, as the guiding rate of interest. Proponents of this argue that if projects do not return at least that much, then the country would be better off if the government repaid the national debt, since this would be equivalent to a public investment returning the rate r_g.

The rates of return of U.S. treasury securities, with maturities of 3 to 10 years, do not differ much from the returns on Aaa corporate bonds listed in Table 16.2, that is around 2.5 percent in real terms. This is due to the fact that the risk of these investments are very similar. Therefore, to raise money, the government must pay a return on its bonds that is comparable to the rate earned in the private sector for secure investments.

Nevertheless, the rate of return on government bonds should be viewed probably as a lower bound on the interest rate applicable to public investments. This is because many people cannot afford to buy such bonds. For a large group of people, current needs are such that they are not willing to trade current consumption for future consumption at the rate r_g (see Sec. 16.2). The guiding rate of interest appropriate for people who cannot buy bonds is not easy to determine. However, the fact that they are many suggests that the rate of discount used to evaluate forestry investments on public lands should be higher than 2.5 percent, perhaps 3 to 4 percent in real terms.

16.7 A COMPUTER PROGRAM FOR INVESTMENT ANALYSIS

The computations needed to calculate the net present value of a project, its benefit-cost ratio and its internal rate of return are simple but tedious. For that reason, computer programs are useful for doing the computations quickly and easily. Although it does not have all of the features of commercial packages, the particular program presented below illustrates how principles and formulas derived in this chapter are applied in such programs.

Computer Code

The computer code of the program is listed in Fig. 16.4; the definitions of the variables are given in Table 16.3. The program is called Invest. The program is interactive, that is, it asks data from the user and the user responds by typing in the data.

The main program calls four subroutines, one to read the data and the other three to calculate the investment criteria. After each criterion has been computed, the main program prints the results.

The subroutine ReadData begins with an INPUT statement that asks the user to type in the guiding rate of interest. It then proceeds with a WHILE

```
'--------------------------------------------
'                    Invest
'--------------------------------------------
'  Calculates net present value, benefit-cost
'  ratio and internal rate of return of project
'--------------------------------------------

main:
   GOSUB readData
       PRINT USING"Guiding rate of interest**.***";rate
   GOSUB netPresentValue
       PRINT USING"  Net present value *****.";npv
   GOSUB bcRatio
       PRINT USING"  Benefit-cost ratio **.** ";bc
   GOSUB rateOfReturn
       PRINT USING"  Internal rate of return **.***";rateReturn
END


'--------------------------------------------
'  read benefits, costs and year they occur
'  input ends by entering a negative year
'--------------------------------------------

readData:
   INPUT"Guiding rate of interest"; rate
   year=0
   nterms=0
   WHILE year >=0
       INPUT "year";year
       IF year>=0 THEN GOSUB benefcost
   WEND
RETURN
```

Figure 16.4 Computer code of program Invest.

loop that prompts the user to type the year when a benefit or a cost occurs. The loop terminates when the user types a negative year. The actual benefits and costs are read by the subroutine BenefCost. This subroutine also counts the number of entries of benefits and costs and the year of the current entry.

The subroutine NetPresentValue applies Eq. (16.4) to calculate the present net worth of the project. Present value of costs and benefits are first initiated to zero. Then, for each entry of costs and benefits, the discount factor is computed. The subroutine then calculates the cumulative present value of benefits and costs. After the last entry, the subroutine calculates the net present value.

The subroutine BenefitCost uses the results of subroutine NetPresentValue to calculate the benefit-cost ratio of the project according to Eq. (16.6).

The subroutine RateOfReturn uses the principle illustrated in Fig. 16.2 to calculate the internal rate of return of a project. That is, it finds the intersection of the graph of the function $NPV(r)$ with the horizontal axis. This

```
'---------------------------------------------
'   save net returns and year they occur
'---------------------------------------------
benefCost:
  nterms=nterms+1
  INPUT "   benefit";benefit(nterms)
  INPUT"   cost";cost(nterms)
  power(nterms)=year
RETURN


'---------------------------------------------
'   compute net present value
'---------------------------------------------
netPresentValue:
  pvBenefit=0
  pvCost=0
  FOR iterm=1 TO nterms
    year=power(iterm)
    discount=(1+rate)^year
    pvCost=pvCost+cost(iterm)/discount
    pvBenefit=pvBenefit+benefit(iterm)/discount
  NEXT iterm
  npv=pvBenefit-pvCost
RETURN


'---------------------------------------------
'   compute benefit-cost ratio
'---------------------------------------------
bcRatio:
  bc=pvBenefit/pvCost
RETURN


'---------------------------------------------
'   compute internal rate of return
'---------------------------------------------
rateOfReturn:
  rate=0
  rateChange=.001
  GOSUB netPresentValue
  WHILE npv>0
    rate=rate+rateChange
    GOSUB netPresentValue
  WEND
    rateReturn=rate-rateChange/2
RETURN
```

Figure 16.4   Continued.

TABLE 16.3 DEFINITION OF VARIABLES IN PROGRAM INVEST

Variable	Definition
rate	Interest rate, per year
year	Year when a cost or a benefit occurs
nterms	Counter of cost and benefit entries
benefit(nterms)	Benefit of a particular entry ($)
cost(nterms)	Cost of a particular entry ($)
power(nterms)	Year of a particular entry
discount	Discount factor
npv	net present value ($)
bc	Benefit-cost ratio
rateChange	Interest-rate changes in search of internal rate of return
rateReturn	Internal rate of return

is done by initiating the interest rate at zero and calculating the corresponding net present value. Then, the WHILE loop increases the interest rate by a fixed step, here a tenth of a percent. The subroutine RateOfReturn then calls the subroutine NetPresentValue to compute the net present value of the project at the new interest rate. The loop continues until the net present value is negative. At that point, the internal rate of return lies between the current

```
guiding rate of interest? 0.03
year? 0
    benefit? 0
    cost? 1460
year? 10
    benefit? 0
    cost? 610
year? 30
    benefit? 2270
    cost? 200
year? 50
    benefit? 2280
    cost? 200
year? 65
    benefit? 15500
    cost? 400
year? -1

Guiding rate of interest 0.030
    Net present value 1624.
    Benefit-cost ratio 1.77
Internal rate of return 0.042
```

Note: Bold characters indicate user's response to program prompts.

Figure 16.5 Interactive session with program Invest. Bold characters indicate user's response to program prompts.

interest rate and the last. The last statements of the subroutine compute a more precise estimate of the internal rate of return by subtracting half of the step increment from the last rate.

There are faster ways to compute the internal rate of return, but this one will do. It takes much longer to just enter the data than it takes the program to do the calculations.

Example of Interactive Session

Figure 16.5 shows an example of an interactive session with the program Invest. The particular project analyzed is the ponderosa-pine reforestation with the sequence of benefits and costs listed in Table 16.1. The first lines of Figure 16.5 show the requests of the program and the responses of the user. The last lines show the results of the computations: for a guiding rate of interest of 3 percent per year the net present value of the project is $1624 and the benefit-cost ratio is 1.77. The internal rate of return is 4.2 percent per year.

16.8 CONCLUSIONS

The basic criterion to evaluate forestry investments is net present value: The difference between the discounted value of returns and costs. Strictly speaking, benefit-cost ratio and internal rate of return lead to decisions that are consistent with net present value only when all projects under consideration can be done.

If only one resource is limiting and projects are divisible, projects can be ranked according to their net present value-resource ratio. Otherwise, the correct choice of projects may require solving a linear- or integer-programming problem.

Investments can be evaluated indifferently in real or nominal terms. However, the guiding rate of interest must be consistent with the price system used: it must be real if other prices are real, nominal otherwise.

The guiding rate of interest is determined for a private firm by its sources of financing and investment opportunities. For a public agency, the rate of return on government bonds can be viewed as a lower bound on the guiding rate of interest.

PROBLEMS

16.1. A Peace Corps forester in Central America must evaluate three short-rotation fuelwood projects. The costs and benefits associated with each project and the years in which they will occur are given below. Assuming a guiding rate of interest of 5 percent per year, what is the present value of the benefits for each project? The present value of the costs? The net present value?

On the basis of net present value, which of the projects should the forester undertake if the projects are independent and there is no capital constraint on the forester's activities? What if the projects are mutually exclusive? (Hint: Work out Probs. 16.1 to 16.3 by hand to make sure you understand the calculations, then check your answers using program Invest.)

	Project A			Project B			Project C	
Year	Benefit	Cost	Year	Benefit	Cost	Year	Benefit	Cost
0	$ 0	$45	0	$ 0	$100	0	$ 0	$41
5	0	20	7	15	30	4	5	15
9	25	10	10	35	15	8	20	5
15	150	25	15	240	45	15	110	10

16.2. Calculate benefit-cost ratios for the fuelwood projects described in the previous problem, still using a guiding rate of interest of 5 percent per year. On the basis of their benefit-cost ratios, which of the projects should the forester undertake if the projects are independent and there is no capital constraint? What if the projects are mutually exclusive? Did you get the same answers as for the previous problem? Why?

16.3. Determine the internal rate of return for each project described in Prob. 16.1. (Calculate the net present value of each project for several interest rates between 3 and 8 percent per year and plot these data.) Still assuming that the guiding rate of return is 5 percent per year, which projects should the forester undertake on the basis of their internal rates of return if the projects are independent and there is no capital constraint on the Forester's activities? What if the projects are mutually exclusive? Did you get the same answers as in the previous two problems? Why?

16.4. A reforestation forester has five clear-cuts that need to be replanted, but has a limited number of seedlings to plant them with. Her company's silvicultural guidelines require that she replant the clearcuts to a density of 300 trees per acre. The area of each clear-cut is given below, along with an estimate of the net present value of the next rotation on each.

Compute the net present value–resource ratio for each clear-cut and rank them on the basis of this ratio. Given only 20,000 seedlings, which clearcuts should the forester replant this year? Given 5000 more seedlings, what additional clearcuts should she replant?

Clearcut	Area (acres)	Net Present Value
A	15	$1275
B	29	2117
C	22	2178
D	34	2346
E	12	1224

16.5. Assume that in addition to having only 20,000 seedlings, the forester described in the previous problem has a $1200 budget for planting labor, and that such labor costs $40 per work-day. Labor requirements to replant each clearcut are given below. (These requirements vary depending on a clearcut's size, slope, soil type, and degree of site preparation.)

Formulate a linear programming model for deciding which clearcuts should be replanted this year, subject to the limited labor, budget and number of seedlings available. How would you modify this model to constrain it to consider only all-or-nothing planting for each clearcut? Solve both formulations with a computer and compare the optimal solutions.

Clearcut	Planting Labor Requirements (days)
A	5
B	7
C	8
D	11
E	5

16.6. The nominal producer price index for softwood lumber was 380 in 1979, but fell to 321.6 by 1982 as the housing market collapsed. Over the same period, the producer price index for all commodities rose from 235.6 to 299.3.

What was the nominal annual percentage price change for softwood lumber from 1979 to 1982? The annual percentage change in the general price level? The real annual percentage price change for softwood lumber?

ANNOTATED REFERENCES

Buongiorno, J., and D. E. Teeguarden. 1973. An economic model for selecting Douglas-fir reforestation projects. *Hilgardia* 42(3):35–120. (Reviews investment criteria, applies linear programming, and net present value-resource ratio.)

Chambers, P. C., S. A. Sinclair, C. C. Hassler, and B. G. Hansen. 1986. Forest products investment model: A microcomputer tool for incorporating risk into capital budgeting. *Forest Products Journal* 36(1):64–68. (Applies the techniques of stochastic simulation studied in Chap. 15 to investment analysis.)

Clark, J. J., T. J. Hindeland, and R. E. Pritchard. 1984. *Capital budgeting*. Prentice-Hall, Englewood Cliffs. 562 pp. (A comprehensive treatment of investment analysis.)

Cubbage, F. W., and C. H. Redmont. 1985. Capital budgeting practices in the forest products industry. *Forest Products Journal* 35(9):55–60. (Survey of criteria used in industry and modes of setting interest rates.)

Fortson, J. C., and R. C. Field. 1979. Capital budgeting techniques for forestry: A review. *Southern Journal of Applied Forestry* 3(4):141–143. (Reviews the key steps in the analysis of forestry investments.)

Gregersen, H. M. 1975. Effect of inflation on evaluation of forestry investments. *Journal of Forestry* 73(9):570–572. (Discussion of proper use of real and nominal prices and interest rates in the analysis of forestry investments.)

Gregersen, H. M., and A. H. Contreras. 1979. Economic analysis of forestry projects. FAO Forestry Paper 17. Food and Agriculture Organization of the United Nations, Rome, 193 pp. (Practical guide to the evaluation of forestry investments in developing countries.)

Gunter, J. E., and H. L. Haney, Jr. 1984. *Essentials of forestry investment analysis*. OSU Bookstores, Corvallis. 337 pp. (A programmed learning guide to interest calculations, decision criteria, and the effects of taxation on forestry investments.)

Klemperer, W. D. 1976. Economic analysis applied to forestry: Does it short-change future generations? *Journal of Forestry* 74(9):609–611. (Presents a justification for discounting in the analysis of forestry investments.)

Leuschner, W. A. 1984. *Introduction to forest resource management*. Wiley, New York. 298 pp. (Part I on forest valuation contains an extensive treatment of interest calculations, decision criteria, capital budgeting, and the effects of taxation on forestry investments.)

Mills, T. J., and G. E. Dixon. 1982. Ranking independent timber investments by alternative investment criteria. U.S. Forest Service Research Paper PSW-166. Pacific Southwest Forest and Range Experiment Station, Berkeley. 8 pp. (Ranking a large number of projects according to their net present value per acre, benefit-cost ratio, or internal rate of return led to similar results.)

Row, C., H. F. Kaiser and J. Sessions. 1981. Discount rate for long-term Forest Service investments. *Journal of Forestry* 79(6):367–369, 376. (Discussion of the appropriate guiding rate of interest for public forestry investments.)

Teeguarden, D. E., and H. L. Von Sperber. 1968. Scheduling Douglas-fir reforestation investments: A comparison of methods. *Forest Science* 14(4):354–367. (Compares capital budgeting, linear programming, and rules of thumb.)

Tufts, R. A., and W. L. Mills. 1982. Financial analysis of equipment replacement. *Forest Products Journal* 32(10):45–52. (A detailed application of investment analysis.)

Williams, M. R. W. 1981. *Decision making in forest management*. Wiley, New York. 143 pp. (Concise treatment of investment analysis for a wide variety of forestry activities.)

Chapter 17

Forecasting the Demand and Price of Wood

17.1 INTRODUCTION

All the models we have studied so far make bold assumptions regarding the context in which the forest operates. For example, we often made assumptions on the future price of the commodities or services produced by the forest. These assumptions are critical; changing them may alter considerably the way the forest should be managed.

Unfortunately, we still do not know how to make accurate economic forecasts, but some progress is being made. Several econometric models have been developed to analyze and predict the markets for forest products. Since these markets influence many forestry activities, forest managers should be aware of these models and understand how they are built. It is important that they appreciate the potential of econometric models, and their limitations.

The purpose of this chapter is to provide a brief introduction to econometric analysis and forecasting. We shall do this mostly with an example, a simple model of the pulpwood market in Wisconsin.

17.2 ECONOMETRICS

An econometric model is a set of equations to provide a quantitative explanation of the changes in economic variables. Econometrics combines economic theory and statistics. The theory suggests the form of the equations relating the variables of interest, while statistics provide the means to estimate the parameters of the equations.

The weakness of existing econometric models is due in part to the limitations of economic theory (we do not know how the economy really works), to limitations of the statistical methods used and to weak data. Economic data are typically poorly defined, inaccurate, or altogether nonexistent.

Nevertheless, econometric modeling of forest product markets is progressing quickly. Rigorous empiricism is one of the best ways to analyze and forecast forestry markets, in part because a formal model is clear: it shows explicitly all the assumptions that have been made. Clarity eases understanding and progress.

17.3 A MODEL OF THE WISCONSIN PULPWOOD MARKET

To avoid too much abstraction we shall use throughout this chapter the case of the market for aspen pulpwood in Wisconsin. The model is a simplified version of a model proposed originally by Leuschner (1973).

The model has two objectives: First, to understand the forces that determine the demand, supply, and price of pulpwood. Second, to forecast the demand for pulpwood and its price in the next 5 years. Forecasts of this kind would be valuable for Wisconsin pulpwood producers. The forecast of demand would help them determine whether they should expand or contract their operations. The forecast of price would help them predict their returns.

Structural Equations

The theoretical model consists of the following equations:

$$Demand: D_t = a + bK_t + u_t \tag{17.1}$$

$$Supply: S_t = c + dP_t + v_t \tag{17.2}$$

$$Equilibrium: D_t = S_t \tag{17.3}$$

where:

D_t is the quantity of pulpwood demanded in year t
P_t is the price of pulpwood
S_t is the quantity of pulpwood supplied
K_t is the capacity of pulpmills in Wisconsin
a, b, c, and d are unknown parameters
u_t and v_t are random disturbances

These *structural* equations describe our view of how various forces interact to determine the supply, demand, and the price of pulpwood. The form of the model may be shaped in part by economic theory, previous studies, and personal experience of the market.

The first equation is our hypothesis concerning the demand for pulpwood. It says that in a given year demand is a linear function of pulping capacity.

One expects demand to increase as capacity of production increases and, therefore, the coefficient b should be positive. Note that the equation suggests that demand for pulpwood is not influenced by price, presumably because the cost of pulpwood is minor compared to other costs when a plant does not run at full capacity. Thus, all the pulpwood necessary, given the mill capacity, is bought, no matter the cost. We shall not try to test whether price does in fact influence demand. Nevertheless, we shall check whether the data are consistent with the proposed hypothesis.

The second structural equation is a classical supply equation: Quantity supplied in a given year is a linear function of the price of pulpwood. As the price of pulpwood increases, one expects the supply to increase and, thus, the coefficient d to be positive. This hypothesis is consistent with pulpwood production in Wisconsin: there are many small independent producers, as in the classical model of supply in a perfectly competitive market.

These first two equations are stochastic. They hold only approximately. This is reflected by the disturbances u_t and v_t which are assumed to be small and random.

The third structural equation instead is an identity, supposed to hold exactly. It states that the quantity of pulpwood demanded within a year is equal to the quantity supplied. This identity allows us to simplify the model. Defining the quantity of pulpwood demanded and supplied as $Q_t = S_t = D_t$ leads to:

$$\text{Demand: } Q_t = a + bK_t + u_t \tag{17.4}$$

$$\text{Supply: } Q_t = c + dP_t + v_t \tag{17.5}$$

Types of Variables

The capacity of pulp production K_t is assumed to be determined by forces not explained within the model. In particular, the price and quantity of pulpwood do not influence capacity. Presumably, capacity is determined by the demand for paper and other factors, but this relationship is not clarified in our model. Capacity is an *exogenous* variable.

The other variables, Q_t and P_t, are determined jointly by the system of equations when the parameters, disturbances, and the exogenous variable K_t are given. They are called *endogenous* variables. That Q_t and P_t are determined jointly is illustrated in Fig. 17.1. For example, an increase in K_t, other things being equal, causes the vertical demand line to move to the right. Quantity increases and, simultaneously, the price increases.

Reduced Form

There is an algebraic analog to this graphic explanation of Q_t and P_t. The system of Eqs. (17.4) and (17.5) can be solved for the endogenous variables, Q_t and P_t, as a function of the exogenous variable, K_t, parameters, and dis-

Price

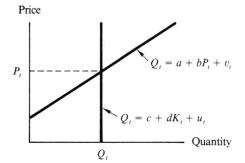

$Q_t = a + bP_t + v_t$

P_t

$Q_t = c + dK_t + u_t$

Quantity

Q_t

Figure 17.1 Demand and supply of pulpwood.

turbances. The two equations lead to:

$$c + dP_t + v_t = a + bK_t + u_t$$

that is:

$$P_t = \frac{a - c}{d} + \frac{b}{d}K_t + \frac{u_t - v_t}{d}$$

Therefore, the structural equations imply the following quantity and price equations:

$$\textit{Quantity: } Q_t = a + bK_t + u_t \tag{17.4}$$

$$\textit{Price: } P_t = e + gK_t + z_t \tag{17.6}$$

where $e = (a - c)/d$
  $g = b/d$
  $z_t = (u_t - v_t)/d$

Equations (17.4) and (17.6) are called the *reduced form* of the model. They show that both Q_t and P_t change simultaneously if K_t changes. Reduced-form equations can be used to predict future values of the endogenous variables Q_t and P_t. It is clear, however, that these forecasts will be inexact. There are three sources of error: (1) predictions of the exogenous variable K_t must be made; (2) the parameters of the reduced form equations must be estimated; (3) forecasts must be made of the disturbances u_t and v_t. It is generally assumed that the future value of the disturbances is equal to their expected value, zero, so that at best we obtain forecasts of the expected values of Q_t and P_t.

The reduced-form equations can also be used to recover the coefficients of the structural equations. Once a, b, e, and g have been estimated, then the supply equation is fully defined by:

$$d = \frac{b}{g} \quad \text{and} \quad c = a - de$$

We shall see below why it is necessary to estimate the supply equation in this indirect way.

17.4 DATA

To estimate the value of the coefficients in Eqs. (17.4) and (17.6) we need data on the variables Q_t, P_t, and K_t. Rarely do we have data that describe exactly the variables of interest. Most of the time, they are only very rough approximations; many sources must be reconciled and often bold assumptions must be made to arrive at some estimate of the desired variables. For the present model, we shall use the following data sources:

1. For the price of aspen pulpwood we shall use the data collected for many years by T. A. Peterson and published in the Wisconsin Forest Products Price Review.

TABLE 17.1   DATA ON THE WISCONSIN ASPEN PULPWOOD MARKET, 1947 TO 1981

t	Q_t	K_t	P_t	A_t
47	187	2796	12.25	0
48	167	2962	12.58	0
49	185	3107	11.25	0
50	195	3004	11.00	0
51	281	3574	14.88	0
52	275	3265	13.00	0
53	305	3618	13.25	0
54	348	3834	12.38	0
55	364	4046	12.50	0
56	507	3820	13.50	0
57	453	3909	12.75	0
58	369	3998	12.67	0
59	431	4152	12.88	0
60	540	4148	13.00	0
61	530	4173	12.88	0
62	572	4198	12.75	0
63	613	4294	13.75	0
67	739	4620	15.62	0
68	629	4725	16.25	0
69	697	4720	16.75	0
70	771	4710	17.12	0
71	736	4670	17.12	0
72	685	4670	17.25	0
73	761	4705	19.75	0
74	797	4760	26.75	1
76	693	4740	24.75	1
77	696	4795	25.25	1
78	669	5200	27.38	1
79	751	5160	29.88	1
80	873	5360	32.65	1
81	965	5300	34.00	1

Note: Q_t is the quantity of aspen pulpwood produced in Wisconsin in year t, in 1000 cords. K_t is the capacity of pulp mills in the state, in tons per day. P_t is the price of aspen pulpwood delivered to the mill, in dollars per cord. A_t is a dummy variable.

2. For the quantity of pulpwood supplied and demanded, we shall use data on the quantity of aspen pulpwood produced in Wisconsin. This quantity is a reasonable approximation of the variable sought because most of the aspen pulpwood produced is indeed used within the state. Production data are published by the U.S. Forest Service (e.g., Blyth and Smith, 1983).
3. For pulping capacity, we shall use the data on daily capacity published in the Lockwood directory of the pulp and paper industry. These data are also reproduced in Blyth and Smith (1983).

All the data used in this chapter are given in Table 17.1. They cover the period 1947 to 1981. Some of the data were not available for the years 1964 to 1966 and 1975. For simplicity, we have kept only the years for which all data were available.

17.5 THE LEAST-SQUARES METHOD

To get accurate forecasts of pulpwood price and quantity with the reduced-form Eqs. (17.4) and (17.6), we need accurate estimates of the parameters a, b, e, and g.

The most common way of estimating equations like (17.4) and (17.6) is the ordinary least-squares (OLS) method.

Consider the reduced-form quantity equation. The OLS method consists in estimating the coefficients a and b, in such a way that the sum of the squares of the residuals, SSR, be minimum. That is, given a series of n observations on the variables Q_t and K_t we compute:

$$\text{SSR} = \sum_{t=1}^{n} u_t^2 = \sum_{t=1}^{n} (Q_t - a - bK_t)^2$$

and determine the values of a and b that make SSR as small as possible. These calculations are performed routinely by computer programs that do regression analysis.

Subject to some assumptions, listed below, the estimates obtained by OLS are best-linear-unbiased estimates of the parameters being sought. This means that:

The expected values of the estimates are equal to the values of the parameters. That is, on average the estimates are equal to the true parameters.

Among all possible linear unbiased estimates of a and b, the OLS estimates have minimum variance. In a sense, then, OLS estimates are the most accurate that we can get.

But these properties of OLS estimates hold only under the following assumptions:

The expected value of the residuals is zero and their variance is constant.

The residuals are uncorrelated over time; in particular, u_t is independent of u_{t-1}.

The independent variable K_t is predetermined; in particular it is independent of u_t.

In addition, to make statistical tests the residuals must be normal. In that case, the ratio of each OLS coefficient to its standard error has Student's t distribution.

Part of the econometric work is to make sure that these assumptions hold. If they do not, the proposed model is incorrect and must be changed, or some other method of estimation is needed.

17.6 ESTIMATION RESULTS AND DIAGNOSTIC CHECKS

The results of estimation of the reduced-form equations by ordinary least-squares, using the data in Table 17.1 are:

For the quantity equation:

$$Q_t = -730 + 0.30K_t$$
$$\quad\quad (77) \quad (0.02)$$

$$R^2 = 0.90 \tag{17.7}$$

For the price equation:

$$P_t = -14.0 + 0.007K_t$$
$$\quad\quad (4.6) \quad (0.001)$$

$$R^2 = 0.62 \tag{17.8}$$

where R^2 is the coefficient of multiple correlation. It indicates how much of the variance of the dependent variable (Q_t in the quantity equation, P_t in the price equation) is explained by the independent variable K_t. Variations in capacity appear to account for 90 percent of the variance in quantity of pulpwood demanded, but only 60 percent of the variance in price.

The numbers in parentheses are the standard errors of the coefficients. The smaller the standard errors, the more accurate the coefficients.

Before trying to infer anything more precise from these statistics, we must check whether the residuals satisfy the OLS assumptions.

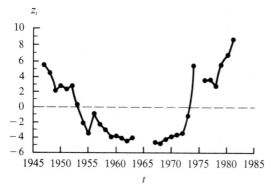

Figure 17.2   Time plot of residuals from the original price equation.

Are Errors Correlated?

One of the most pervasive problems of econometric analysis when time-series data are used is *autocorrelation*. Here, we shall deal only with first-order autocorrelation, the case where the residual in any year is not independent of its value in the previous year.

Autocorrelation can be detected by plotting the residuals in chronological order and watching for systematic patterns. For example, the estimated residuals for the price equation are the differences between the observed and predicted prices, that is:

$$z_t = P_t - (-14.0 + 0.007 K_t)$$ (17.9)

The plot of these residuals over time is shown in Fig. 17.2. The residuals are strongly correlated. From 1947 to 1953, all residuals are positive. From 1954 to 1973, all are negative. From 1974 to 1981, all residuals are positive again. Equation (17.9) clarifies the meaning of this autocorrelation. During the period 1947 to 1953, the estimated price equation underestimates systematically the true price. In the period 1954 to 1973, the equation overestimates the true price, and in the last period, it underestimates the true price again. Because these errors are systematic, the model is not a good approximation of the true price equation.

A similar plot for the quantity equation, not shown here, does not have that problem. The assumption that the residuals of the quantity equation are uncorrelated seems to hold.

Is the Variance of Errors Constant?

One of the assumptions of OLS is that the variance of the residuals is constant. This is sometimes violated by a tendency of the residuals to become larger in absolute value as the value of the variables increases. This phenomenon can be checked by plotting the residuals against the predicted value of the dependent variable. For example, for the quantity equation we plot u_t against $(-730 + 0.30K_t)$, the predicted value of Q_t.

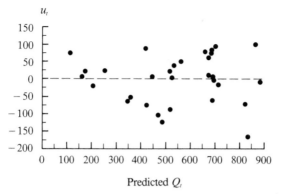

Figure 17.3 Plot of residuals against predictions from the original quantity equation.

Figure 17.3 shows this plot. The scatter of residuals tends to become wider as the quantity predicted increases. The plot for the price equation, not shown here, has a similar problem.

17.7 REVISED MODEL

The checks of the residuals suggest that the original model of the Wisconsin pulpwood market is wrong. The new model must solve the problems of autocorrelation and unequal variance. There is a simple, though not universal, solution to the latter problem. Express the equations as functions of the logarithms of the variables. This scaling changes greatly the range of the variables. For example, while Q_t varies from 167 in 1948 to 965 in 1981, $\ln Q_t$ varies only from 5.12 to 6.87. This, in turn, will reduce the changes in the variance of the residuals. Therefore, the new expression of the quantity equation is:

$$\ln Q_t = a + b \ln K_t + u_t \tag{17.10}$$

and the OLS estimate is:

$$\ln Q_t = -16.60 + 2.73 \ln K_t$$
$$(1.16)\quad\ \ (0.14)$$

$$R^2 = 0.93 \tag{17.11}$$

The plot of residuals against the predicted value of $\ln Q_t$ is shown in Fig. 17.4. The residuals seem to have constant variance. Thus, Eq. (17.11) is accepted as the final form of the quantity (and demand) equation.

The autocorrelation of the residuals in the price equation is not solved as easily. Many ways have been suggested to correct for autocorrelation. Here, we shall recognize the fact that autocorrelation is often due to omitted variables.

There may be other variables, besides capacity, that influence the price of pulpwood. Suppose that something occurs that increases considerably the cost of harvesting and transporting pulpwood, other things being equal. Then,

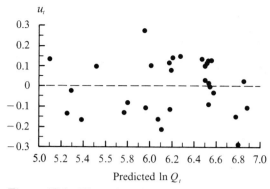

Figure 17.4 Time plot of residuals from the final quantity equation.

the supply equation in Fig. 17.1 would shift upward (remember that a supply curve reflects marginal costs or production). This would lead to an increase in price.

Now, between 1947 and 1981 an event did occur that increased considerably the cost of pulpwood procurement. This was the oil embargo of 1973 that was followed by strong increases in energy costs. We shall not investigate in detail what changes this led to in pulpwood production in Wisconsin, but only recognize the fact that changes are likely to have occurred. To recognize these possible changes we rewrite the supply equation as:

$$\ln Q_t = c + d \ln P_t + fA_t + v_t \qquad (17.12)$$

where A_t is a *dummy variable* that takes the value 0 up to 1973 and 1 thereafter. We expect the coefficient f to be negative, reflecting the fact that, other things being equal, Wisconsin loggers would have produced less after 1973 than before, at a given price. Dummy variables are very useful to reflect qualitative changes when variables are unavailable to measure those changes. Like K_t, A_t is exogenous, not explained within our model.

Substituting the demand equation (17.10) in this new supply equation leads to a new reduced-form price equation, namely:

$$\ln P_t = e + g \ln K_t + hA_t + z_t \qquad (17.13)$$

where $e = (a - c)/d$
 $g = b/d$
 $h = -f/d$
 $z_t = (u_t - v_t)/d$

Estimation of the reduced form with the data in Table 17.1 leads to:

$$\ln P_t = -3.45 + 0.74 \ln K_t + 0.54A_t$$
$$\quad\quad\;\; (1.04) \quad\;\; (0.13) \quad\;\; (0.05)$$
$$R^2 = 0.91 \qquad (17.14)$$

The plot of the residuals over time are shown in Fig. 17.5. The pattern, though not perfectly random, represents a big improvement over that in Fig. 17.2. We shall accept Eq. (17.14) as the final version of the price equation.

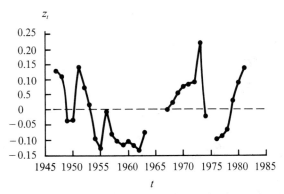

Figure 17.5 Plot of residuals against predictions from the final price equation.

17.8 INFERENCES, FORECASTING, AND STRUCTURAL ANALYSIS

Now that we have equations with residuals that satisfy the assumptions of OLS, we can (assuming that the residuals are distributed normally) make inferences from them, with a stated probability of being right.

Interpretation of Coefficients

First, we note that the coefficients of the variables expressed in logarithms are elasticities. For example, differentiating the demand equation (17.11) gives:

$$\frac{dQ_t}{Q_t} = \frac{2.73 dK_t}{K_t}$$

where dQ_t/Q_t and dK_t/K_t are the relative changes in quantity and capacity. The equation implies that a relative change of 1 percent in pulping capacity leads, on average, to an increase of 2.73 percent in the quantity of aspen pulpwood demanded by (and supplied to) Wisconsin mills. In other words, the elasticity of pulpwood demand with respect to capacity is 2.73.

Test of Hypothesis and Confidence Intervals

Equation 17.11 shows that the standard error of the elasticity of demand with respect to capacity is 0.14. The ratio of the coefficient to its standard error is $2.73/0.14 = 19.5$. This ratio has a t distribution. There is approximately a 5 percent chance that the elasticity be zero if its t ratio is 2. Since the actual t ratio is much larger, the chance that the elasticity be zero is indeed very small.

Viewed in another way, a 95 percent confidence interval for the elasticity of demand with respect to capacity is:

$$(2.73 - 2 \times 0.14, 2.73 + 2 \times 0.14) = (2.45, 3.01)$$

There is a 95 percent chance that the true elasticity lies in this interval.

Applying the same principles to the price equation (17.14), we observe that the elasticity of pulpwood price with respect to capacity is 0.74. Thus, other things being equal, an increase in capacity of 10 percent leads to an increase in pulpwood price of 7.4 percent. This elasticity is significantly different from zero at the 95 percent confidence level. The 95 percent confidence interval is:

$$(0.74 - 2 \times 0.13, 0.74 + 2 \times 0.13) = (0.48, 1.00)$$

The coefficient of A implies that, other things being equal, the price of pulpwood increased after 1973 by a factor of $\exp(0.54) = 1.7$. This change is statistically significant.

Forecasting

The American Paper Institute publishes annual forecasts of capacity of the pulp industry in different regions of the United States. This is essentially a compendium of the expansion plans of most pulp mills for the next 4 years. In particular, the Institute publishes forecasts of pulping capacity in the eastern North-Central region. Wisconsin is by far the largest producer in that region, so that it is fair to assume that the expected rate of growth of capacity for Wisconsin is similar to that of the region.

Given the estimates of the reduced-form equations (17.11) and (17.14), it is a simple matter to forecast the implications of the expected growth of capacity on pulpwood demand and price.

For example, let us assume that it is 1981 and that the American Paper Institute predicts a growth of pulping capacity in the eastern north-central region of 2.4 percent per year during the next 4 years. Applying this rate of growth to Wisconsin alone, the expected capacity in that state in 1985, K_{85}, would be:

$$K_{85} = K_{81}(1 + 0.024)^4$$

where K_{81}, the capacity in 1981 is 5300 tons per day, so that $K_{85} = 5827$ tons per day.

The forecast of the quantity of Wisconsin aspen pulpwood that will be demanded in 1985 is obtained by substituting K_{85} in equation (17.11):

$$\ln Q_{85} = -16.60 + 2.73 \ln K_{85} = 7.07$$

so that $Q_{85} = \exp(7.07) = 1176$ thousand cords.

Similarly, the forecast of the price of pulpwood in 1985, P_{85}, can be obtained from the reduced-form price equation (17.14):

$$\ln P_{85} = -3.45 + 0.74 \ln K_{85} + 0.54 A_{85}$$

where $K_{85} = 5827$ and $A_{85} = 1$, since 1985 is after 1973, leading to $P_{85} = \$33.31$ per cord, delivered to the mill.

It is clear that the quality of the forecast depends not only on the quality of the model but also on the accuracy of the forecasts of capacity. Because capacity plans may not be realized, one would usually compute several conditional forecasts of price and demand, for different values of future capacity.

Structural Analysis

The reduced-form equations do not show how Wisconsin loggers respond to changes in the price of pulpwood. To learn this, we must go back to the supply equation (17.12) in the revised structural model. In that equation, the coefficient d is the elasticity of Wisconsin pulpwood supply with respect to price. The value of this coefficient can be recovered from the reduced form, since $g = b/d$, and since $b = 2.73$ and $g = 0.74$, we get $d = 2.73/0.74 = 3.69$. This shows that the Wisconsin supply of aspen pulpwood is elastic with respect to price.

One can also recover the other coefficients of the supply equation from the reduced form since:

$$f = -hd = -1.99 \quad \text{and} \quad c = a - ed = -3.87$$

so that the estimate of the supply equation is:

$$\ln Q_t = -3.87 + 3.69 \ln P_t - 1.99 A_t$$

A keen reader may wonder why the supply equation was not estimated directly by OLS using Eq. (17.12). The reason is that in that equation, the price P_t is not independent of the residual, u_t. This is made clear by the reduced form (17.13). A change in u_t changes w_t, which changes $\ln P_t$. Thus, one of the assumptions of OLS is violated. Applying OLS to the reduced-form equations avoids that problem because the independent variables K_t and A_t are exogenous, thus, by definition, independent of the residuals in our model.

17.9 CONCLUSIONS

To make forecasts of the demand for and price of pulpwood in Wisconsin we developed a quantitative model of that market. We started with structural equations of demand and supply. From them we derived reduced-form equations that expressed quantity demanded and price as functions of exogenous variables. We then estimated these equations by ordinary least squares, using annual data. Next, we checked if the residuals of each equation satisfied the OLS assumptions. If they did not, we revised the structural equations to arrive at a more plausible model. The final reduced-form equations were used to make conditional forecasts of price and demand, given published forecasts of the exogenous variables. The accuracy of the forecasts we got depended on the quality of the model developed and on the accuracy of the forecasts of the exogenous variables.

There are many ways of building models of markets for forest products. They do not necessarily rely exclusively on econometrics. For example, useful models have been constructed that use econometrics to represent the demand side of a market and linear programming for the supply side. Similarly, forest management models can be enhanced with econometric methods. For example, the demand equation used in the forest-simulation model of Chap. 14 could very well be estimated by econometrics. For the sake of simplicity, the methods of this book appear in separate chapters. With experience and good judgment you may combine them in ways suited to your own needs in order to solve interesting and challenging problems.

PROBLEMS

17.1. Assume that it is 1981, and a pulp industry analyst has just announced that to comply with recent environmental legislation the pulp industry will have to spend more on pollution control. The analyst estimates that the net effect will be to lower the rate of growth in pulping capacity in the North-Central region from 2.4 to 2.0 percent per year for the next 4 years. Other things being equal, how would this affect the 1985 forecasts of price and quantity demanded made in Sec. 17.8?

17.2. Consider the set of structural equations (17.1–17.3) for a simple model of the market for aspen pulpwood in Wisconsin. Modifying the demand equation (17.1) to allow price to affect the quantity demanded results in the new set of structural equations:

$$Demand: D_t = a + bK_t + eP_t + u_t$$

$$Supply: S_t = c + dP_t + v_t$$

$$Equilibrium: D_t = S_t$$

where: D_t is the quantity of pulpwood demanded in year t
P_t is the price of pulpwood
S_t is the quantity of pulpwood supplied
K_t is the capacity of pulpmills in Wisconsin
a, b, c, d, and e are unknown parameters
u_t and v_t are random disturbances

This set of equations can be simplified by substituting $Q_t = D_t = S_t$ (from the equilibrium equation) into the demand and supply equations. Make these substitutions, and solve for the reduced-form equations, expressing the endogenous variables P_t and Q_t as functions of the exogenous variable K_t and the five unknown parameters. How do these reduced-form equations differ from those in equations (17.4) and (17.6)? Under what circumstance are they the same?

17.3. For some multiple-equation models, it is impossible to use OLS estimates of the coefficients of the reduced-form equations to estimate the unknown parameters of one or more structural equations—the structural equations are then said to be unidentified. Given OLS estimates of the coefficients of the reduced-form equations derived in Prob. 17.2, can you derive estimates of all, some, or none of the structural equation parameters a, b, c, d, and e? (*Hint*: Think of each estimate of a coefficient in a reduced-form equation as providing an equation of the form $f(a, b, c, d, e)$ equals the estimated coefficient. Do the number of equations and unknown parameters match?)

17.4. (This problem requires the use of an OLS regression program.) A large forest products company needs to decide between investing in a new lumber mill or a new plywood mill. Since either mill will have a long life, the company's officers have asked their forest economist to evaluate the relative strength of future demand for lumber and plywood. To do this, she will try to forecast national trends in per-capita consumption of lumber and plywood with the following models:

$$L_t = a + bt$$
$$P_t = d + et$$

where: L_t is the per capita consumption of lumber in year t
P_t is the per capita consumption of plywood
a, b, d, and e are unknown parameters

Use the data given below to estimate the unknown parameters in each of these equations. How much of the variation in per capita consumption of lumber and plywood is explained by these simple models? What do the signs of the estimates of parameters b and e indicate? What are the 95 percent confidence intervals for each of these parameters? Does either model seem to have a problem with autocorrelation? With unequal variance of the errors? What forecasts do you obtain for per capita consumption of lumber and plywood in the year 1990 using these models?

Year	Lumber / capita (ft^3)	Plywood / capita (ft^3)	Housing starts (1000s)
60	30.8	4.2	1296
61	29.9	4.5	1365
62	30.9	4.7	1493
63	32.0	5.0	1635
64	32.9	5.4	1561
65	32.6	5.8	1510
66	31.9	5.8	1196
67	29.9	5.7	1322
68	31.5	6.4	1545
69	30.7	6.0	1500
70	29.1	5.7	1469
71	30.6	6.6	2085
72	32.1	7.4	2379
73	32.2	7.1	2058
74	27.8	5.9	1353
75	25.8	5.9	1171
76	29.7	6.9	1548
77	32.4	7.3	2002
78	33.5	7.4	2036
79	31.7	6.8	1760
80	26.4	5.6	1313

17.5. (Requires the use of an OLS regression program.) The forecasting models estimated in Prob. 17.4 ignore the effects of variables that do not display a simple time trend. For example, the number of housing starts in a given year tends to vary in cycles, yet housing starts have a strong influence on the use of both lumber and plywood. Reestimate both models using both time and housing starts as explanatory variables. That is to say, estimate the models:

$$L_t = a + bt + cH_t$$

$$P_t = d + et + fH_t$$

where: L_t is the per capita consumption of lumber in year t
P_t is the per capita consumption of plywood
H_t is the number of housing starts
a, b, c, d, e, and f are unknown parameters

How much more of the variation in the per-capita consumption of lumber and plywood is explained by these models? What do the signs on the estimates of parameters b and e indicate? What are the 95 percent confidence intervals for each of these parameters? What do the signs on the estimates of parameters c and f indicate? Does this make sense? What are the 95 percent confidence intervals for each of these parameters? Does either model seem to have a problem with autocorrelation? With the variance of the errors? Assuming 1500 thousand housing starts in 1990, what forecasts do you obtain for per-capita consumption of lumber and plywood in that year using these models?

ANNOTATED REFERENCES

Adams, D. M. 1983. An approach to estimating demand for National Forest timber. *Forest Science* 29(2):289–300. (Uses econometrics to estimate the demand for timber from National Forests in the western United States.)

Adams, D. M., and R. Haynes. 1985. Changing perspectives on the outlook for timber in the United States. *Journal of Forestry* 83(1):32–35. (A good example of application of a market-model in forecasting and policy analysis.)

Armstrong, J. S. 1985. *Long-range forecasting: From crystal ball to computer.* Wiley, New York. 687 pp. (A good comparative guide to many different forecasting methods.)

Blyth, J. E., and W. B. Smith. 1983. Pulpwood production in the North-Central region by county, 1981. U.S. Forest Service, Resource Bulletin NC-69. North Central Forest Experiment Station, St. Paul. 21 pp. (Source of the data on pulpwood production used in this chapter.)

Bulkley Dunton and Company. Various dates. Lockwood's directory of the paper and allied trades. Bulkley Dunton, New York. (Source of the data on pulping capacity used in this chapter.)

Buongiorno J., and T. Young. 1984. Statistical appraisal of timber with an application to the Chequamegon National Forest. *Northern Journal of Applied Forestry* 1(4):72–76. (A single-equation regression model to predict the value of auctioned timber.)

Chow, G. C. 1983. *Econometrics.* McGraw Hill, New York. 432 pp. (This is an advanced text in econometrics, but pages 27 to 36 and pages 47 to 58 contain excellent simple examples of demand analysis and forecasting.)

Gilless, J. K., and J. Buongiorno. 1986. PAPYRUS: A model of the North American pulp and paper industry. *Forest Science Monograph* (forthcoming). (Example of a market model that combines econometrics and linear programming.)

Larsen, M. W. 1980. Developing an econometric planning model for the wood product firm. *Forest Products Journal* 30(9):14–20. (Simple econometric models to forecast sales, costs, and net income.)

Leuschner, W. A. 1973. An econometric analysis of the Wisconsin aspen pulpwood market. *Forest Science* 19(1):41–46. (An earlier, simple model of the market studied in this chapter.)

Levenbach, H., and J. P. Cleary 1984. *The modern forecaster: The forecasting process through data analysis*. Lifetime Learning Publications, Belmont 537 pp. (An introductory treatment of econometric methods. Requires little mathematical background.)

McKillop, W. 1967. Supply and demand for forest products, an econometric study. *Hilgardia* 38(1):1–132. (One of the pioneering analyses of forest product markets using econometrics, with applications to forecasting.)

Peterson, T. A. Various dates. Wisconsin forest products price review. University Wisconsin-Extension, Madison. (Original source of price data used in this chapter.)

Elements of Matrix Algebra

The purpose of this appendix is to explain the matrix notations and operations used at the end of Chap. 8. In that chapter, we described the growth of an uneven-aged stand with the following equations:

$$y_{1,t+1} = 0.92\,y_{1,t} - 0.29y_{2,t} - 0.96y_{3,t} + 40.$$
$$y_{2,t+1} = 0.04\,y_{1,t} + 0.90\,y_{2,t}$$
$$y_{3,t+1} = \phantom{0.04y_{1,t} +} 0.02\,y_{2,t} + 0.90\,y_{3,t} \tag{A.1}$$

To simplify further manipulations, we shall write this system of equations with matrices and vectors. A matrix is a table of numbers, variables, or algebraic expressions. A vector is a matrix that has only one row or one column.

For example, the coefficients of $y_{1,t}$ $y_{2,t}$, $y_{3,t}$, in Eq. (A.1) constitute the following matrix of three rows and three columns:

$$\mathbf{G} = \begin{bmatrix} 0.92 & -0.29 & -0.96 \\ 0.04 & 0.90 & 0 \\ 0 & 0.02 & 0.90 \end{bmatrix}$$

while the variables and the constant term constitute the three following column vectors:

$$\mathbf{y}_{t+1} = \begin{bmatrix} y_{1,t+1} \\ y_{2,t+1} \\ y_{3,t+1} \end{bmatrix} \qquad \mathbf{y}_t = \begin{bmatrix} y_{1,t} \\ y_{2,t} \\ y_{3,t} \end{bmatrix} \qquad \mathbf{c} = \begin{bmatrix} 40 \\ 0 \\ 0 \end{bmatrix}$$

with these notations, the system of Eqs. (A.1) can be written as:

$$\mathbf{y}_{t+1} = \mathbf{G}\mathbf{y}_t + \mathbf{c} \tag{A.2}$$

where $\mathbf{Gy}_t$ is the product of matrix $\mathbf{G}$ by vector $\mathbf{y}_t$, that is:

$$\mathbf{Gy}_t = \begin{bmatrix} 0.92 & -0.29 & -0.96 \\ 0.04 & 0.90 & 0 \\ 0 & 0.02 & 0.90 \end{bmatrix} \begin{bmatrix} y_{1,t} \\ y_{2,t} \\ y_{3,t} \end{bmatrix}$$

The general law of multiplication of matrices is as follows:

Given a matrix $\mathbf{A}$ of m rows and p columns, and a matrix $\mathbf{B}$ of p rows and n columns, the product $\mathbf{C} = \mathbf{AB}$ is a matrix of m rows and n columns such that each entry $c_{i,j}$ of $\mathbf{C}$ is obtained by multiplying each entry of row i in $\mathbf{A}$ by the corresponding entry in column j of $\mathbf{B}$ and adding up the products. That is:

$$c_{i,j} = a_{i,1}b_{1,j} + a_{i,2}b_{2,j} = \cdots + a_{i,p}b_{p,j} \qquad \begin{aligned} &\text{for } i = 1,\ldots,m \\ &\text{and } j = 1,\ldots,n \end{aligned}$$

Therefore, the product $\mathbf{Gy}_t$ is the following column vector:

$$\mathbf{Gy}_t = \begin{bmatrix} 0.92\,y_{1,t} - 0.29y_{2,t} - 0.96y_{3,t} \\ 0.04y_{1,t} + 0.90y_{2,t} \\ 0.02\,y_{2,t} + 0.90y_{3,t} \end{bmatrix}$$

Furthermore, matrices with the same number of rows and columns are added by adding their corresponding entries. Thus, the right-hand side of Eq. (A.2) is obtained by adding vector $\mathbf{c}$ to vector $\mathbf{Gy}_t$, entry by entry, leading to the following vector:

$$\mathbf{Gy}_t + \mathbf{c} = \begin{bmatrix} 0.92\,y_{1,t} - 0.29y_{2,t} - 0.96y_{3,t} + 40 \\ 0.04y_{1,t} + 0.90y_{2,t} \\ 0.02\,y_{2,t} + 0.90y_{3,t} \end{bmatrix}$$

Equation (A.2) means that each entry of this vector is equal to the corresponding entry of vector $\mathbf{y}_{t+1}$. Therefore, (A.2) is indeed equivalent to the system of Eq. (A.1).

Equation (A.2) implies that the condition of the stand at time $t + 2$ is:

$$\mathbf{y}_{t+2} = \mathbf{Gy}_{t+1} + \mathbf{c} = \mathbf{G}(\mathbf{Gy}_t + \mathbf{c}) + \mathbf{c} = \mathbf{G}^2\mathbf{y}_t + \mathbf{Gc} + \mathbf{c}$$

By applying the rules of matrix multiplication and addition we get:

$$\mathbf{Gc} = \begin{bmatrix} 0.92 & -0.29 & -0.96 \\ 0.04 & 0.90 & 0 \\ 0 & 0.02 & 0.90 \end{bmatrix} \begin{bmatrix} 40 \\ 0 \\ 0 \end{bmatrix} = \begin{bmatrix} 36.8 \\ 1.6 \\ 0 \end{bmatrix}, \qquad \mathbf{Gc} + \mathbf{c} = \begin{bmatrix} 76.8 \\ 1.6 \\ 0 \end{bmatrix}$$

$$\mathbf{G}^2 = \begin{bmatrix} 0.92 & -0.29 & -0.96 \\ 0.04 & 0.90 & 0 \\ 0 & 0.02 & 0.90 \end{bmatrix} \begin{bmatrix} 0.92 & -0.29 & -0.96 \\ 0.04 & 0.90 & 0 \\ 0 & 0.02 & 0.90 \end{bmatrix}$$

$$= \begin{bmatrix} 0.83 & -0.55 & -1.75 \\ 0.07 & 0.80 & -0.04 \\ 0 & 0.04 & 0.81 \end{bmatrix}$$

Having $\mathbf{G}^2$ one can then compute $\mathbf{G}^3 = \mathbf{G}^2\mathbf{G}$ and higher powers of $\mathbf{G}$ by reapplying the same rules.

Elements of BASIC Programming

The programming language BASIC is the most widely used on microcomputers, probably because it is one of the easiest to learn. There are many different, though similar, versions of BASIC. This appendix summarizes the features of the version used in writing the programs in this book.

A BASIC program consists of an ordered sequence of instructions for the computer, each of these instructions being a BASIC *statement*. To write these statements, one use constants, variables, subscripted variables and functions.

Constants and Variables

A *constant* may be an integer number like 2, 3, 11, 25,000, or it can be a decimal number, such as 10.05 or 1.00.

A *variable* is a symbol, or name, which represents a quantity that may take different values at different times. Variables may be integer or real. Examples of variable names are:

tlast,   year,   rate,   iclass,   pval,   fcost

A *subscripted variable* is a variable that has a subscript. The subscript is an integer constant or variable given in parenthesis. Examples of subscripted variables are:

trc(1),   volume(iclass),   cost(year)

If you change one of the programs in this book so that a subscript may take a value greater than 10, then you must declare the maximum dimension of the subscripted variable at the beginning of the program. For example, the statement:

DIM trc(13), cost(25)

indicates that the subscript of the variable *trc* may take a value up to 13 and that of cost up to 25. All words shown in bold are reserved words of the language that must be spelled as shown.

Functions

Common elementary mathematical functions are a feature of the BASIC language. The functions used in the program of this book are:

LOG(x)	The natural logarithm of the variable x
SQR(x)	The square root of the variable x
RANDOMIZE 3333	initiates the seed of random number generator to 3333, or some other constant
RND	Function that takes a new random value between 0 and 1 every time it is called

Arithmetic Expressions

In BASIC the arithmetic operators $+$, $-$, $*$, $/$ and $^\wedge$ are used to combine constants, variables, subscribed variables, and functions into arithmetic expressions. The following are examples of mathematical expressions and of their BASIC counterparts:

Mathematical expression	*BASIC expression*
$v_j/(1 + r)^j$	v(j) / (1 + r)^j
$\dfrac{x - c(y + b)}{g - h}$	(x − c*(y + b)) / (g − h)
$a + b \ln(x)$	a + b**LOG**(x)

Assignment Statements

An example of assignment statement in BASIC is:

Cost = 10 + 2.5 *** LOG**(x)

which means that the variable on the left of the equal sign is assigned the value of the arithmetic expression on the right, based on the current value of the variable x.

Loops

Loops permit the repetition of certain statements and are make computer programs so useful. The programs of this book use two forms of loop structures, the **FOR**...**NEXT** and the **WHILE**...**WEND** loops. An example of the **FOR ... NEXT** loop is:

```
val = 0.
FOR iclass = 1 TO 7
  val = val + 5.0
NEXT iclass
```

Here, the statement between **FOR** and **NEXT** is repeated seven times. After the first pass through the loop, *iclass* has the value 1 and the variable *val* is assigned the value 5.0. After the second pass *iclass* has the value 2 and *val* has the value 10. The loop ends when *iclass* has the value 7. Then, *val* has the value 35.0.

An example of the **WHILE ... WEND** loop is:

```
year = 0
volume = 0
WHILE year < = 5
  year = year + 2
  volume = volume + 10
WEND
```

This executes the statements between **WHILE** and **WEND** as long as the condition year $< = 5$ is true. In this case, volume has the value 30 when the **WHILE** loop is terminated.

Input Statements

The following statements:

```
READ age, area, cost(1)
DATA 12.0, 50, 326
```

read the values 12.0, 50, 326 from the **DATA** statement and assign them to the variables *age*, *area* and *cost*(1), respectively. The statements:

```
FOR iclass = 1 TO 7
  READ trd(iclass)
NEXT iclass
DATA 250, 100, 40, 20, 5, 0, 0
```

read the values $250, 100, \ldots, 0$ and assign them to $trd(1)$, $trd(2), \ldots, trd(7)$.

Output Statements

The statement:

```
PRINT "year"; thisyear
```

displays on the computer's screen the word "year," followed on the same line by the current value of the variable *thisyear*. The statements:

```
FOR iclass = 1 TO 10
  PRINT USING "****.**"; trb(iclass),
NEXT iclass
```

Print the current values of the variables $trb(1)$, $trb(2)$, ..., $trb(10)$ on the same line. Each variable printed has two digits to the right of the decimal point and up to four on the left.

Subroutines

A subroutine is a self-contained section of a program doing a specific thing. Good programmers divide their programs into several well-defined subroutines. A subroutine starts with a label (any name followed by :) and ends with the word **RETURN**. An example of a subroutine is:

```
Pvalue:
disc = (1 + rate)^year
FOR iclass = 1 TO 7
  pval = pval + trv(iclass) * trc(iclass) / disc
NEXT iclass
pval = pval - fcost / disc
RETURN
```

The execution of subroutines is controlled by **GOSUB** statements within the program that calls the subroutines. For example, a program using the subroutine Pvalue could be:

```
Main:
  . . .
pval = 0.0
GOSUB Pvalue
returns = returns + pval
  . . .
END
```

In this case, the **GOSUB** statement in the program Main causes the execution of the subroutine Pvalue. The **RETURN** statement at the end of the subroutine Pvalue causes the program to branch back to the statement returns = returns + pval after the subroutine is finished.

The **END** statement is the last statement of the main program.

Control Statements

The control statement used in programs in this book is **IF ... THEN ... ELSE**. It directs program execution to a particular statement based on the result of a *logical expression* that is either true or false. An example of a control statement is:

> **IF** tnFire < = tnHarvest **THEN GOSUB** burn **ELSE GOSUB** harvest

This statement directs the program to execute subroutine Burn if the variable *tnFire* is less or equal than *tnHarvest*, and to execute subroutine Harvest otherwise. The **ELSE** clause is optional. For example, the statement:

> **IF** trc(iclass) < 0 **THEN** trc(iclass) = 0
> trb(iclass) = 50 + trc(iclass)

will set the variable *trc(iclass)* to zero if it is negative and then calculate *trb(iclass)*. On the other hand, it will calculate directly *trb(iclass)* if *trc(iclass)* is positive.

Index